The Kiplinger / CHANGING TIMES Guide to

# BUYING
# AND
# SELLING
# A HOME

## By the Editors of
## CHANGING TIMES Magazine

Published by
The Kiplinger Washington Editors, Inc.
1729 H Street, NW
Washington, DC 20006

Distributed by
Select Magazines, Inc.
8 East 40th Street
New York, NY 10006

This book is available in bulk quantities at discount. For more information,
contact the Circulation Department, The Kiplinger Washington Editors, Inc.,
at the above address.

ISBN: 0-938721-02-X

Printed in the United States of America

First Printing: April, 1987

# Contents

# Introduction

By Knight A. Kiplinger
Editor in Chief, *Changing Times* magazine

When we published the first edition of *Buying and Selling a Home*, in the spring of 1983, the housing market was still recovering from the severe recession of 1981–82. Inflation was coming down, home prices were generally flat, but mortgage rates were still high enough to price many would-be homeowners out of the market.

Exotic kinds of mortgages and seller-financing deals had sprung up to bridge the affordability gap, and this book devoted as much space to shopping for a mortgage as it did to shopping for a home.

Our approach was apparently found useful by many house hunters; *Buying and Selling a Home* became a national bestseller, with more than 150,000 copies sold.

Much has changed in the past four years. Many of the innovative mortgages of 1983 are no longer offered today, chased from the market by falling interest rates and their own complexity. The fixed-rate mortgage—declared dead forever just a couple of years ago—stormed back to become the dominant kind of home financing once again. Home prices are once again rising at their traditional, better-than-inflation rate, except in parts of the country that still haven't recovered from hard times in energy and agriculture.

But there are new rules in the game, too—most importantly,

the 1986 Tax Reform Act. Homeownership—of not just one, but two personal residences—emerged largely unscathed from tax overhaul. The tax advantages of owning your own home have been diminished only by a trimming of marginal tax rates and a few limitations on mortgage interest deductions.

Every chapter of *Buying and Selling a Home* has been fully revised to reflect the new realities of lower inflation, stable interest rates, and the effects of federal tax reform.

We have also added lots of new material, including chapters on buying a vacation home and investing in residential real estate. Both of these activities have been heavily affected by tax reform, as you will see in these chapters.

The book is divided into two sections: Part One, for buyers, and Part Two, for sellers. Whichever you are (and many people are both simultaneously), carefully read the part addressed to the other party. You'll gain insight into the concerns and strategies of all the major players in a transaction, and the knowledge will help you get a better deal for yourself.

Recognizing that the vast majority of real estate transactions are handled by brokers and agents who receive a commission on the sale, *Buying and Selling a Home* tells you the right way to select and deal with these professionals. It also describes how buyers can often benefit from using a "buyer's broker," who is clearly working for the buyer, not the seller. And for homeowners who want to try their hand at selling without an agent, we give realistic, step-by-step advice on how to do it.

The second edition of *Buying and Selling a Home* is the work of many talented people. Some of the text was picked up intact from the first edition, written by Joan Meyers, a veteran real estate journalist, lecturer and former broker. The lead author for the new edition was Priscilla Brandon, a *Changing Times* research associate who also worked extensively on the first edition. Kevin McCormally, senior editor of *Changing Times*, wrote the new material on the tax angles of real estate. Facts in the entire manuscript were checked by freelance researcher Camilla Luckey.

We hope that this book helps guide you through the murky and often turbulent waters of real estate deals in America today—and tomorrow. Real estate has long been a core subject of *Changing*

*Times*, the first magazine of personal-finance guidance, so the subjects in this book will be periodically updated in monthly issues of the magazine.

Don't hesitate to write us with your questions or comments about *Buying and Selling a Home*. Your ideas will help us strengthen the book in future editions.

—K.A.K

Washington, D.C.
April 10, 1987

# PART ONE

# FOR BUYERS

# 1

# To Buy or Not to Buy

Homeownership has long been regarded as one of the key elements of the "American dream." America has one of the highest proportions of homeownership in the world, with more than six out of every ten families living in owner-occupied housing.

The reasons for America's love affair with homeownership are many. Some are financial. Our tax code continues to subsidize heavily the ownership of homes, making it more attractive than renting for most people. Homeownership is also America's favorite forced-savings and investment plan, with an increasing share of the monthly mortgage payment going into the building of equity for future uses—another home, college expenses, retirement, etc. A home is, truly, the only investment you can live in, and over the past 40 years, it has been a generally well-performing investment, relative to alternative uses of money.

But much of the motivation behind homeownership is psychological. This country was founded on principles of individual destiny, personal control over one's life and surroundings, and freedom of individual expression. A home of one's own helps fulfill all of those promises, giving the owner freedom from rent hikes and the whim of the landlord, and the freedom to live life as he or she wishes. A home can provide a sense of security and pride. A home gives a feeling of stability and commitment, not to

7

mention autonomy and privacy. It is often the first step in an owner's putting down roots in a community.

But like most freedoms, the benefits of homeownership also carry heavy responsibilities—financial obligations and duties of maintenance, recordkeeping, and planning.

## THE INTANGIBLES

It's no wonder that psychologists rank buying a home high on the list of stress-producing events. Not only is it the biggest purchase most people make in a lifetime, but it also forces a wholesale examination of goals, commitments and lifestyle. It's an emotional as well as a financial investment.

People buy homes for lots of different reasons. Before you go into the market for a home, examine your motives, clarify your wants and needs, and focus your investigation.

With so much at stake, don't rush into the market without thoughtful preparation. If you join the ranks of buyers charging about searching for answers without knowing the right questions, you may, by luck, end up with a house you can live with. Then again, you may spend weeks, even months, looking at houses only to end up feeling thwarted and confused.

Before you take the plunge, address questions like these:

What does being a homeowner mean to you? To your spouse? What do you really want in a home, and from a home? If you have children or plan to some day, how will your choice of home affect them? Your home determines where children will go to school and what facilities will be nearby for recreation, shopping and worship. What about proximity and convenience for friends? Its location or design can make it a favorite gathering place for your friends or extended family.

How will becoming a homeowner change you and the way you live? Who hasn't heard stories about the totally unhandy new buyer who ends up renovating his or her home from top to bottom; the successful business that had its beginning in a spare room or basement; or the irrepressible free spirit who is transformed into a model of financial responsibility by homeownership?

## FINANCIAL BENEFITS

Treating a home solely as an investment probably is impossible. Financial calculations alone fall short of giving you the perspective you need for such a big decision. Still, a home is a major investment, and the financial aspects of homeownership should not be ignored.

Here are some of the key financial benefits of homeownership:

### Budgetary discipline

Accumulating the down payment on a home is often the goal that creates a family's first real savings program. Later on, paying the mortgage is a strong inducement to creating and sticking with a budget. Depending on your personality and level of discretionary income, this form of enforced savings (and consequent equity buildup) can be an important factor in boosting family net worth. Stripped to its essentials, equity is the difference between what you would get if you sold your home and any debt outstanding. Equity includes the down payment, all payments against the principal balance, and any appreciation in the market value of your home that occurs after you buy it.

### The power of leverage

Buying a home offers you the opportunity to magnify the purchasing power of your money through what is called leverage—the use of borrowed money to purchase an asset that is likely to appreciate, magnifying your profit.

Normally, you buy property—whether it's a home or a commercial building—with some of your own funds plus a long-term mortgage. That use of borrowed money enables you to profit from price increases on property you haven't yet paid for.

The larger your loan as a proportion of the home's value, the greater your leverage and potential gain. Say you purchase a $100,000 single family house with no loan and sell it three years later for $125,000. The $25,000 gain represents a 25% return on your $100,000 outlay.

Suppose, on the other hand, that you had invested only $20,000 of your own money, while borrowing the other $80,000. When you sell (ignoring for the sake of simplicity the cost of the loan, tax angles, commissions and other costs) you have made $25,000 on your $20,000 investment, a spectacular 125% return on your investment over the three years of ownership.

Using maximum leverage—with a very small down payment and very large mortgage—isn't prudent or advantageous for everyone, but most first-time buyers will need all they can get just to open the door.

## Appreciation

If your home is worth more now than when you bought it, that's appreciation. When you sell it you can use the profit as a springboard to a better home. Or you can tap the equity/appreciation build-up to pay college tuition, to buy a vacation hideaway, to take a long dreamed-of ocean cruise. For many people, the equity in their homes becomes a major source of retirement funds.

## Tax benefits

Homeowners benefit from the tax deductibility of mortgage interest and property taxes. When you sell, you can defer federal taxes on all the profits if within two years you buy another home of equal or greater value. When you reach 55, you can sell the home and keep up to $125,000 of profit completely free of tax.

## THE RISKS AND HARD WORK OF HOMEOWNERSHIP

So far, it may sound like there's no way to lose. But homeownership is not for everyone. There are risks—as well as burdens.

## Financial risks

The value of your home is not guaranteed to go up, and it could go down. The leverage that is so alluring when real estate values are on the rise can act to magnify losses as well as gains. For example, suppose you invested $20,000 in a home valued at $100,000 in a booming economy. Then recession hits your community, you lose your job and you're forced to sell for $80,000; the $20,000 loss wipes out 100% of your investment, and you'll probably have to dig into your pocket to cover commissions and other expenses. Real estate is not a liquid asset. You can lose if you have to sell in a hurry, because of a divorce or job loss, for example.

You lose, too, if you invest in a home a sum of money that could have been invested elsewhere for a better return. If alternative investments—such as stocks or bonds—are rising in value faster than homes in your area, you might do better, in the short run, as a renter/investor rather than a homeowner.

Even if you buy a home, you may want to hold back some of your cash to invest in income-producing assets, rather than pour it all into your new home; this is especially relevant for the trade-up home buyer who has substantial cash from the sale of the previous home.

Homes cost money to maintain. You have to be prepared to pay for routine maintenance (usually with time and money) and for the inevitable replacement of big-ticket items, such as the roof or furnace.

### Reduced mobility

Homeowners have less freedom of movement; it's not as easy to pack up and move for a change of scenery or a new job. And a hefty mortgage payment may make it hard to maintain any other savings and investment programs for retirement, vacations and other things.

### Rent vs. buy

In the short run, renting often makes more financial sense than buying, in terms of how much shelter one can afford for a given price.

Rents tend to be an accurate reflection of the free-market pricing of housing simply as *shelter*. But the ownership cost of a house or condominium is a combination of both *shelter* value and *investment* expectation.

So at any given moment, you can usually rent an apartment or house for less than the monthly carrying costs that a buyer of that property would have to pay to carry it through the early years of ownership.

This explains why many young people can't afford to own the very condominium that they've been renting with no financial strain, or why a young family might be able to rent a much fancier, more spacious house than they would be able to buy.

That's the short-run picture, but the long-range view is different. Over time, rents tend to rise, but the basic cost of owning your own home—the monthly payment of principal and interest—stays the same. Combined with a record of price appreciation, this is what makes homeownership financially attractive in the long run.

Until the "long run" arrives, however, you may have to make some sacrifices to become a homeowner. You may have to put up with less space if you have to pay more to own a small home than to rent a larger one. To find a house you can afford, you might have to move to a location farther from your job and favorite haunts; that means extra traveling cost and possibly two cars for your household, where one used to suffice.

## BUYING A HOUSE WITH OTHERS

The vast majority of houses are either solely owned by individuals or jointly owned by married couples.

But with a surge of unorthodox living arrangements in the 1970s came a new variety of ownership arrangements among unrelated individuals sharing the same principal residence or vacation home. Single people living as couples or just groups of friends wanted the advantages of homeownership, too.

Many lenders are still cool to such arrangements, but some are not.

There are proper ways to go about buying property jointly with relatives or unrelated friends, the two most common being tenancy in common and partnership. A good real estate attorney can explain them to you.

Owning in a group can create problems. When a tenancy-in-common ownership share changes hands, the lender may declare the loan due. The only recourse, if you don't want to sell the property, is to refinance.

Setting up a general partnership to own the place can head off many of those problems by anticipating and dealing with them in the partnership agreement. Use your lawyer to draw up the agreement.

Make sure the partnership agreement addresses the following points:

▶ How ownership will be divided, which in turn determines who pays how much of the down payment, monthly payment, maintenance and repairs. The contract should also describe how any profits or losses from rent or sale of the place will be divided and how tax benefits will be distributed.

▶ How use of the house's space is to be divided.

▶ What constitutes a deciding vote and under what circumstances such a vote is considered necessary.

▶ Which owner will act as managing partner and thus be responsible for signing checks and paying routine expenses.

▶ How much advance notice a withdrawing partner must give and how the buyout price will be set.

A partnership may also protect the existing mortgage when a new owner enters the picture if the lender agrees that it is an interest in the partnership—not an interest in the property—that is being transferred.

Ideally, a general partnership should try to find a lender who is willing to limit each partner's liability on the loan to his or her respective percentage of ownership, even though such agreements are unusual. Otherwise, each partner is responsible for 100% of the loan, so a lender could single out any partner to sue for the money if there's a default, instead of going through complicated foreclosure proceedings. Regardless of this protection, you'll want to be confident that each member of the buying group is financially responsible, creditworthy and stable in his or her career.

The legal and financial techniques associated with ownership by unrelated individuals are just the beginning of your consideration of this issue.

Just as important, or even more so, is compatability of lifestyle and the prospects of a durable friendship among all involved. As for investment value, keep in mind that partnership interests in a commonly owned house are not highly liquid. To get full value for anyone's share, the group may have to sell the whole house.

There are a lot of obstacles to overcome in such an arrangement, but with careful planning and thoughtfulness among friends, it can work out well both socially and financially.

# 2

## Assessing Your Resources

Once you know you're serious about buying a home—and before you start looking at houses—gather the information you will need to present to lenders. Review your financial situation to determine what you can pay down and how large a load you can carry monthly.

When you've completed that task, visit with lenders to get your figures plugged into the available mortgage formulas to yield an affordable price range. This kind of preparation—called "prequalifying"—will give you a financial comfort zone within which to shop. You'll know what's easy, what's possible and what's out of the question.

### FIGURE YOUR NET WORTH

If you don't have a net worth statement already, it's time to put one together. An inventory of your assets and liabilities will help you determine the maximum down payment you can make. If money you will need is tied up in such illiquid assets as your current home, land or collectibles, you must allow yourself plenty of time either to sell or borrow against them.

# NET WORTH WORKSHEET

| WHAT YOU OWN | | WHAT YOU OWE | |
|---|---|---|---|
| **CASH:** | | **CURRENT BILLS:** | |
| Cash on hand | $ | Rent | $ |
| Checking accounts | | Utilities | |
| Savings accounts | | Charge accounts | |
| Money-market funds | | Credit cards | |
| Life insurance cash value | | Insurance premiums | |
| Money owed you | | Alimony | |
| | | Child support | |
| | | Other bills | |
| **MARKETABLE SECURITIES:** | | | |
| Stocks | $ | | |
| Bonds | | **TAXES:** | |
| Government securities | | Federal | $ |
| Mutual funds | | State | |
| Other investments | | Local | |
| **PERSONAL PROPERTY (RESALE VALUE):** | | Taxes on investments | |
| Automobiles | $ | Other | |
| Household furnishings | | | |
| Art, antiques, other collectibles | | | |
| Clothing, furs | | **MORTGAGES:** | |
| Jewelry | | Homes | $ |
| Other possessions | | Other properties | |
| | | **DEBTS TO INDIVIDUALS:** | |
| | | | $ |
| **REAL ESTATE (APPRAISED VALUE):** | | | |
| Homes | $ | | |
| Other properties | | | |
| | | | |
| **RETIREMENT FUNDS:** | | | |
| Vested portion of company plan | $ | **LOANS:** | |
| Vested benefits | | Auto | $ |
| IRA/Keogh | | Education | |
| Annuities (surrender value) | | Home improvement | |
| **OTHER ASSETS:** | | Other | |
| Equity in businesses | $ | **TOTAL LIABILITIES:** | $ |
| Partnership interests | | | |
| **TOTAL ASSETS:** | $ | | |
| | | What you own minus what you owe equals your net worth: | $ |

## THE DOWN PAYMENT

Now figure your maximum down payment, if you wanted to put all your liquid assets into the home purchase. Take your total *liquid* net worth (including the equity you'll get from the sale of your present home), and subtract from that figure 1) settlement and moving costs; 2) savings for emergencies, educational expenses or retirement; and 3) cash you'll need for decorating and furnishing your new home.

---

### WHAT YOU CAN PUT DOWN

Estimating your available cash for a down payment

| | |
|---|---|
| Net worth (total assets minus liabilities): | $_____ |
| Less funds reserved for college expenses, savings, retirement, emergency needs, etc.: | −$_____ |
| Less cash needed for costs related to the new home: | |
| Settlement expenses: $_____ | |
| Sales expenses for current home: _____ | |
| Moving and relocating expenses: _____ | |
| Immediate improvements to new home: _____ | |
| Decorating, furnishing new home: _____ | |
| | −$_____ |
| NET ASSETS AVAILABLE: | $_____ |
| Plus gifts from parents, relatives: | +$_____ |
| TOTAL AVAILABLE CASH FOR DOWN PAYMENT: | $_____ |

The bottom line will be the sum that you *could* put down on the new house, if you wish to use it all. The more cash you pay up front, the less you will have to pay month by month on the mortgage, and the lower your total interest costs will be over the term of the mortgage.

Conversely, the less you put down, the greater will be your leverage, tax deductions for mortgage interest, and available funds for other expenses, including decorating and furnishing your new home. Also keep in mind that the money you hold back from your down payment, if invested wisely, might earn you more than the appreciation on your property will add to your equity.

As you figure the amount of your liquid assets, remember that you don't have to put it all into the down payment. The minimum required will be determined by the type of loan, the lender and whether the mortgage will be sold in the secondary market.

Mortgage lenders, of course, prefer a big down payment to a minimal one. That tells the lender that the new homeowner has a major stake in the property and won't be tempted to default on the loan and walk away from the house. The larger the down payment the less risk of foreclosure and the less chance the lender will suffer any financial loss on the property.

In most cases you will need to pay from 10% to 20% down on the purchase price of the property. If you plan to buy with a down payment of less than 20%, you will be expected to have a higher income relative to mortgage debt than someone putting down more than 20%.

If your calculations indicate that you can't put at least 20% down,

1) Consider buying a less expensive home.

2) Find out whether you are eligible for a VA-guaranteed or FHA-insured loan, with little or no down payment.

3) Try to get help from family or friends. As a general rule, you'll be expected to make at least a 5% cash down payment in addition to any funds received as a gift toward the purchase price of the home.

A relative or friend may be willing to make you a second-trust loan (at a competitive market rate, not subsidized) to close the gap between down payment and the first mortgage. But "simultaneous second trusts" are not allowed by many lenders, and even if acceptable, the lender will scrutinize your finances carefully to make sure you can afford to carry both mortgages.

Some lenders will regard this loan as a gift and require you and the lender to sign a form saying the money is a gift that need not be repaid; if you and the "giver" want to later convert the gift to a loan—after the purchase—that's up to the two of you; there may be gift tax and estate considerations, so consult an attorney.

4) Look for property where the seller is willing to take back a second mortgage.

5) Inquire from lenders about private mortgage insurance (PMI). For a full discussion of PMI, see Chapter 11.

## HOW BIG A LOAN?

How much you can borrow will depend on your income and the size of your down payment. Job stability, credit references, payment histories and other indications of creditworthiness also are factors.

The old rule of thumb about qualifying for a loan up to twice family income is just that. Using that outdated guideline, $50,000 of income should translate to a $100,000 mortgage. Sound too simple? It is. A family with $50,000 of annual earnings, three children, $5,000 in savings and a new car loan just won't stack up the same way with lenders as a childless couple with the same income, no debts and a $30,000 stock portfolio.

You'll get closer to reality by applying some of the same tools lenders use to evaluate the creditworthiness of prospective buyers. One common method is to apply a number of ratios to gross monthly income. For example, if you are making a 20% down payment, you may be allowed to devote up to 28% of gross, pre-tax monthly income to housing expenses (including mortgage, property taxes, insurance, condominium fees, utilities and maintenance). However, your combined housing expenses and installment debt obligations may not exceed 36%.

If your down payment works out to 10% of the sales price, most lenders will reduce the amount they are willing to finance so that monthly payments and other housing expenses don't exceed 25%

## HOW MUCH CAN YOU PAY MONTHLY?

**I. Family income**

annual salaries (before deductions)  _____

bonuses, commissions  _____

interest, dividends  _____

other  _____

total annual income  _____

monthly income (divide annual total by 12)  _____

**II. Family expenses other than housing costs**

food  _____

clothing  _____

debt payments  _____

alimony or child-support payments  _____

education  _____

home furnishings  _____

life, health, auto insurance  _____

recreation  _____

transportation  _____

medical  _____

charities, other contributions  _____

other  _____

amount you would like to save  _____

total annual expenses  _____

monthly expenses (divide annual total by 12)  _____

**III. Housing budget**

monthly income, from Section I  _____

monthly expenses, from Section II  _____

maximum amount available for housing
(subtract expenses from income)  _____

of gross monthly income. Total monthly debt payments then must not exceed 33%.

To help you calculate the debt burden of hypothetical mortgages at various interest rates and terms, buy yourself a paperback book of mortgage amortization tables that will show the monthly principal and interest expense. If you have a personal computer, you can purchase software that will run amortization tables, and some real estate analysis programs will do much more. (One widely available book is *Interest Amortization Tables,* by Jack Estes, published by McGraw-Hill.) Then add in a monthly amount for your probable real estate taxes, homeowners insurance and utilities.

Loantech (P.O. Box 3635, Gaithersburg, MD 20878) sells pocket-sized 15- and 30-year mortgage loan slide charts for estimating maximum mortgage payments. It also sells, among other things, amortization schedules, a prequalifying service, and adjustable-rate mortgage analyses.

## CLEAN UP YOUR CREDIT FILE

Any lender is going to scrutinize your monthly income and outgo at the time you apply for the loan. Debts and other obligations reduce the amount of cash you can spend on housing, so try to clear the decks as much as possible before applying for a mortgage loan. Pay off as many high-interest consumer loans as possible. If you are planning to buy a new car, boat, or major furniture (paying by either cash or credit), postpone the purchases until after you've bought your home.

On the other hand, a good credit record requires that you have used credit in the past. Some people who have always been cash-only buyers find themselves hampered by their own prudence when it comes time to buy a home. If you have been diligently saving up a down payment and haven't been borrowing for two or three years, it's a good idea to create a record of credit activity during the year in which you are planning to buy a home. Stick to small-ticket items and make minimum payments promptly.

If you have a question about whether anything in your credit record might present a problem when seeking a loan, it would be wise to check on it before making your application. At best such problems cause delays. At worst, you can be turned down for a loan. A long delay after you have filled out a loan application could cause you to lose out on the interest rate commitment from a prospective lender.

Federal law gives you the right to know what's in your credit report. Get the names of the credit reporting agencies doing residential loan reviews in your area by writing to the Associated Credit Bureaus (P.O. Box 218300, Houston, TX 77218). Or ask real estate brokers and major lenders for the names of credit bureaus in your area. In most cases, you will need to write a letter including your full name, names of current and past spouses, your social security number and current and previous addressses going back five years. Expect to pay anywhere from $8 to $15.

If you discover an unfavorable report has been turned in by a creditor with whom you have disagreed, now is the time to seek a settlement. Depending on the problem, your record may still contain information on the case when you apply for a loan. However, a lender may view it more objectively if the file shows that the matter recently has been satisfactorily resolved. If your credit application is turned down, you are entitled to know why.

If you feel you have been tagged unfairly for nonpayment or slow payment, you should write a well-documented letter setting forth your understanding of the facts and file it with the credit bureau or bureaus in your area. If you aren't sure which bureaus have a file on you, find out from the problem creditor. Or, if the problem has been completely resolved, request in writing that the creditor inform all the reporting services to which it had sent information. This could take from 30 to 90 days.

When you finally make a loan application, the lender will request a complete update on your file, and you may be charged up to $100 or so for this credit check. In most cases, the credit agency will be asked by the lender to reverify your employer, salary, address, etc. If your company ordinarily does not release income and other personal data on employees, you should instruct your personnel office in writing to cooperate with the credit checker who calls.

Typically, your credit file will contain information covering the preceding three years. No adverse credit information, except bankruptcy, can be kept on file for more than seven years. Lenders look for these red flags: late payments, overextension, liens, garnishments and, the biggest flag of all, bankruptcy.

## PREQUALIFYING YOURSELF

Rules and formulas used to evaluate the creditworthiness of borrowers vary depending on the type of loan being sought. But whether you are seeking a conventional loan from a savings & loan or a government-backed VA or FHA loan from a mortgage company, the less you pay down, the more closely your finances will be examined. In the case of VA and FHA loans, the lender will want to know how many people you are supporting and their ages. Government rules require lenders to estimate your living costs, rather than take your word for it.

As you work through these worksheets and examine your budget, try to assess the impact homeownership will have on you and your family's spending patterns. Will you take fewer vacations? Will you spend less on clothing? Will the cost of commuting to work rise or fall?

Most importantly, how much will your tax bill go down—and your monthly take-home pay rise—once you begin taking big deductions for mortgage interest, which constitutes most of your monthly mortgage expense early in the term of the loan? Study the next chapter carefully to get a full appreciation of the range and variety of tax breaks you'll get from the purchase and ownership of your new home.

### How much down, how much borrowed?

In deciding how much cash to put down, remember that getting settled in a new home always costs more than people realize. You'll want to hold back some cash for furnishing, and add an extra cushion of cash if you're buying an older home that might surprise you with a plumbing or roofing expense.

Should you borrow as much as you can? When inflation was running as high or higher than mortgage interest rates, and you were paying back what you borrowed with dollars that were steadily loosing their purchasing power, the answer was easy: "The bigger the mortgage the better." Many homeowners and speculators in single-family residences made a killing in the 1970s by putting down miniscule down payments and then trading up to larger (or more) houses as inflation made their equity grow enormously. But is that still the best strategy in a climate of lower inflation, relatively low interest rates and lower marginal tax rates?

For most first-time buyers, there's no point in weighing the various trade-offs. Most will have to borrow to the hilt and scrape hard to come up with the minimum down payment. However, many so-called move-up buyers will come into a substantial sum of money when they sell their old homes. Their decision will be tougher: whether to invest the cash in the new home and take out a small mortgage, or invest the money and borrow a large amount.

Nationally, investment returns on average single-family homes recently have been modest compared with returns on such financial investments as stocks and bonds. Home values on average may continue to keep pace with inflation, and in some areas may do significantly better. But don't expect a repeat of the boom of the late 1970s.

You've got to assess the future of the economy in your home area and the demand for homes of the type, location and price range of the one you'll be buying. For example, within a given metropolitan area, some neighborhoods have appreciated very well, while othes have stagnated. And high-priced homes often go up relatively more than middle-market houses in the same city. In the mid-1980s, home prices were escalating rapidly in a boom area like Boston, but were depressed in many agricultural and oil-production cities of the Midwest, Texas and Oklahoma.

If you have unusually good job security, you may want to gamble on a bigger mortgage than someone in a precarious field of work. Job security will affect the kind of mortage you choose, too. If your job is safe in high-inflation or recessionary times and your earnings will likely keep pace with the cost of living, you'll be more comfortable with an adjustable mortgage than someone who lost ground in the last period of high inflation and high interest rates.

Remember that home equity—unlike financial assets such as bonds, CDs and dividend-paying stocks—pays no current income whatsoever, so you shouldn't pour everything you have into your home unless you have to. For example, if the stock market is moving upwards, your cash will be tied up in a home that is not paying you any income and which may be appreciating less rapidly than good-quality stocks. If you do put all your cash into your home and then need some money later, you can borrow against it, but you'll be paying at least 1.5% to 2% over the prime lending rate for a home equity loan, and usually more for a fixed-rate second mortgage.

## PREQUALIFYING WITH A LENDER

Now that you've got your financial affairs in order and checked out your credit record, the next step is a visit with a lender—mortgage company, savings & loan, bank or credit union—where you can translate all the data into hard facts about the types of mortgages suited to your particular needs and what your upper price limit will be.

A real estate agent also can prequalify you. Some agents will do a professional job—one that will give you the same information you would get from a lender. Just keep in mind, however, that the more costly the home you buy, the more an agent stands to earn in commission from the seller.

The prequalifying interview should be free to the potential borrower. And you are not obliged to use the lender who does the prequalifying interview. When you're ready to borrow, you'll need to talk with several competitive lenders, and you may make more than one loan application (even though each one will cost you some fees). Take all of your basic financial data to the prequalifying interview—the cash flow and balance sheets you've already prepared at home.

## KINDS OF LOANS

You'll want to find out how much mortgage debt you can carry under the most commonly available mortgages.

''Conventional mortgages'' are transactions between borrowers and institutions operating in the private sector of the economy. They are not insured or guaranteed by the government.

Traditionally they featured set monthly payments, fixed interest rates, extended loan terms and full amortization.

Because the 30-year fixed-rate mortgage is still the benchmark against which other loans can be compared, find out what size conventional 30-year loan you can qualify for under the guidelines issued by secondary-market mortgage buyers like Fannie Mae (the Federal National Mortgage Association) or Freddie Mac (the Federal Home Loan Mortgage Corporation). Because these institutions buy only loans that meet their criteria, such mortgages are often referred to as "conforming" loans.

Get information on a conforming 30-year fixed-rate mortgage, a one-year adjustable-rate mortgage, and perhaps a 15-year fixed-rate loan as well. Knowing what you can afford within these commonly used parameters is a useful starting point.

If you are planning to get a VA-guaranteed or FHA-insured mortgage, you may be able to get a bigger loan. However, keep in mind that sellers in a hot market are usually not eager to do business with buyers using this type of financing. They may expect to have plenty of would-be buyers using conventional mortgages, so it's not uncommon for sellers to put the phrase "no FHA and no VA financing" right in the sales contract.

Due to the extra paperwork and appraisal delays these loans often entail, it may take longer to reach settlement, and some sellers won't put up with that. In addition, under VA financing, the buyer is permitted to pay no more than a 1% loan origination fee ("point"), so if the lender is asking for more discount points, the seller will have to pay. For these reasons, it's a good idea to see if you can manage a home purchase without resorting to a FHA or VA mortgage.

When interest rates are changing rapidly, home shopping can be frustrating. What you can afford may vary from one week to the next. In such a market you can ask the institution prequalifying you to provide a computer list of the various size mortgages for which you qualify at the widely varying interest rates. Another option would be to figure it out yourself with a paperback book of amortization tables or real estate analysis software for your personal computer.

## GET YOUR EARNEST MONEY READY

Some people are short on liquid assets, but have substantial equity in their homes. This could pose a problem when they have to write a check for earnest money to submit to a seller along with their purchase contract. Earnest money shows the seller that you're a serious, qualified purchaser. (Of course, if the contract is not accepted or the deal later hits a snag through no fault of yours, you'll get the earnest money back, with interest if you specified in your offering contract that the money be held in an interest-bearing escrow account.)

If after assessing your resources you find that you'll be short on earnest money when it comes time to begin house hunting, consider getting a home equity loan—a line of credit secured by the equity in your current house.

Under a typical plan, the lender establishes a credit limit that won't exceed 70% to 90% of the appraised market value of your property, minus what you still owe on the mortgage and any other debts against the house. You pay some closing costs (appraisal, title search, attorney's fees) and, in many cases, an annual fee to maintain the account. The variable interest rate, adjusted monthly on the current balance, may run a margin of 1% to 4% above the base rate, usually the prime lending rate.

The handy thing about a home equity line of credit is that it's a loan you don't have to use until it's needed. Once established, it is ready for you to write a check against for the earnest money on your next purchase or to consolidate current debts at a lower interest rate. The balance owed will be repaid, along with your first mortgage, out of the sale proceeds from your current house.

To reiterate what we said above: As you prepare for the mortgage application process, you'll want to avoid adding to your current debt, so don't succumb to the temptation to use your new equity credit line for unneeded things.

The market for home equity loans has been very competitive in recent years, so shop carefully for the best terms on base rate, margin and closing costs.

# 3

# Home Sweet Tax Shelter

Your home—probably the biggest investment of your life—is likely to be the best tax shelter you'll ever enjoy, too.

Uncle Sam is standing by to serve as a generous partner in your investment, ready to subsidize your mortgage payments while you're paying for your house and willing to turn a blind eye to profit you make when you sell it—so long as you invest the money in your next principal residence.

Given the favored status of homeownership in America, it was no surprise that the sacrosanct deductions for mortgage interest and local property taxes survived the tax-break-busting Tax Reform Act of 1986. Homeowners not only held their own at a time many tax breaks were being sacrificed in the name of lower overall tax rates, they actually won a valuable new tax-saving right: the opportunity to use their homes for protection against the law's crackdown on the deduction of consumer interest.

There is no doubt that buying a home will cut your tax bill. But it will also complicate your tax life. If you don't itemize deductions now, you're almost sure to begin once you have mortgage interest and local property tax expenses to write off.

Consider that the interest portion of the first 12 monthly payments on a $100,000, 10%, 30-year mortgage is nearly $10,000—several times the 1987 standard deduction of $2,540 on an individual return or $3,760 on a joint return. Even when the standard deduction jumps to $3,000 and $5,000 in 1988, the interest outlay will still easily surpass it. You'll also get to deduct whatever you have to pay for state and local property taxes.

And once you begin itemizing, other expenses that are of no value to non-itemizers—such as charitable contributions and, if the totals exceeds certain thresholds, medical bills and certain employee and other miscellaneous costs—are transformed into tax-saving write-offs.

The interest and tax deductions just scratch the surface of the tax benefits attached to owning a home. While becoming a homeowner doesn't demand that you memorize chapter and verse of the tax law, you do need a general awareness of the rules if you are to take advantage of them. As is true with many areas of the tax law, what you don't know can hurt you.

This review is designed as a refresher for veteran homeowners in the process of moving, as well as a primer for first-time buyers. For a discussion of the tax implications of selling a home, see Chapter 17.

## POWERFUL TAX DEDUCTIONS

The opportunity to trade nondeductible rent payments for mostly deductible mortgage payments is a powerful lure for homeownership.

When doing the number crunching and budget squeezing to determine how much house you can afford, you have to study two sets of books: one for your actual monthly outlays, the other for the true, after-tax cost. In the early years of a home mortgage, nearly all of every monthly payment is interest. That's disappointing from one standpoint: it means you are paying off only a tiny bit of the loan principal. But it's great in terms of tax savings. Look again at the $100,000, 30-year, 10% mortgage cited above. Each year, interest and principal payments total $10,530. In the first year, $9,975 of that amount—95% of it—would be deductible as interest. Even in the 15th year, 79% of your payments would be deductible. In fact, only in the unlikely event that you live in the house for 24 years would the scales tip so that less than half of the total paid during the year would be tax-deductible interest.

Just what those deductions are worth depends on your marginal tax bracket which, in turn, depends on your income. The tax rates for 1987 and 1988, when the full tax cut ordered by the Tax Reform Act of 1986 will be in effect, are listed in the table below.

To judge the value of the tax deductions to you, estimate your taxable income for the year and find your tax bracket. If you fall in the top 38.5% tax bracket in 1987, for example, $1,000 in deductions saves you $385 in taxes. In other words, of each $1,000 of housing payments consisting of interest and property taxes, Uncle Sam pays $385 by reducing your federal income tax bill by that amount. When figuring the true after-tax cost of your house payments, remember to count any state income tax savings you'll pocket because of your deductions.

## Your tax bracket

The figure for taxable income is your income after all exemptions, adjustments and itemized deductions. If your taxable income on an individual return is $50,000, for example, you fall in the 35% tax bracket in 1987. That does not mean the government takes 35% of all of your taxable income. Only dollars that fall in the 35% tax bracket—those between $27,001 and $54,000—are taxed at that rate. The dollar amount shown in the right-hand column is the tax due on income that falls in lower brackets. On a $50,000 taxable income, then, the tax bill would be $5,301 (the tax due on the first $27,000) plus $8,050—35% of the $22,999 that falls between $27,001 and $50,000. The total bill would be $13,351.

*1987 tax rates*

**Taxable Income Tax—Individual Returns**

| | |
|---|---|
| Up to $1,800 | $0 plus 11% |
| $1,801 to $16,800 | $198 plus 15% |
| $16,801 to $27,000 | $2,448 plus 28% |
| $27,001 to $54,000 | $5,304 plus 35% |
| Over $54,000 | $14,754 plus 38.5% |

**Taxable Income Tax—Joint Returns**

| | |
|---|---|
| Up to $3,000 | $0 plus 11% |
| $3,001 to $28,000 | $330 plus 15% |

$28,001 to $45,000....................................$4,080 plus 28%
$45,001 to $90,000....................................$8,840 plus 35%
Over $90,000.......................................$24,590 plus 38.5%

*1988 tax rates*

**Taxable Income Tax—Individual Returns**
Up to $17,850...............................................$0 plus 15%
$17,851 to $43,140....................................$2,678 plus 28%
$43,141 to $100,480*.................................$9,759 plus 33%
Over $100,480......................................$28,678 plus 28%

**Taxable Income Tax—Joint Returns**
Up to $29,750...............................................$0 plus 15%
$29,751 to $71,900....................................$4,463 plus 28%
$71,901 to $171,900* .............................$16,265 plus 33%
Over $171,900......................................$48,998 plus 28%

*The top of the 33% bracket is extended by $10,920 for each dependent claimed on the return in addition to the personal exemptions for yourself and your spouse.

## The effects of tax reform

There is no denying that as tax reform brings down rates, the value of homeownership tax breaks—and all other deductions—is diluted. It's true that as the federal subsidy slips, home-ownership becomes more expensive, but that shouldn't scare you away from buying a home.

The key question for a potential homebuyer: "More expensive than what?" Renting? Hardly, because there are good reasons to believe the cost of renting will rise as a result of other parts of the tax reform package. The fact is, laments about the higher cost of owning a home are based on comparisons with what it *used* to cost, not on meaningful comparisons with today's or tomorrow's alternatives.

The National Association of Home Builders contends that tax reform hikes the cost of owning a home by an average of 10%. The argument goes something like this: Say a family's annual housing outlay is $13,920, of which $10,000 is deductible as interest and property tax. If they were in the 38% tax bracket in the pre-reform days of 1986, the deductions saved $3,800 in tax, leaving a $10,120 after-tax cost. In 1988, their expenses remain the same but they fall into the 28% tax bracket, providing a mere $2,800 subsidy. The after-tax cost of ownership rises to $11,120, or about 10% higher than in 1986.

When viewed in isolation, it appears that, despite all the talk to the contrary, homeowners took it on the chin. But if you take the total effect of tax reform into account, the lower rate at which all of your income is taxed will in most cases more than reimburse you for the "loss" you suffer because Congress cut tax rates. If you pay no more in pre-tax dollars for your house and you pay no more of your total income in taxes, the effect of reform is a redistribution of your tax burden, not an increase in living costs.

## Adjust your withholding

But what good are tax-saving deductions if you're worrying about coming up with the needed cash each month to make a mortgage payment? Fortunately, you don't have to wait until the following year when you file a tax return to cash in on the savings. As soon as you purchase your first home, or buy a new house that involves higher deductible expenses than your previous place, you probably can direct your employer to begin withholding less tax from your paychecks.

If you're self-employed, it's likely you'll be able to scale back your quarterly estimated tax payments beginning with the next one due.

To reduce withholding, you have to file a revised W-4 form with your employer. Get a copy of the form and its instructions from your personnel office or a local IRS office. The form can be complicated, but basically, for each $1,900 of added itemized deductions, you earn one extra withholding allowance. And each allowance you claim trims withholding from each paycheck, leaving you with more take-home pay to cover your mortgage.

## The record-keeping burden

Buying a home may be your first introduction to the endearing term "tax basis." The basis of your home is its value for tax purposes. It is the figure you will compare with the amount you get when you sell the place to determine whether you have a taxable profit in which the IRS is interested.

Although the basis of a home begins simply enough—as what you agree to pay for the house—it will change often between the day you buy and the time you sell. And, as discussed in Chapter 17, the basis of each home you own will affect the tax basis of the next one you buy. You have to keep track of all adjustments—for your entire life as a homeowner—to ensure that you are not overtaxed.

This record-keeping chore begins with sorting out the tax consequences of the closing costs you pay at settlement. (Those fees are discussed Chapter 13). Although a few of these expenses may be deducted in the year of the purchase, most are considered part of the cost of acquiring the house and are added to the basis.

First, consider the deductible closing expenses, since they have the most immediate financial consequences.

## Closing costs

**Points you pay to get your mortgage:** A "point" is a fee—1% of the loan—that the mortgage lender will charge you up front. Whether called a "discount point," "loan origination fee," or something else, it's really prepaid interest; for the buyer of a principal residence, it's fully deductible in the year paid, provided the points are for the use of the borrowed money rather than a fee to cover loan-processing costs.

Assume, for example, that to get a 9.5%, $100,000 mortgage you have to pay the lender three points (3% of the loan amount). You can write off that $3,000 on the tax return for the year of the purchase. The IRS even provides a special line for the deduction on Schedule A, in addition to the space for deducting the interest paid on your mortgage.

The right to deduct points fully in the year paid applies only to points paid on a mortgage to buy or improve you principal residence. Points paid on a mortgage to buy a vacation home, for example, don't get this special treatment. Neither does the one-point loan-processing fee charged on a VA or FHA mortgage, because it is assumed to be for services rather than use of the borrowed funds.

In cases where the points are not fully deductible in the year paid, the expense is deducted ratably over the life of the loan. On a 30-year mortgage, for example, 1/30th of the points would be deducted each year. If the house is sold before the mortgage is paid off, any as-yet-undeducted points are fully deductible in the year of the sale.

To protect the deduction in the year you buy, get a written statement from the lender listing points separately from fees for specific administrative services. Also, write a separate check to pay the points, rather than having the charge rolled into the mortgage proceeds.

**Prepaid interest or property tax adjustments:** If your costs include reimbursing the seller for interest or taxes he or she paid in advance for a period you will actually own the home, you may deduct those amounts as though you paid the interest or taxes directly. Even if such adjustments don't show up on the settlement sheet, you can deduct them. If the seller has made such prepayments but you are not required to reimburse him at settlement, the prepayments are considered to be included in the price you're paying for the house. In that case you can still deduct the prepaid interest and taxes, and reduce your basis in the house by the same amount.

**Additional closing costs** and other acquisition expenses are generally not deductible unless you qualify to write them off as job-related moving expenses, which are discussed later. Instead, many of these out-of-pocket costs are added to the purchase price to hike your basis. Since additions to basis don't produce any immediate tax savings, you might be tempted to ignore them. But that would be a costly mistake. Sooner or later you are going to have to know the adjusted basis of your home, and the higher you can prove it to be, the better. The bigger your basis when you sell, the smaller any potentially taxable profit you have to report to the IRS.

Maintaining detailed records from the beginning is not only the best way to assure accuracy. It's also a lot easier than trying to reconstruct your basis later on. After you acquire a home, set up a file immediately to keep a running tab on your adjusted basis.

Besides the purchase price, the following acquisition costs can be included in the basis of your home:

▶ Appraisal and credit report fees
▶ Mortgage origination and assumption fees
▶ Attorney and notary fees
▶ Recording and title examination fees
▶ State and county transfer taxes
▶ Property inspection fees
▶ Title insurance premiums
▶ Utility connection charges
▶ Amounts owed by the seller that you agree to pay, such as part of the real estate agent's selling commission or back taxes and interest.
▶ The cost of an option if you purchase under a rent-with-option-to-buy deal. It is also possible that part of the rent payments made prior to closing may be added to the basis if they were applied to the purchase price. Check with a tax attorney or accountant about how payments under your contract should be treated.

## THE TAX SIDE OF OWNING

It's easy to take advantage of the basic tax benefits—the write-offs for mortgage interest and property taxes. If your mortgage is held by a financial institution, you will receive a statement early each year showing how much deductible interest you shelled out in the previous year. (The IRS gets a copy, too, so make sure the figures are square on your 1040 form.) The statement will also show the amount you can deduct for property taxes if you make those payments through your lender. Otherwise, copies of tax bills and your canceled checks provide the information you need to complete your tax return.

Your tax situation is more complicated if your mortgage is held by an individual or you are buying with the help of "creative financing" (a loan from the seller). The specifics of your arrangement control what part of your payments is deductible and what portion is not.

Assume, for example, that the seller holds a $10,000 second mortgage that calls for interest-only payments for three years and a balloon payoff of the entire principal at the end of that period. In that case, all of your payments on the note during the three years would be deductible as interest. Unfortunately, not all arrangements are so straightforward.

Consider a "zero interest" deal involving seller financing at the best of all interest rates: 0%. The IRS doesn't believe such generosity exists, so the law assumes that the financing costs are actually built into the price of the home. The result is that the buyer's basis is reduced by subtracting the value of interest-free financing from the sales price. Also, the buyer gets to treat part of each payment—after payments made during the first six months—as tax-deductible interest. Just how much the buyer/borrower can deduct depends on the repayment schedule and IRS tables listing "imputed interest" rates.

Other special rules apply to graduated payment mortgages, shared-appreciation mortgages and other "creative" financing plans. The more you stray from conventional financing, the more you need to consult with an attorney or accountant to discuss any tax twists and turns attached to your home buying plans.

## Local assessments

In addition to real estate taxes, it is not unusual for local governments to assess homeowners for services or benefits provided during the year. Such fees are becoming more and more common in some areas, as local officials search for ways to hold down property taxes. These bills should go into your tax file because, depending on what the charge is for, it could be either a deductible expense or an addition to your basis.

In general, assessments for benefits that tend to increase the value of your property—sidewalks, for example—should be added to the basis of your property. Special charges for repairs or maintenance or local benefits, such as sewers or roads, however, can be deducted as additional local taxes. Fees for specific services, such as garbage collection, are neither deductible nor additions to basis.

## Improvements and repairs

Monthly payments are just the beginning of the costs of owning a home. You can count on spending plenty of money over the years maintaining, repairing and improving your property. Here, too, Uncle Sam gets involved.

Work around the house is divided between projects considered repairs and those constituting capital improvements that enhance—rather than just maintain—the value of your home. The distinction is critically important. The cost of repairs is a nondeductible personal expense. The cost of improvements is nondeductible, too, but such expenses are considered additions to the basis of your property.

To qualify as a capital improvement, the expense has to be for something that adds value to you home, prolongs its life or adapts it to new uses. Adding a bathroom or deck, replacing a furnace or water heater, putting in new plumbing or wiring, and landscaping the yard are examples of improvements that increase your basis.

Repairs, on the other hand, merely maintain the home's condition. Fixing a gutter, painting a room or replacing a window pane, for example, would be considered repairs rather than capital improvements. In some cases, though, the cost of projects that would ordinarily be considered repairs—such as painting a room—can be added to basis if the work is done as part of an extensive remodeling or restoration of your home. Also, some major repairs—such as extensive patching of a roof—may qualify as improvements.

There is no laundry list of what the IRS considers an improvement. But the better your records, the better your chances of pushing up your basis to reflect improvements on your property. Keep detailed records of any work done that might qualify as an improvement. It's better to keep papers you might not need than to toss out a receipt that could save you money. In addition to saving receipts and canceled checks, keep notes to remind yourself exactly what was done, when and by whom.

When toting up the cost of improvements, be sure to include any incidental costs. If you pay to have your lot surveyed as part of installing a fence, for example, the cost of the survey can be added to your basis. Although you can count what you pay hired workers, you are not allowed to add anything for your own time and effort if you do the work yourself.

### The latest tax break

Keeping track of basis-boosting improvements is more important than ever now that Congress has given homeowners a loophole in the general crackdown on the deductibility of consumer interest. The Tax Reform Act of 1986 ordered a gradual phase-out of the right to deduct "consumer interest," a category that includes interest on car loans, student loans, credit card accounts . . . just about every kind of loan—except mortgages. For 1987, taxpayers may deduct 65% of their consumer interest; 40% in 1988; 20% in 1989; and just 10% in 1990. For 1991 on, there will be no deduction at all for consumer interest.

However, homeowners have a safety valve. If you borrow against your home—via either a second mortgage or a home-equity line of credit—interest on the loan is deductible regardless of what you use the money for. There is a limit, though, on how much you can borrow and preserve the interest deduction. Tax deductible borrowing may not exceed the cost of your home plus the value of any improvements. Basically, the limit forbids the deduction of interest when you borrow against appreciation-generated equity in your home.

There is an important exception to the cost-plus-improvement cap: You can exceed it, and still get to deduct the interest, if the borrowing is to pay educational or medical expenses. The deductibility of mortgage interest—whether on regular mortgages or home equity line of credit—applies to your principal residence and a second home.

Here's how it works: Say you bought your home a few years back for $50,000 and have made improvements costing $15,000, but, thanks to appreciation, the place is now worth $115,000. The most you can borrow with full deductibility of interest is $65,000, and that amount includes any remaining balance on your first mortgage. You may borrow more, of course, and a lender would probably be glad to lend you up to 80% of your unencumbered equity, but the IRS won't let you deduct the interest on borrowings exceeding the $65,000 cost-plus-improvement amount.

If you add another $10,000 in improvements, your reservoir of tax-deductible borrowing would rise to $75,000.

This new tax benefit may be of little use to first-time homebuyers. Assume you buy a $100,000 home with 20% down. Your deductible-borrowing limit is $100,000 but it's doubtful any financial institution will permit you to borrow more than the 80% loan already outstanding on your first mortgage. But over the years, as the home's value appreciates, you will find yourself in a position to make interest-deductible borrowing against your $20,000 down payment. When the home is worth $125,000, it is likely that a lender would approve a $10,000 to $15,000 line of credit, all of the interest on which would be deductible.

The real value of the new tax benefit will become apparent as you trade up to more expensive homes. Although the rules do not permit deductible borrowing against appreciation equity, whenever you roll the profit from one home into another, your cost-plus-improvement cap jumps to include all of the appreciation from the former home. Assume, for example, your first home cost $50,000 and you made no improvements. As long as you own it, $50,000 is your limit for tax-deductible borrowing, even if the house appreciates in value to $100,000. But if you sell that house and buy another for $100,000, you can instantly borrow against that amount and deduct the interest.

## Refinancing

There are two important tax points regarding refinancing— trading in one mortgage for another. Homeowners refinance either to reduce their monthly payments with a new lower-rate mortgage, or to tap equity in a home with a larger first mortgage, rather than by adding a second trust.

For whatever reason you refinance, if the lender holding your original mortgage slaps on a prepayment penalty, the amount is considered interest and is fully deductible in the year you pay it.

The second issue involves points you pay when you refinance. In a controversial 1986 decision, the IRS announced that points paid on refinancing are not fully deductible in the year paid, except to the extent the funds are used for home improvements.

Here's an example of the IRS position: A homeowner with a $100,000 mortgage refinances at $120,000 and uses $20,000 to build a swimming pool. Assume also that two points ($2,400) were charged. Since one-sixth of the money went for a home improvement, one-sixth of the points—or $400—may be deducted in the year paid. The rest must be deducted evenly over the life of the loan. On a 30-year mortgage, that would mean one-thirtieth or the remaining $2,000—$66.66—would be deducted each year, assuming the homeowner remembers to do so.

This issue bears watching by all homeowners. In the spring of 1987, legislation was pending in Congress to reverse the IRS position and permit the deduction of points on refinancing, just as with points on a mortgage for original purchase of a principal residence. Also, it was considered inevitable that some taxpayers would challenge the IRS in court, in an effort to win the full deduction.

# 4

## Defining Your
## Housing Needs

Now that you know *how much* home you can afford, it's time to do some hard thinking about *what kind* of home you want and need. This chapter and the next two—dealing with location and kinds of housing—will help you narrow the choices.

Buying a piece of real estate is a science. Buying a home is an art. The science is getting the legal and financial parts right. The art is finding a property that you can be happy living in.

You can hire all the help you need with the technical side. The nontechnical part is another matter. Only you know what you like. If you don't decide what you like before wading into the market, someone out there will try to make up your mind for you.

Your best preparation for home buying is to be clear about your needs, your financial ability, your preferences and your prejudices. The central questions: What kind of home do you want, and where do you want it? If you are sure about those things, you will be immune to pressure tactics and hype.

At any given time in a metropolitan area of a million inhabitants, thousands of residential properties are for sale. With a little thought you could divide them into a dozen or more categories: homes falling within various price ranges, those within certain types of neighborhoods, new or resale homes, townhouses, homes within a particular school distict and so forth. Unfortunately you still would be left with several hundred potential homes in each category. Start with the general—your price range and approximate location—and then move to the specific: neighborhood, age and type of home, and kind of ownership (condominium or co-op).

Shopping only within your chosen location can scale down the range of properties to be inspected. Finally, examining only selected properties within your price range should bring the operation within manageable proportions.

Knowing your financial limits is a good beginning. However, you probably will find 10 or 15 entirely different sorts of homes within your price range. Decide now whether you want to be on the east or west side of town, whether you will accept a cookie-cutter housing development or will go to any length to avoid that, whether you can handle a "fixer-uppper." Otherwise, you're in for an emotional tug of war when you find the living room you want in a house on the west side and the school district you want on the east side.

It can't be overstated: Focus on the location and general quality of the property. Don't go chasing an exact price or a particular feature, be it a deck, a high-efficiency furnace, or a finished basement. Price can be worked out in negotiation with the seller (given the right general ballpark), and a good-quality home in a good location can be tailored to your specific needs later.

There are two phases to a home-seeking strategy. In the first you are getting the feel for different areas and an idea about what is being offered at what price. From that you draw up a list of specifications. The second phase is the search to fill those specifications.

## MAKE A LIST OF NEEDS AND WANTS

Most buyers are in search of something they cannot describe. They may be trying, often unknowingly, to replicate a childhood home, if it was a happy one. If it wasn't happy, whatever stands out about that home goes on the buyer's negative list. This doesn't mean that they are looking for the same red-brick house with privet hedge, but rather they seek a feeling, an ambience. It could be a feeling of spaciousness, warmth, airiness, the amount of daylight, the quality of the light, coziness, the abundance of nooks and crannies, a parklike backyard.

If you're looking for a home with the help of an experienced agent, he or she should be able to help you define your needs and wants. However if you are too vague, a really good agent may decide not to waste time on you and you could end up with someone who is more a hindrance than help. He or she may have endless patience, but no direction.

Start your want list by recalling houses you have liked and write down a description of each. Since you have already determined your price range, that combined with the want list below, will give you a sieve through which to sift the dozens of ads you will read in conducting your search. Keep in mind, though, that the final choice of a home almost always requires compromising.

| | MUSTS | WANTS (rank) | | |
| --- | --- | --- | --- | --- |
| | | high | medium | low |
| Commuting time: | | | | |
| less than one hour | _____ | ____ | _____ | ___ |
| less than half-hour | _____ | ____ | _____ | ___ |
| Setting | | | | |
| suburban | _____ | ____ | _____ | ___ |
| urban | _____ | ____ | _____ | ___ |
| country | _____ | ____ | _____ | ___ |
| Particular neighborhood | _____ | ____ | _____ | ___ |
| Particular school district | _____ | ____ | _____ | ___ |
| Public transportation | _____ | ____ | _____ | ___ |
| Zoning laws (parking, pets, in-law suites, etc. | _____ | ____ | _____ | ___ |
| Particular architectural style | _____ | ____ | _____ | ___ |
| 1 story, 2 stories, split level | _____ | ____ | _____ | ___ |
| Yard | _____ | ____ | _____ | ___ |
| Number of bedrooms | _____ | ____ | _____ | ___ |
| Number of baths | _____ | ____ | _____ | ___ |
| Bath in master bedroom | _____ | ____ | _____ | ___ |

| | | | | |
|---|---|---|---|---|
| Eat-in-kitchen | _____ | ____ | _____ | ___ |
| Separate dining room | _____ | ____ | _____ | ___ |
| Basement | _____ | ____ | _____ | ___ |
| Expandability | _____ | ____ | _____ | ___ |
| Fix-up house | _____ | ____ | _____ | ___ |
| Energy efficiency | _____ | ____ | _____ | ___ |
| Fireplace | _____ | ____ | _____ | ___ |
| Garage | _____ | ____ | _____ | ___ |
| Other: | _____ | ____ | _____ | ___ |

## MAKE A "DON'T WANT" LIST, TOO

Say you have a well-defined want list, you screen ads carefully, you carefully instruct every agent you work with, and you refuse to look at any property that doesn't have the requisite family room, master bath or whatever your firm requirements are. After weeks of looking, the seemingly perfect home shows up. It has every one of the items on your list.

First there is euphoria over finding all the desired features in one package. Then, to the bewilderment of the agent or the seller of this perfect home, you go silent. You may announce, "I need more time to think it over." That thinking-it-over time might take hours, days, possibly even a week. At last your final answer is no.

Why does the perfect home fail to win the only test that counts: whether, when it comes right down to crunch time, you are willing to plunk down a deposit? The reason may be that you failed to identify your "don't wants."

Finding a home with all the desired features is only half the challenge. The property must also be free from objectionable features.

Objections, which constitute your don't want list, are of two major types: personal prejudice and economic fear. And there's plenty of overlap between the two.

To avoid getting into a situation where you have to veto a house that has everything you say you want, do some systematic soul searching.

Go back through your past again, and this time think of all the homes you have not liked, whether you lived in them or merely visited them. Include the ones occupied by friends, acquaintances, family—all the houses and apartments that for one reason or another made a negative impression on you.

If they gave you a "I wouldn't want to live here" feeling, now is the time to identify the causes. Make a written list of the things you didn't like.

Identify your personal objections, whatever they are: windowless inside kitchens, small bathrooms, northern exposures, frame construction, casement windows, dormers, fake brick siding, floor plan, scary neighborhood, too little daylight, house incongruous with its surroundings, too far out, too close to the road, too much of a child-rearing neighborhood, proximity to a commercial zone, deadend street, heavy traffic, street with no trees, street with overgrown trees, whatever.

Also consider things that other buyers might object to. Heavy traffic on the street might not bother you, but it's legitimate to be concerned that it might make resale tougher.

Other buyers might also balk at buying your house if it's overimproved. A home may have great entertaining space, a swimming pool and extensive landscaping—all features that are normally attractive to upscale buyers. But if the house is the only upgraded home in an area of ordinary homes, it will not be attractive to the typical high-income buyer. That makes it an interesting white elephant, and it could be a terrific bargain if you can negotiate the price down to reflect the home's wrong location. Such bargains can be deceptive though: sweet on the buying end and sour on the selling end.

After you have your list of things you don't want in a home, assign them weights. Decide which objections are negotiable and which aren't. You might, for example, give in for a house with a western garden when you really wanted a southern one, but you would not give in on a heavily trafficked street.

If you are buying a home with a spouse or a partner, compare your don't-want lists. Frequently, the person with the strongest objections is the silent partner of the team. The more vocal one may take the lead in putting together the "want " list, but when it comes down to crunch time, it is often the silent one who produces a veto, often for an objection not voiced previously or not even thought about until then.

Besides harming the home-hunting process, these out-of-the-blue vetoes can put terrific strains on a relationship. Agents, mortgage loan oficers and escrow agents never cease to be amazed at how a couple may know all about each other's tastes in food, vacations, cars, clothes and entertainment and not be aware of strongly held prejudices and opinions about what makes a permanent place to live a home. Since rental apartment living is so often a matter of expediency or convenience, it doesn't offer an adequate test.

Objections are much more elusive than demands because they don't get thought about or talked about as much. But if you know yours, as well as their relative importance, you will be ahead in the home-hunting game.

# 5

# Choosing a Neighborhood

You've probably heard the old cliché that the three major determinants of housing value are 1) location, 2) location, and 3) location. Like many cliches, it's basically true.

When an agent rushes into the office with news of a hot new listing, the first question colleagues ask is not "How much?" or "How big?" but "Where is it?".

No single factor affects the value of a home as much as location. If you can't afford what you want *where* you want it, sacrifice something inside the house rather than sacrifice the location. You can add a second bathroom or install hardwood floors to bring a house up to your standards, but you can't improve the neighborhood singlehandedly. Better to take a house that needs work in a good neighborhood than to take one at the same price (or even a bit lower) that's all dolled up but in a marginal location.

Price doesn't guarantee a fine location either. Just because a builder puts a $150,000 house on a particular site doesn't mean the market will justify that price. Some builders, in an effort to fatten their profit, can't resist gambling on a cheap piece of land, often to their later regret.

Obviously, everyone can't live behind the country club overlooking the seventh fairway—nor would many buyers want to. A good location, like many other features of a home, is relative. Confirmed city dwellers won't be put off by a restaurant or corner deli on the block. But suburbanites might find the same low-key establishments intrusive.

## WHAT IS "LOCATION" ANYHOW?

Depending on the market, "location" can be a city, a town or a county. Location also is a neighborhood. It may be a home on a particular plot of land. Consider all three in choosing your home. Pick a town or community with a character and style that match your own. Then, scout out the town's best neighborhood—within your price range. Finally, zero in on the best home on the best lot within that neighborhood.

Much of the value of a home rests in its surrounding economic and social environment—its neighborhood. In general, the more defined a neighborhood, the more likely that homes located there will maintain their value. You are looking for more than just a cluster of homogeneous properties. A few blocks of carefully tended homes otherwise surrounded by blight isn't a viable neighborhood. Typically, it takes at least a dozen blocks, marked off by recognizable boundaries, for a neighborhood to sustain its character. The boundary might be a park, a highway, a campus, a river, a county line, a string of stores—anything that interrupts the pattern. One highly visible boundary gives residents a sense of belonging within it. Several make the neighborhood identification even stronger.

In addition to being located in the right neighborhood, a home must not clash with its surroundings. A poor fit imposes a harsh penalty on any home's value. Pick any $1,000,000 home in the poshest neighborhood of your city. Mentally move it to the worst slum you can imagine and guess what it would be worth.

Next pick a setting in between—say a nice middleclass community. If you have an appraiser's eye for value, you will recognize that bringing that $1,000,000 mansion from the slums where it is unsalable to a mid-way location won't restore even half its value. What's true for a transplanted mansion is just as true for a $250,000 house in a $70,000 neighborhood. Be especially wary of the over-improved house in a neighborhood of less houses; even if you love it, it may be hard to find others who feel just as you do when the time comes to sell.

Some homes command premium prices because of the special cachet of their neighborhoods. Even the plainest, smallest homes on Beacon Hill in Boston, Nob Hill in San Francisco, Beverly Hills in Los Angeles, and Georgetown in Washington, D.C., command high prices on a per-square-foot basis. Professional appraisers call such premiums "caprice value."

In any city, some neighborhoods enjoy inflated values because the "right" people live there. By comparison, other neighborhoods with strong schools or other highly desirable features may be undervalued because they aren't "in." A buyer who is indifferent to fashion can find good values in neighborhoods that offer desirable amenities and services—and end up with a lot more house for the money.

Deliberately choosing to pay caprice value can be a perfectly sound investment, if social prestige is very important to you. If you want to buy a home with a socially desirable address, make sure the high price is in line with the market. Get a professional appraisal. Properties in prestige areas sometimes attract speculators who hope to make exhorbitant profits off unwary buyers, especially wealthy newcomers from out of town. And not all residents of such neighborhoods are above doing a little "fishing" for gullible buyers.

### CHECK IT OUT

If you're looking for a new home in an area where you already live, you'll have a good sense of the strengths and weaknesses of various parts of town, and you can do your neighborhood scouting on your own, without an agent.

But if you're coming from out of town, you'll need help, especially if you're relocating on short notice. Try to find acquaintances or friends of friends in the area you're moving to, and get their opinions of neighborhoods. If you're being relocated to a branch office of your current employer, talk to your new colleagues and secure the services (at your employer's cost) of a relocation firm that works with real estate agents in your new area. Long-distance house-hunting is very difficult, and it can be smoothed by the services of professionals. Try to schedule several lengthy house-hunting trips, allowing enough time to drive around the whole area and get a feel for neighborhoods.

Don't overlook the obvious. Make sure you choose a place you'll enjoy living in six months after moving in. If you like it, others will in the future when you're ready to sell.

The look and feel of a community as you drive around its neighborhoods can't be quantified, but it's important. Trees, shrubs, cul-de-sacs, curved streets and landscaping around small retail stores are good signs. But unless you already live there, you need to probe deeper.

Read up on the local politics and history. It will offer clues to the future. The chamber of commerce, the town hall and the local library are other good sources for background. They also may have information on population and income trends. County and city governments also can provide critical tax information and zoning regulations.

Start your research by getting a detailed map. It should indicate schools, fire departments, parks, lakes and shopping areas. Ask the local real estate board or title company for prices of homes in the desired neighborhoods and jot them down to give you a base for comparison shopping. Use the map to familiarize yourself with the area, and to get a general feel for the proximity of individual homes to schools, stores and the like, once you begin househunting.

If time permits, attend a community meeting. A political fundraiser, a PTA meeting, a zoning hearing or church or synagogue service will enable you to meet some of the residents.

Visit the schools! Schools affect the taxes you pay on your property. And good schools increase property values for parents and non-parents alike. Even if you aren't a parent, don't neglect to inquire about the quality of neighborhood schools. What schools are nearby? How many elementary schools are operating? What is the average class size in grades 1 through 6? How do most children get to school? How do students in the town or county rate on standardized tests? What enrichment courses are offered? Where do graduating high school seniors go to college? Parents may want to meet the neighborhood school principal.

Shop the stores. Note the kind of stores and the quality of the merchandise. Merchants have to be responsive to subtle changes in the socioeconomic level of their patrons. They buy what they perceive their customers want. For example, the mix of staples to "luxury" items in a supermarket might tell you something about whether it's a neighborhood you'd feel comfortable in.

Do at least one rush-hour practice commute. Make it on a weekday at the time you normally would be en route. Use the public transportation system. How often do buses and subways run during morning and evening rush-hours? What is the weekend and off-peak schedule? If you are depending on buses or trains to get to work, or for other commuting, try to determine whether there are proposals to reroute or drop the line.

Consider your travel patterns. Figure what roads you might travel to deliver children to day-care centers or school. Will it be convenient to stop after work to pick up groceries, or will buying bread and milk entail a lengthy side trip? Does the surrounding community offer recreation and entertainment that suits your interests, or will you find yourself facing frequent lengthy drives for a movie, concert, or athletic contest?

## WEIGH THE NEGATIVES

A town or neighborhood can decline, or take off toward renewal before home sales figures reflect it. Before you take a fancy to a home, rule out locations where negative factors outweigh positives.

**Crime.** Pass up casual conversations here and go to the police precinct station for records of robberies, break-ins, vandalism, assaults and drug-related problems. Is crime increasing, decreasing or staying about the same? Parents with young children will want to know how safe their children will be going to and from school and playing in the neighborhood.

**Traffic.** Heavy traffic is a major drawback in any residential area. It generates noise and pollution. Of course, being on a busy street is less a problem for highrise condominium dwellers than for families in detached one- and two-story homes. Even so, a unit on the quiet side of the building certainly is more desirable than one where you can hear the steady roar of automobiles.

**Visual pollution.** Look for public utility substations and transformers, radio or television broadcasting towers, gas stations, auto dealerships, salvage yards, overnight parking for commercial auto fleets, bus stops, ball fields where night games are played.

**Smells and sounds.** Does the commuting pattern create air pollution or smog in the area? What about food-processing or chemical plants? Even something as delightful in small doses as the smell of bread wafting from a bakery is a nuisance when you never can escape it.

Visit the area during the day and at night, and on weekdays as well as weekends. Does it lie in the flight pattern for airplanes? Is it too close to a bus stop, fire station or school?

**Overcrowding.** Are roads, parks, stores, and pools too crowded? Are there too many cars parked on streets and in driveways? Is there any sign that homes are being used as rooming houses or broken into multiple housekeeping units?

Full-blown blight is easy to spot. What you need to be alert to are the earliest signs of neglect or decay. A neighborhood that appears slightly down-at-the-heels may not reveal any other signs of decline . . . yet. Perhaps nothing is broken, littered or really shabby. You still should try to find out why the level of maintenance has slipped. Is the ratio of owners to renters shifting? Are such municipal services as sidewalk and road repairs being postponed or reduced?

## EXAMINE THE LOT

Give some thought to whether you will enjoy living on a lot before you fall in love with the house on it. Do you spend a lot of time outdoors? How much privacy do you want? Will you maintain the grounds yourself, or will you hire someone for such routine chores as mowing the lawn and trimming hedges? Do you want to be involved with landscaping, or would you prefer an established yard with mature trees and shrubs?

Once you find a home you like, give the land it sits on more than a perfunctory once-over. Step back and notice the overall pattern of blocks and streets in a neighborhood. Most subdivisions are laid out in lots and blocks. A section of land is blocked off and divided into lots. Use a map to determine the physical layout of a community that has piqued your interest. Common street patterns are: gridiron, curvilinear, loop, and Radburn Plan. (See illustrations on next page.) In addition, many newer developments use what is called a cluster plan.

**Gridiron.** Lots generally are rectangular, and homes face the street. In neighborhoods where lots are large, traffic is limited and back alleys are safe, the pattern works best. But such a layout can be monotonous, and the design doesn't provide for open spaces and recreational areas.

**Curvilinear.** When done well, this system is an improvement over the gridiron. Traffic patterns are improved by meshing major roads with secondary streets and cul-de-sacs. Small parks often are placed at intersections.

**Loop streets.** This pattern reduces the traffic on residential streets while still providing good access to the main highway. Compared to the gridiron system, fewer lots face busy roads, and there is more open space.

**Radburn Plan.** Named after Radburn, N.J., where the plan originated, it clusters units into large cul-de-sac blocks. There is open space between each cluster, and pedestrians are well separated from auto traffic.

**Cluster.** This plan groups homes around cul-de-sacs. Street patterns are more varied, and there can be a dramatic increase in the amount of land available for recreation and other community uses.

Each system has its pluses and minuses. An older neighborhood may not have an ideal layout or the best traffic flow, but those drawbacks may be more than offset by its proximity to downtown offices, theaters and restaurants. Similarly, a new development offers a quiet cul-de-sac for bike riding and roller skating but requires a long commute to work. Which of these features are more important to you?

Finally, don't overlook the physical dimensions and composition of the lot itself. Shape, size, slope, and soil composition should be noted.

**Shape.** Look for a basically rectangular or square lot with adequate road frontage and enough land behind the house. Lots with unusual shapes can make it harder to sell your home.

## COMMON STREET PATTERNS

GRIDIRON

CURVILINEAR

LOOP

RADBURN

CLUSTER PLAN

**Size.** A lot that falls pretty much within the average for the neighborhood probably is the best bet. Bigger isn't necessarily better. Many couples don't have time for large-scale grounds-keeping, and help is expensive and hard to find. Acreage that can't be subdivided can keep a property on the market.

**Slope.** The contour of a lot determines not only what already was built on it but what could be added after you move in. A home built on a steep hillside may preclude the addition of two extra bedrooms that might be needed later by a growing family. Slope and the ability of the soil to absorb water combine to determine where and how fast water drains from it. Low areas that hold water can mean trouble inside and outside the house. Muddy spots are a nuisance, particularly just outside the back door. They may be only a symptom, however, for the real problem inside. A wet basement goes beyond the nuisance level. Drying it out permanently will likely be expensive. It may even be impossible.

**Soil composition.** Look for a good layer of topsoil that will support a healthy lawn and border plantings. Is there an established vegetable or flower garden? An inexpensive soil analysis can provide you with answers about soil quality. Some lots are scraped bare in construction and extensive preparation may be needed for a top-notch garden. Soil composition also affects settling of a house. Unstable soil conditions can make settling a never-ending process, leading to cracked walls and other eyesores or even damaging foundations and other structural components in the home. Contaminated soil can raise health anxieties or even cause illness.

# 6

# Many Kinds of Homes

The population size, land, climate, history, and even ethnic heritage of a region determine the kinds of homes in its local housing inventory. So by targeting a particular locale and price range, you've already made some preliminary decisions about the kind of housing you'll eventually select.

If you've chosen a particular school district in a small county, for example, your choice may not include condominium townhouses or cooperative apartments. You may be restricted to finding the single-family detached dwelling that best suits your needs.

If you've been thinking about a mobile or manufactured home, local zoning law will dictate where you live, and the choices will usually be very few. A large metropolitan area should offer a good mix of all kinds of homes. But in many expensive locales, like the New York metro area, the middle-budget homebuyer will find the choice limited to a very small condominium close in or a slightly larger detached home at a lengthy commute.

Here's a run-down on the major kinds of housing, with their pros and cons:

## SINGLE-FAMILY DETACHED HOUSES

The single-family detached house is the essence of homeownership, with all its joys and headaches. You have four walls to call your own, and often a yard or garden, too. These offer privacy, but they also present a burden of upkeep (painting, planting, mowing, snow removal, etc.) that would be less or non-existent in a condominium townhouse or apartment.

The big choice in detached housing is the older home or something new.

## THE NEW HOUSE

### Advantages:

**Predictable cost and low maintenance.** Assuming competent design and craftsmanship in the new house (which is not always a good assumption today), the major mechanical systems—plumbing, wiring, heating and air-conditioning systems—as well as structural members should hold up for a long time after purchase. You can expect a minimum of repair and fix-up headaches, so the monthly mortgage payment and utilities should be the entire cost of maintaining the property into the near future.

**Modernity.** New homes may have the latest in floor plan designs, kitchen and bathroom layouts, as well as adequate storage and closet space.

**Cheaper to furnish.** Decorating costs can be reduced because many new homes come with wall-to-wall carpeting and window treatments, as well as more installed appliances and fixtures.

**Energy efficiency.** A new house should be well insulated and should come outfitted with storm windows. It should be less expensive to heat and cool than a comparably sized older home.

**Recreational features.** Community swimming pools, craft workshops and fully equipped gymnasiums often are found in large, new developments. Some even have tennis courts and bridle paths for residents' use.

### Disadvantages:

**Location.** Communities tend to grow from the center out, so new developments usually are located on the fringes of suburbia. That means a long commute to downtown jobs, museums, restaurants and theaters.

**Uneven quality.** Shoddy construction always is a concern when buying a new home, because many structural flaws take time to show themselves. They may be the result of a marginal builder looking for ways to cut costs, but they can surface in houses built by large well-known firms, too.

**The raw look.** In all but the most carefully planned and expensive projects, developers tend to skimp on trees, foundation plantings and lawns. New developments can look downright barren. And, if substantial sections are yet to be built, graded and paved, buyers should expect to encounter noise, dust, mud and a good deal of general nuisance.

**Look-alikes.** Brick chimney, stone chimney; white shutters, brown shutters; garage on the left, garage on the right—those may be your only choices among the houses in a new development. Some people might like the consistency such look-alikes give to the character of a development. Others detest it, preferring to own a house with at least a few unique characteristics.

## THE OLDER HOUSE

### Advantages:

**Location.** An older home often is situated near work, schools, shopping and transportation.

**Size.** Many older houses have large rooms with high ceilings, or lots of rooms that can be remodeled to suit your needs. You often get a lot more square feet (and often cubic feet) for your money in an older home.

**Individuality.** If you want a house with character, and perhaps even a history of its own, consider an old home. Middle-aged houses often reflect the love and care that have been lavished on them through such owner-added touches as crown moldings, carved fireplace mantels and built-in bookcases.

**Better construction.** This is often, but not necessarily, true of older homes. It's something you have to check out case by case. If you respect the quality of slate roofs, copper gutters and chimney flashing, hardwood floors, and plaster walls, you're more likely to find them in an older house than in a new house in the same price range.

**Lower property taxes.** Property taxes on an older home may be less than on a comparable new home. Then again, they could be more, but be less likely to rise as rapidly as they might in a new community or development where streets, sewers, schools and public utilities have yet to be built.

**Ambience.** Mature trees and lawns and a variety of architectural styles, as well as a range of color and texture of materials, present a more varied environment.

## Disadvantages:

**Functional inferiority.** Unless an older house has been modernized, its floor plan and traffic flow may not suit modern living as well as that of a new home.

**Unpredictable expenses.** If the older house needs renovating, you can get estimates of the cost before you make a purchase offer, but don't be surprised if the eventual work ends up costing significantly more. In addition, it is difficult to predict exactly when such items as a roof, furnace or hot water heater will need replacing.

**Remodeling costs.** If you plan to update the kitchen or modernize a bathroom, you will have to finance the job with a home improvement loan, a home equity loan or a second mortgage. All of these typically carry a higher interest rate than on a first mortgage.

Sometimes, however, if you submit detailed plans and contractor bids for improvements that you intend to do immediately after settlement, your first-mortgage lender will give you enough to cover both purchase and renovations with one loan. A more common financing deal involves temporary construction financing until the renovation is finished, when a permanent mortgage will be placed after a fresh appraisal.

For both of these arrangements, the lender will require blueprints and cost estimates in advance, so buyers of houses needing renovation should get moving on design plans as soon as the purchase contract is accepted.

## CONDOMINIUM OWNERSHIP

The term *condominium* refers to a legal form of ownership, not a particular type of property. Under such a plan, the owners of individual dwelling units in a housing development also own undivided proportional interests in such common facilities as the grounds, hallways, elevators and recreation areas.

Just about any kind of development you can think of comes in condominium form: converted older apartment houses, townhouse complexes, elegant old mansions divided into luxury apartments, commercial lofts and office buildings in busy downtown areas, apartments fitted into former schools and farm silos, and virtually self-contained villages of free-standing houses, complete with tennis courts, golf courses, pools and community houses.

Condominiums give owners virtually the same financial advantages as single-family houses. The federal income tax breaks are identical: Mortgage interest and property taxes on your home are deductible. You may be able to defer part or all of any profit made on the sale by buying another home. And when you are 55 or older, you may be able to exercise a once-in-a-lifetime right to exclude from income as much as $125,000 of gain on the sale or exchange of the condo unit.

The track record of price appreciation by condos and co-ops is so variable from city to city and building to building that it is hard to generalize. When the price of single-family detached homes soared in the late 1970s, many apartment building owners converted their units to condos and sold them for high prices to buyers who thought prices would rise at a fast clip forever. (Condo conversions were also boosted by rent control laws, and before long some cities also enacted laws restricting condo conversions; both kinds of governmental policy have a strong bearing on the market and price performance of condos.)

Some of those eagerly purchased units have performed badly as investments in the decade since, while others have done very well. In general, condos tend to appreciate faster than average right after a project is sold out, then the rate of price growth tapers off.

In some very overbuilt areas, such as southern Florida in the early-to-mid-1980s, there were many good bargains in condos for those who didn't mind the problems of under-occupied, under-maintained buildings, and who were looking for a moderately priced, long-term residence, not a quick killing on a fast turnover.

Condos typically offer a trade-off: less cost for less space. Instead of having your own backyard, you may share one with 200 or so other residents. In place of your own full basement or attic for storage, you get a storage bin in the basement. You may have to share coin-operated washers and dryers. And you can't keep a bike and workbench in your parking space.

On the other hand, less space is precisely what many buyers are looking for. They want the enjoyment of an indoor swimming pool an elevator ride away, or having ready access to a tennis partner on Saturday mornings. They don't want to rake leaves and mow the lawn. If all you want is a one- or two-bedroom apartment, and yet you'd like to cash in on the benfits of ownership, a condo or co-op may fit your requirements perfectly.

While cost may be your first priority, a condo's facilities and the lifestyle it requires—especially interaction with other owners—should not be ranked too far behind. You may buy for one reason and end up disliking what you've bought for another reason. Your neighbors may be noisy, or otherwise objectionable. You will be subject to rules adopted by other owners. Certain activities and hobbies may be restricted or banned. Pets may be forbidden. Whether it's a garden apartment, townhouse or high rise, a condominium locks you into community living.

Before you shop, learn as much about condominium ownership as possible. Line up a good lawyer who understands condos. And start making a list of questions to ask.

### What's the area like?

You want your unit to be a good investment, as well as a good place to live.

Generally, look for residential areas with good quality apartment buildings and homes in the middle- to upper-price range. Assess convenience to public transportation, stores, schools, hospitals and parks.

Find out if units have been appreciating. Compare recent selling prices with original purchase prices. How much of that appreciation occurred in the months or year after the development sold out? How much is occurring now? Information on sales is available from county land transfer records.

Try to visualize the neighborhood in five, ten or 15 years. What are the zoning rules covering nearby unbuilt areas? Could the view be obstructed by a future high rise? Could a highway be constructed nearby?

## Is it financially sound?

What debts does the condo association owe, and to whom? Are there adequate funds held in reserve to handle routine maintenance, as well as replacement of expensive items, such as boilers and roofs? Has the association tended to rely on special assessments for emergency needs?

## Will you fit in?

Do you desire compatability with other tenants, in terms of lifestyle, occupations, age, or any other characteristic? How are problems resolved? Will you be expected to vote on every little detail—like what color to paint the halls—or will routine decisions be made by the elected board?

## What's the vacancy rate in the region?

An oversupply of condo units in an area can depress prices generally. Too many vacant units in a particular building not only can depress prices, it can, among other things, reduce the funds available to the condo association for maintenance and repairs and increase the pressure on the developer or current owners to rent rather than sell.

## How many units are rented?

Some units usually are rented out by investors; others by owners who have moved away temporarily. In resort areas, most of the units in a project may be on rental during the vacation season, but that's a special case. A high proportion of renters is undesirable, so much so that the FHA won't insure condo loans in projects with less than an 80% owner-occupancy rate. Renters, it's charged, are less concerned than owner-occupants with preserving the building and grounds, and investors are less likely than homeowners to upgrade and renovate their units.

## Is there a heavy sales turnover?

You expect turnover in a resort project. But heavy turnover in a year-round residential community can create an uncomfortable feeling of impermanence; increase the wear-and-tear on elevators, hallways and other common elements; weaken security controls; and discourage compliance with rules.

## Who owns the common facilities?

Developers sometimes hang on to such facilities—laundry room, the parking areas, the pool and other recreational facilities—for the income from rental fees. Avoid a project in which important amenities are not owned by the condominium owners. Otherwise, you become a captive user, exposed to uncontrollable fee increases and inconveniences.

## Are the facilities adequate?

Inspect the pool, tennis courts, parking area and other facilities at times of peak usage. A pool that's big enough for a 200-unit building occupied mainly by working couples and singles could prove an overcrowded mess with the same number of apartments filled largely by families with small children. Free parking may be limited or unavailable. You may have to pay to use a party room or gym.

## What are the restrictions?

There are sure to be some, so read the declaration or master deed, the bylaws and house rules before you sign a contract. Ironically, you may find it best not to buy if the condo does not impose enough controls.

## Are you adequately insured?

Does the condominium board have enough liability insurance? There have been suits brought by both condo owners and visitors against condo associations, especially involving violent crime on the premises. Find out if you as an owner would be personally liable in such a suit, and if so, does the association carry insurance that would cover you?

## Answers to these questions

Answers to many of these questions can be found in the following documents, which you should examine before you buy:

▶ *Master deed.* Also called an enabling declaration, a plan of condominium ownership or declaration of conditions, covenants and restrictions, the master deed is the most important document. When recorded, it legally establishes the project as a condominium. It also, among other things, authorizes residents to form an operating association and describes individual units and commonly owned areas.

▶ *Bylaws.* These spell out the association's authority and responsibilites, authorize the making of a budget and the collection of various charges, and prescribe parliamentary procedures. They may empower the association to hire professional managers or contain other special provisions. The bylaws may also set forth insurance requirements and authorize the imposition of liens against the property of owners who fail to pay monthly charges, although these provisions sometimes may be included in the condo's master deed.

▶ *House rules.* They state what owners can and can't do. Any restrictions on pets, children, decorations, use of facilities and such will be found here. The rules may be incorporated in the bylaws or set apart in a separate document.

▶ *Sales contract or purchase agreement.* It's basically similar to other real estate contracts, but there are differences. In signing, you may acknowledge receipt of the other documents. Check whether there is a cooling off period during which you can back out of the contract. Will you be able to get out of the deal if you can't get financing? There should be written assurances, if necessary, that the project will be completed as promised, and you should have the right to make an inspection prior to settlement. Your deposit should be placed in an escrow account.

▶ *Other papers.* No less important, these could include a copy of the operating budget, a schedule of current and proposed assessments, a financial statement on the owners' association, any leases or contracts, a plan or drawing of the project and your unit and an engineer's report if one was done. One of the financial documents should show how much money has been reserved for unforeseen or emergency outlays. Some states require developers to give each potential buyer a prospectus that details the important facts about the offering.

Ideally, the board should include in monthly condo fees a realistic contribution to reserves for large repairs and replacements. Otherwise you may be confronted with repeated emergency assessments at times that may be inconvenient to your budget.

Ask the board treasurer for copies of recent budget reports and obtain an engineer's summary of the physical condition of the building, including projections for major repairs.

Find out what assessments have been made during the past five years in addition to the regular condo fee. While some associations deliberately choose to operate with minimal reserves, relying on special assessments as needed, good management is generally associated with a healthy reserve to make special assessments unnecessary.

### Study and ask questions

You and your lawyer should take the time to evaluate all this material before you decide to buy, no matter how onerous the job appears. If you live in a state that does not require the delivery of documents before you sign a contract, insist on your right to obtain and examine them.

If you've never lived in a condo, you may be astonished by the power held by the board of directors. It can put a lien on your unit if you don't pay your monthly fee or you are late coming up with the money for a special assessment. It may have the license to spend tens of thousands of dollars on a repair or improvement without prior approval of the other owners.

The board is elected by the condo owners and serves as a miniature government. Even if it turns the day-to-day operating details over to a resident manager or outside management company, the board retains the ultimate authority for running the project.

Request information on the background of each board member, and plan to attend at least one board meeting. If you are serious about condo ownership, you should plan to participate in a certain amount of organizational activity in order to protect your interests.

## Getting financing

You may be asked to make a larger down payment on a condo than on a comparable single family property. But, otherwise, getting a mortgage for a condo is no different than getting a loan on a single family house.

Lenders in some areas may be reluctant to give you a loan if you plan to put down less than 10%, and FHA-insured mortgages are not available to prospective owners of condo projects less than a year old. In recent years, high foreclosure rates on condominiums purchased with very low down payments and on units in smaller buildings have caused many lenders to reexamine their lending requirements in such cases.

For more information, see *Condominiums & Cooperatives* (2nd edition), by David Clurman, F. Scott Jackson and Edna Hebard (John Wiley & Sons, Inc.). This comprehensive book discusses important areas of condominium and cooperative living, including buying, selling and investing, the legal structure of condos and co-ops, assessing a community, and operation and management.

## COOPERATIVE APARTMENTS

The "stockholder in 202-F" may sound like someone with a seat on a securities exchange, but if you live in a cooperative apartment, that's how you might describe your neighbor.

Unlike condominium ownership, which gives you title to a particular unit and an undivided interest in common areas, purchasing a co-op entitles you to a share in a corporation. Owning stock or a membership certificate in the corporation in turn grants you the right to live in a particular apartment. You become a tenant-stockholder of the corporation, and, in most states, your collateral is considered personal property rather than real property. Typically, the corporation owns the co-op property, is responsible for management and property taxes and finances the project with a "blanket" mortgage.

Tenant-stockholders are allowed to deduct their proportional share of real estate taxes and mortgage interest for federal tax purposes, providing that at least 80% of the cooperative's income comes from the shareholders, and no more than 20% comes from parking fees, interest on reserve funds and the like.

Because a new co-op owner is a fellow shareholder in the whole building, current co-op tenants tend to be very choosey about new owners. It is common for a co-op governing board to require prospective owners to appear before them for an interview and to submit personal references in addition to statements of financial resources. Most co-op boards zealously protect the lifestyle of their buildings, and prospective owners are sometimes rejected because the board believes they would be too noisy, reclusive or sloppy, or might throw large boisterous parties. However, co-op boards are prohibited by federal law and many state statutes from rejecting or discouraging a prospective buyer on the basis of that person's race, gender, creed or national origin.

Co-ops have been operating in the U.S. since the end of the 19th century, but for years they took a back seat to condominiums as the preferred method of apartment ownership. Now co-ops are making a comeback in Boston, Chicago, New York and Washington, D.C., thanks in part to local caps on condominium conversions. The most important impetus behind the recent rise in popularity, however, is the availability of financing. These days, conversions from rental property are almost equally divided between condos and co-ops.

## Financing a co-op

In the past, it was nearly impossible to get a loan to buy a co-op. Few banks offered them, mainly because there was no secondary market for them. Prospective co-op owners simply paid cash or took out personal loans with high interest rates. This tended to make co-op ownership more suitable for upper-income people, with the exception of some co-ops sponsored by state housing agencies.

Then, in 1984, the Federal National Mortgage Association began buying co-op "share loans." These Fannie Mae loans are secured by the stock and occupancy rights of co-op ownership, with terms similar to those of mortgage loans. They are still not as easy to get as mortgages, however, and they are slightly more expensive, with interest rates about 0.25 percentage points higher. Closing costs on this kind of loan are generally less than with a regular mortgage.

Many banks, savings and loans and mortgage companies offer share loans. If you are having difficulty locating a lender in your area, contact the Share Loan Service Corporation (1630 Connecticut Avenue, N.W., Washington, D.C. 20009). This organization is backed by the National Cooperative Bank, a national bank specializing in cooperative lending. Once a cooperative meets the standards set by the National Cooperative Bank or Fannie Mae and becomes a participating shareholder of Share Loan Corporation, share loans are available to individuals wishing to buy a co-op unit there and to current owners wishing to refinance.

Lenders who want to sell share loans they originate into the secondary market usually must make sure a project meets Fannie Mae's minimum underwriting and legal standards. Among the requirements are structural soundness, restricted commercial use, fiscally responsible operating budget and appropriate management.

Share loan and cooperative documents of projects meeting Fannie Mae's legal requirements must include various legal safeguards to protect the interests of the tenant-stockholders, the corporation and the lender.

The following are common cooperative documents you will need to study before you buy:

▶ *Articles of Incorporation.* A cooperative is incorporated under state law and the corporation's purpose, powers and obligations are described in the Articles of Incorporation.

▶ *Bylaws.* These spell out the duties and responsibilities of shareholders, officers and directors.

▶ *Stock, Shares or Membership Certificate.* Shares or membership certificates are your proof of ownership in the corporation.

▶ *Proprietary Lease or Occupancy Agreement.* The lease sets up the terms and conditions by which you occupy your co-op unit. In it, you are obligated to pay your pro rata share of the corporation's expenses, including real estate taxes, operating costs and debt. Rules on using your unit, subleasing and maintenance also are found in the agreement.

▶ *Recognition Agreement.* A share loan lender and the cooperative corporation enter into this agreement in order to document the lender's rights and the corporation's responsibilities and obligations to the lender. A corporation may enter into recognition agreements with more than one lender.

▶ *Security agreement.* In this document, the share loan borrower assigns the proprietary lease (or occupany agreement) and pledges his or her stock, shares or membership certificate to the lender in return for a loan.

## THE RIGHT QUESTIONS TO ASK

### Is it financially sound?

Is there adequate income to meet expenses? Income comes from three primary sources: the tenant/stockholders, commercial use—for example, rental income from parking, and from interest or dividends earned on reserve funds. Expenses include debt repayment, real estate and income taxes, building maintenance and operations and reserve fund pay-ins for replacements and capital improvements.

A cooperative financed with an FHA-insured blanket mortgage is required to have reserve funds that meet the agency's criteria. In addition to collecting money for taxes and debt, adequate sums must be set aside to replace structural elements and major components, such as heating, cooling, plumbing and electrical systems. In addition, a general operating reserve must be established for other contingencies and for resale problems. These reserves are established under the cooperative's regulatory agreements and documents should be available to prospective owners.

Fannie Mae's project approval standards give lenders the tools they need to evaluate cooperative projects. Typically, they require, among other things, that each project have an adequate cash flow and that monthly assessments be structured to handle operating expenses and to build sufficient reserves.

### Age and condition of the building?

The answer to that question sets the stage for what kind of financial experience you will have once you become a tenant-stockholder. Is there an engineering report on the condition of the project? If you discover that the galvanized plumbing in the building is nearing the end of its anticipated 40-year life span, you know it will have to be replaced, not repaired. How does the board of directors plan to pay for the job? From the reserve fund? With a special assessment? By refinancing the mortgage?

## How will you fit in?

How old is the average shareowner? What is the financial status and philosophy of the majority? A building full of up-and-coming professionals in their early forties may have a very different money management philosophy than one filled with retired or soon-to-be retired people. Likewise, if you can afford to buy into a particular cooperative only by living in the smallest unit, you may be at odds with affluent neighbors who insist on a uniformed doorman—regardless of the cost.

## Composition of the board and its financial philosophy?

Is there a fair amount of consensus among board members on how to conduct the corporation's affairs? Do their views on important issues reflect those of other tenant-stockholders? Do they jibe with yours?

## Are you prepared to participate in cooperative living?

Many of the problems of condo and cooperative living are similar. How willing are you to be involved in meetings and group efforts?

## How many units are rented?

A possible concern for would-be tenant-stockholders in new cooperatives is a 1986 change in the tax law that permits shares held by partnerships, trusts, estates and corporations to count toward the 80% of income that by law must derive from tenant-stockholders. In the past such stockholders were required to weigh in on the 20% side of the ratio.

Conceivably, a majority of a cooperative's units could be occupied by tenants or "nominees" of partnerships, trusts, estates and corporations rather than by shareowners who have joined together as "cooperative homeowners." If a building is dominated by tenants rather than owners, it changes the nature of cooperative living. It also may have tax and resale consequences for individual tenant-stockholders.

Existing co-ops probably will not be affected by the change unless they wish to alter their articles of incorporation and bylaws to permit investors to become stockholders.

## May you sublet your apartment?

Some cooperatives forbid it. Others allow it, but may impose a one-time sublet fee or impose an additional monthly maintenance surcharge.

### FOR MORE INFORMATION

For more information about cooperatives and co-op financing, write to the National Association of Housing Cooperatives, 2501 M St., N.W., Suite 451, Washington, D.C. 20037, and to the National Cooperative Business Assocation, 1401 New York Ave., N.W., Suite 1100, Washington, D.C. 20005. And take a look at the following books:

▶ *Going Co-op: the Complete Guide to Buying and Owning Your Own Apartment*, by William Coughlan, Jr. and Monte Franke (Beacon Press).

▶ *A Member's Guide to Cooperative Living*, by Multi-Family Housing Services, Inc. (available from NAHC at the above address).

▶ *A Consumer Guide to Financing a Cooperative Using Share Loan Financing*, free from the Share Loan Service Corp. (1630 Connecticut Avenue, N.W., Washington, D.C. 20009).

### MOBILE HOMES

The house that gets delivered to you on wheels has come a long way in recent years. Mobile homes—or "manufactured homes," as the industry now prefers to call them—first gained popularity as permanent residences with the retirement and resort crowd and with GIs returning home from World War II. Today, they are an important source of affordable housing for the elderly, for first-time homebuyers and for low- and moderate-income families.

A nationwide construction code that took effect in 1976 and is supervised by HUD has improved mobile home safety, quality and durability. Nevertheless, mobile homes that are built only to the minimum requirements of the HUD code will appear strikingly different than conventional homes. For example, ceilings in a mobile home may be built at the 7-foot level rather than the 7½-foot height required in most local building codes. And a 28-inch hallway just won't feel like a 36-inch one.

What about price appreciation? In many cases, mobile homes secured to permanent foundations and situated on lots owned or being purchased by their owners have held their value or even appreciated, as have those located on rented sites in desirable communities. On the other hand, many mobile homes depreciate in value, like a car, a boat or any object that gets worn out with use.

Many zoning restrictions that kept mobile homes out of desirable residential areas in the past have been eased. But they remain a problem and can cut down on your choices of where to live. Many subdivisions are well-designed and attractive places to live. Upper echelon mobile home models may feature wood siding, pitched roofs, cathedral ceilings, fireplaces, bay windows and drywall interiors.

In addition to getting a home that looks very different from the flat-topped, metal-sided box we visualize when the word "mobile home" is used, residents may have a ready-made community, complete with swimming pools, recreation centers and nearby schools and shopping. Condominium mobile home developments allow residents to own part of the common facilities as well as their own units and lots.

## Cost

"Single-section" (or single-wide) mobile units provide up to 1,000 square feet of space. Two or more single-wides can be joined to make double-wide, triple-wide or even larger combinations. The more luxurious multisection models can be hard to distinguish from their conventional counterparts.

The industry says the average mobile home sells for 25% to 50% less than the average site-built homes, not counting the cost of buying the land or renting the site. An average-price new single-section unit cost about $18,000 in 1987, the average multisection about $30,000. That price nearly always includes some furniture, major appliances, draperies and carpeting, but not delivery. Nearly all such homes are mobile only once—when they are transported from the factory to a lot, space or slab. Only a very small percentage ever are moved a second time, and it usually takes a truck tractor to haul them.

## Financing a mobile home

One thing hasn't changed much: the way you pay for a mobile home. Most still are financed as if they were motor vehicles, using personal property (chattel) loans. Interest rates are two to three points above conventional home mortgage rates and payoff periods are shorter, usually 10 or 15 years. The down payment typically is 10%.

Until recently, the way you paid for your mobile home—whether with a real estate mortgage loan or with a personal property loan—made no difference as far as your federal tax obligation was concerned. Either way, the interest was fully deductible from gross income. No more. Beginning in 1987, consumer interest on credit cards, auto loans or any other kind of loan not secured by the collateral of a principal or secondary residence will be phased out over four years. For 1987 you'll be able to write off 65%. In 1988 that drops to 40%; in 1989, 20%; in 1990, 10%. Thereafter, none will be deductible.

This change adds to the cost of mobile home ownership with non-mortgage financing, and it makes it all the more important to try to get a mortgage secured by the home and lot.

Mobile home dealers, like car dealers, arrange most financing. They sell insurance, too, giving buyers the convenience of a one-step, one-payment transaction. But, as in buying a car, you may pay a premium for the dealer's package. Check your other options. You may be able to get a government-backed loan, a bank loan or even a mortgage loan.

Some banks and savings and loans will finance mobile homes with a conventional or FHA-insured mortgage loan of up to 30 years, if the home is permanently set up on land owned by the borrower, or on land to be financed with the mobile home.

Mobile home loans are subject to the federal truth-in-lending law, which means you must be informed in writing of the finance cost expressed as an annual percentage (APR). If somebody quotes you an unusually low figure, it's probably an "add-on" or "discount" rate, neither of which reflects the true cost. Always insist on being told the APR, as the law requires, and make sure that it is the figure in the contract.

### Government-backed mortgages

The Department of Housing and Urban Development's Federal Housing Administration insures loans made by approved lenders to purchasers who are able to make a small down payment and meet the monthly payments. The unit must be used as a principal residence, and you must have an acceptable site for it, either owned or rented. The FHA insures 20-year loans up to $40,500 for the mobile home only, while loans for the combination home and site are insured up to $54,000 for 25 years.

For eligible veterans, the VA will guarantee $20,000 or 50% of the loan, whichever is smaller, for 20 to 23 years. A home purchased with a VA guarantee may not require a down payment.

### Warranties

Once you've bought your unit, you may get warranties from the retailer, the transporter, the installer and the appliance manufacturer as well. Make notes on what each warranty covers and doesn't cover. How long does each warranty last? Who will actually do any work necessary under the warranty? And where will it be done?

### For more information

See the following two information sources:

▶ *The Manufactured Housing Industry Directory of Financing Services and Other Housing Related Organizations* (Meetings + Plus, P.O. Box 1981, Palm Springs, CA 92263). It gives you, among other things:

1. Names, addresses and phone numbers of the lending institutions providing manufactured home/land financing;

2. Names, addresses and phone numbers of major lenders offering VA and/or FHA financing;

3. Names, addresses and phone numbers of housing and finance agencies in the federal government;

4. Information about manufactured housing appraisal services;

5. Names and locations of the various state and national manufactured housing trade associations.

▶ *How to Buy a Manufactured Home*, by the Manufactured Housing Institute, in cooperation with the Federal Trade Commission's Office of Consumer & Business Education; single copy, 50 cents (Consumer Information Center, Department 453P, Pueblo, CO. 81009). Includes information on warranties and other consumer protections; home selection and placement; site preparation, transportation and installation; and home inspection.

# 7

# House Hunting Strategies

If you've gone through the steps outlined in previous chapters—assessing your resources, prequalifying for a mortgage, deciding on your needs and wants—you're ready for some serious house hunting.

To be successful, your house hunting strategy must adapt to the mood and economic realities facing buyers and sellers in your targeted location and price range. The "hot" or "cold" condition of the market at the time you begin looking will determine how you approach the task—with or without the help of a real estate agent; with intensity or at a leisurely pace; relying on classified ads and open houses, or using the grapevine to give you a jump on other buyers when a desirable house first comes on the market.

The biggest determinant of the housing market, of course, is the national, regional and local economy. But within every kind of economy, there are also recurring seasonal differences in market strength. If possible, shop when other homebuyers are not out in force.

Across the country, many properties come on the market in April and May, and homebuyers swarm into the market. Sellers generally don't feel pressured to cut a deal right away. Some will feel differently by June, and more will be downright eager to sell by the time the July/August summer doldrums descend.

Fall usually brings a brisker pace, so September, October and Novermber are generally good months for both buying and selling. From Thanksgiving on through the winter, holiday activities and cold weather generally combine to slow activity. Buyers will find sellers more interested in dealing, but offsetting this is the smaller number of houses on the market in mid-winter.

Naturally, the seasonal ebb and flow of market activity varies from one part of the country to another. You may live in a winter ski area or in a beach resort town where investors and second-home buyers dominate the market. Each region will have its own seasonal pattern. A seven-year seasonal analysis of prices and sales activity in Texas, for example, showed that July, August and September were the best months for selling a home in that state; by contrast, the first quarter—January, February and March—is usually a buyer's market in Texas. Learn the local pattern and, if possible, exploit it to your advantage.

You might be able to swing a good deal by finding a corporate seller trying to unload the home of a transferred employee. Companies want to avoid the cost of carrying unsold houses. When sales are slow, most will reduce listing prices, often below appraised values. How to find those bargains? Ask local real estate brokers. Major corporate relocation management firms, such as those of Equitable and Coldwell Banker, use their own relocation brokerage networks. Since corporate homes are often vacant, chances of working a deal are that much better if you can close quickly.

## THE BUYER'S MARKET

In a buyer's market, there are many houses for sale relative to the number of serious lookers. Houses will sit on the market for some time, and sellers are often willing to cut their asking price and even assist the buyer with cut-rate financing by taking back a second trust.

As a qualified buyer, you have time on your side. You can be more deliberate, and you can bargain harder. You can ask the seller for an appraisal of the house before you submit an offer, and even ask the seller to pay all or part of the cost. You can take your own time to check comparable sale prices in the neighborhood. You can load your offering contract with contingency clauses that protect only you—inspection, financing at a specified interest rate, seller's help with mortgage points, even the condition that you be able to sell your current home before closing on this purchase. In a hot market, the seller wouldn't touch so one-sided a contract, but in a slow market, the seller may have to swallow it.

In a buyer's market, the diligent house hunter can do reasonably well without the aid of a real estate agent. Although you won't have access, without an agent, to new listings in the local multiple listing service computer (the real estate trade's clearinghouse of properties for sale), you won't miss much; most houses will remain on the market long enough to be advertised in the newspaper and shown at a weekend open house.

## THE SELLER'S MARKET

A seller's market is the situation when prices are firm or rising and every new listing is snapped up fast, even those that seem at first to be over-priced. In a truly hot market, good houses are often sold before they're advertised or even punched into the MLS computer; several contracts are submitted on the same property; and buyers vie with each other by offering more than the asking price. In a hot market, there will be more sale-by-owner properties, too.

If this is the kind of market you're working in as a buyer, you had better be ready—financially and emotionally—to move fast when you spot something that meets your needs.

The seller won't give much attention to timid or unprepared buyers, or buyers who load their offering contract with lots of protective contingencies. The would-be buyer who must have the contract reviewed by a not-yet-selected attorney, and the buyer with insufficient earnest money who wants the seller to take a personal note for a few days, probably won't get serious consideration from owners of desirable properties.

In a seller's market, select in advance the attorney and home inspector who will be needed as soon as you decide to submit a contract. If you don't know a good real estate attorney, get names from friends, lenders, title company and real estate agents. If you are buying a condo, co-op or farm, find a lawyer who specializes in that type of transaction.

You will save precious time if you and your attorney are familiar with the contract to be used. Have contingencies you definitely plan to insert drawn up by your attorney in advance, but remember that a "clean" contract—one not littered with lots of escape clauses for the buyer—will be treated with more respect by the seller.

## Financial readiness

As you begin a serious house hunt in a hot market, be prepared to write a check for the earnest money, which usually accompanies your contract offer as evidence of serious intentions, good faith, and ability to close the deal. Arrange for cash tied up in certificates of deposit (CDs) or in stocks and bonds to be moved to your checking account. If you own a home now, consider putting a home equity line of credit on it well before you begin looking for your next home. (See the discussion of home equity loans in Chapters 2 and 16.)

In a hot market, one of the things that might set your offer above other bids will be your ability to go to settlement fast (if that's what the seller wants). If you already own a home, this could mean settling on the new house before you've closed the sale of your current one. If the money you're putting down on the new house is tied up in the current one, talk to your banker about ways to bridge the gap between selling and buying with a short-term advance. The solution may be a bridge loan. Also known as a swing, equity-advance or gap loan, a bridge loan amounts to a short-term advance against the equity in your present property.

## The search for houses

In a hot seller's market, you must use every tool at your disposal to spot good new listings as soon as the seller decides to sell—or even before.

It is not enough just to watch the newspapers every day for advertisements of houses just put on the market. It is especially not enough to wait for weekend open houses. Many fine offerings will be sold by word of mouth, without ever being advertised in the paper or being registered with a multiple listing service.

Some of these unpublicized sales will be "by owner," with no agent involved. Some will be transactions started and completed within one real estate firm, where one agent's new listing is sold to a buyer assisted by another agent in the same office.

For the reasons above, it is necessary in a hot market for the house hunter to use the scouting services of at least one aggressive, experienced agent who knows the targeted neighborhoods. In many cases, it is useful to have several agents in different firms helping you simultaneously. In addition, you should use your own energy and ingenuity in combination with the help of an agent.

For example, ask all your friends who live in or near your ideal neighborhood to let you know if they hear anything that suggests a house might be coming on the market soon. It could be news of an executive's relocation, a split marriage, a retirement move, or the recent death of an elderly person living alone. As ghoulish as it sounds, some house hunters watch the obituary pages and look up the address of the deceased to see where he or she lived; after a suitable period of time, they write or phone an heir listed in the obituary and inquire respectfully if the house will be for sale.

Many smart house hunters will approach the owners of houses they admire, even if the house is not for sale. They do this by driving through the target neighborhood and jotting down the addresses of houses they like the look of, then using a criss-cross directory (available at many public libraries) or public land records at the courthouse to determine the owner's name and phone number. A note or phone call sometimes yields the information that the owner is, indeed, contemplating sale. Sometimes the owner has never thought of selling, but is surprised to hear what his house might be worth; suddenly, you've got an interested seller.

If you're looking at houses with a particular agent, the agent can make this "cold" contact for you and work with both interested parties to make a deal, earning a commission in the process. If you're going it alone, you'll want to encourage the owner not to call an agent until you've had a chance to tour the house, get an appraisal, and make an offer. Point out that a private transaction, without the seller paying a 6% commission, could net him or her substantially more than through a conventional realty listing. Of course, the savings of that commission could be split in some proportion between the seller and buyer, benefitting you both.

Perhaps the seller will be reluctant to sell to you without first finding out how much an agent could get for the house. Here's your strategy for dealing with that: Ask the seller to add a clause to the agent's listing contract specifying that the seller may sell the house to you directly (you must be named in the listing contract) without payment of a commission. The seller should be happy to go along with this, because he has nothing to lose and the possible gain of all or part of the commission.

If you are initiating a negotiation with an unprepared seller, for the seller's protection and your own, suggest that a professional appraisal be done, with the cost shared by you and the seller.

## SHOPPING WITH A REAL ESTATE AGENT

Some people like to look for houses on their own, unaccompanied by a real estate agent. Other people wouldn't think of venturing into the housing market without the help of an agent scouting out new listings, accompanying them on tours of open houses, and offering advice.

Most houses for sale are listed with realty agents, so the house hunter who calls to inquire about an advertised house or who visits an open house on Sunday is going to encounter agents at every turn. If you identify yourself by name—for example, by signing the registry book at an open house—you'll soon start getting calls from agents offering to help you find your dream house. At this point, it's "choose or be chosen." If you are interested in being helped, take the initiative and do the selecting, by contacting agents with proven reputations in the neighborhoods and price range in which you're looking. If you are not interested, be firm and avoid entanglements until you're ready.

Keep in mind that the house hunter who is looking on his own, without an agent's help, is at a considerable disadvantage. Unless very knowledgable about the market in a given area, this house hunter will miss the agent's deep knowledge. More significantly, this looker will have no access to the MLS computer listings of houses for sale. That might be alright in a slow market, but in any kind of active market, the solo house hunter will simply miss a lot of good houses that sell quickly.

Most real estate agents are compensated from the commission sellers pay on the sale price, so why does an agent who doesn't have the listing want to help you find and buy a home? Because the sales commission is split between the seller's listing broker (and the broker's agent) and the broker (and broker's agent) who brings in the buyer. Real estate agents make money from finding both houses to sell and people to buy them, so a well-qualified, serious house hunter represents a paycheck to the agent—but only if the sale goes through. There will usually be no compensation for all the hours of accompanying a buyer through houses unless that agent submits the buyer's successful contract.

If an agent takes you to a house and tours it with you the first time you see it, you should submit your contract offer through that agent. Even if you don't, that agent may be entitled to a share of the sales commission from the seller in the event that you buy the house.

If an agent merely mentions to you that a given house is for sale, but you first tour the house by yourself or with another agent, the first agent will probably not have any claim on part of the commission. That's why agents are often coy about giving house hunters the address of a listing when they first call. Instead, they'll offer to pick you up and drive you to the house for an appointment to tour it. The agent who tells you about a new listing doesn't want to risk that you'll cross the threshold with another agent, costing the first agent a piece of the sale.

Remember that unless you hire your own agent (a so-called "buyer's broker"; see below), an agent works for a seller and is paid by a seller. This is true even when an agent spends hours and hours working with you, the buyer. It is true even if "your" agent has never met the owners of the home you ultimately buy. When an agent works with a buyer, they are both gambling. The agent gambles that in return for his time you will be loyal and buy a home through him. You gamble that your loyalty will reward you with service and produce a suitable property.

So why would a buyer consider using several agents to help in the house hunt, as suggested above? Perhaps because the house you're looking for is very special in some way, and you don't want to risk missing the few possible listings. The best reason for using several agents is to extend your reach in a hot market. When houses move very quickly, the buyer needs more eyes and ears and scouting energy than one agent can supply. Some good listings will be sold within one firm, with the seller's commission being shared by the listing agent and a colleague in the firm who brought in the buyer. The listing won't ever show up in the MLS computer, so if you don't have a relationship already with an agent at that firm, you wouldn't hear about the house in time to see it or bid on it.

In short, you want to be the first person to hear about every good new listing on the market, so you must encourage agents at different firms to compete for your patronage. Tell each agent that you'll reward hustle by accompanying him or her immediately to see the new listing—providing that agent is the first one to call and tell you about it.

You'll be loyal to that agent for all dealings relating to that particular house, but the next day you might go see another house with a different agent who happened to be the first to call you about it.

Pretty soon, you'll start getting calls from several agents within minutes or hours of each other, each trying to be the first to tell you that something good has just shown up in the MLS computer, or even better, that a new listing has just come into the firm and won't go into the computer for 24 hours—a typical period after which the firm is obligated to enter the new listing for other agents to see. (Some privacy-minded sellers specifically ask their agent to keep the listing unadvertised and strictly "in house" for a while, with no notice to the MLS computer.)

## HOW TO PICK AN AGENT

There are only two functions in the real estate business. They are broker and agent (or sales associate.) A broker is licensed by the state to conduct a real estate business and to negotiate transactions for a fee. An agent is a broker's representative and is usually an independent contractor rather than an employee. He or she is permitted to sell real estate under the supervision of a licensed broker. Both brokers and their representatives are properly called agents because they act as agents for their clients.

Contrary to public impression, not all brokers and agents are Realtors. A Realtor (capital "R"—it's a trade name) and a Realtor Associate (who works for a Realtor) are members of the National Association of Realtors, a trade and lobby organization.

If location, location, location are the watchwords for picking a property, experience, experience, experience are the watchwords for picking an agent.

Most buyers, however, don't pick an agent; they acquire one at an open house, or by responding by telephone to an ad. Many select an agent who is a friend, relative or neighbor. You could be lucky; such an agent may turn out to be skilled, experienced and resourceful. On the other hand, you could end up with an amateur.

There is a better way to acquire an agent:

Obtain the names of brokers and agents active in the area where you want to buy. The classified ads are a good place to start. Brokers with agents that list and sell homes in a particular neighborhood will advertise regularly. Ask friends, associates, lenders and attorneys for recommendations. And by all means, consider using a buyer's broker, who will be paid with a fee from you, not from the sales commission. (See the full discussion below.)

Check the broker's reputation in the community. In the case of an agent, find out who the broker is, then check out the firm. Inquire about complaints or problems at the local real estate board and the state real estate commission. Survey some of your prospective neighbors.

Call the most promising brokers. Ask them to put you in touch with one or two of their most experienced agents. Tell each broker what kind of buyer you are and what kind of property you want. For example, a novice buyer may need an agent who is especially intuitive and patient, while a much-transferred corporate executive needs one who lists exclusive homes and has sophisticated negotiating skills.

Interview the agents. Find out what each knows about the community. Ask how many years he or she has been selling real estate and for whom. Determine what kind of service you can expect.

After your screening, select one or more agents to work with, and be candid with them about what degree of service you're expecting, and whether you'll be looking at houses with them alone or with other agents, too. Give them good guidance on how much variation from your ideal specifications—size, price, location, etc.—you'll tolerate. Do you want them to narrowly screen new listings or tell you about everything that is remotely similar to your target house?

## USING A BUYER'S BROKER

When the market is brisk, it may be hard to find an agent to give you a lot of special counsel and hand-holding. This is because most agents are working primarily for the seller, not the buyer. This fiduciary relationship between seller and agent sometimes causes buyers to wonder whether they can trust the agent—even an agent who is ostensibly helping them find a house to buy. How can an agent who is going to be paid by the seller, and whose pay will be based on how *high* the sale price is, negotiate in the buyer's best interest?

This concern is the reason that savvy buyers study the art of real estate negotiation, so they can rely on themselves, not the agent. And it's the reason that smart buyers always retain an impartial attorney to review the contract and settlement papers. This concern about conflict of interest in real estate sales is also the reason that buyer's brokers came into existence.

The only way you can command an agent's undivided loyalties during a house hunt and price negotiation is by entering into a buyer's brokerage contract. It then becomes your responsibility, not the seller's, to pay that agent's fee. This fee should be set in advance and ideally should not be tied to the selling price of the house.

Peter Miller and Douglas Bregman in their manual *Buyer's Brokerage: A Practical Guide for Real Estate Buyers, Brokers and Investors* (Tremont Press, P.O. Box 2307, Silver Spring, MD 20902) list six advantages that they believe buyers have when they are represented by their own agent:

1) A broker employed and paid by a purchaser is obligated to get the best possible price and terms for the buyer. This means that a broker can openly suggest a smaller deposit, better financing terms, the use of a contract form more favorable to the purchaser and an offering price far below the listing figure created by the seller.

2) Because the fee for a buyer's broker is not tied to the selling price of a property, a major source of conflict between the buyer and broker is eliminated.

3) Buyer's brokers can assist with the purchase of properties outside the brokerage system, such as homes offered for sale by self-sellers.

4) Buyer's brokerage gives purchasers access to the same skills, training and services that have been monopolized by sellers in the past.

5) With buyer's brokerage there is a clarity of relationships since one broker openly represents the purchaser and another can represent the seller. The problem of confused representation, where a single broker appears to somehow be concerned with the conflicting interests of both buyer and seller, is eliminated.

6) Buyer's brokerage gives purchasers more control over real estate marketing costs and, ultimately, over acquisition costs as well.

But things are not always so neat and clean in the real world. Some buyer-brokers' fees are tied to the sale price of the home, just like sales commissions; this situation raises conflict-of-interest issues that should be hashed out before you sign on with an agent. And some buyers ask their lenders to fold the buyer-broker fee into the mortgage loan; most lenders agree to this, but lenders making VA loans are not permitted to do so.

Before you enter into a buyer's brokerage contract, check the reputation and experience of the firm and agent. Set up a meeting with the broker to discuss your needs. In most situations you should not expect to pay for this initial consultation. A buyer-broker may require a non-refundable fee as a condition of starting work; the fee will vary with the difficulty of the search and with the overall compensation plan.

## The agreement contract

The compensation plan you agree on is spelled out in the brokerage contract, your equivalent of the seller's listing agreement. It should address the following points:

▶ Will you pay the agent an hourly rate, a set fee, or a percentage of the purchase price?

▶ Will there be an incentive commission for getting a price lower than the asking price—say, 10% of the savings? (But remember, the lowest price is not necessarily synonymous with the best overall deal for the buyer.)

▶ Will you pay an initial retainer and will it be applied against the total fee due?

▶ Is there a minimum fee? Is there a cap on total cost? This is specially important if you are paying by the hour.

▶ How will conflicts of interest be handled?

▶ What will happen should a buyer buy a property shortly after the brokerage agreement ends? Should the broker get a commission? If so, under what conditions?

▶ Exactly what kinds of services and advice will the broker provide?

▶ How will disagreements be handled? For example, both parties could agree to submit to binding arbitration, using a neutral third party.

## Who pays whom

When you buy a house with a buyer's broker, the seller's agent should be willing to cut the 6% sales commission. If the total cost of two separate fees—one paid by you to your buyer's broker and one paid by the seller to the listing broker—is held to an amount equivalent to the 6% commission the seller expects to pay anyway, your agent should have no difficulty persuading a seller to accept your offer.

Here's an example: Say the owner lists her property for $104,000 and agrees to pay a 6% commission. If the house sells for $100,000, and commission is $6,000, the seller will get $94,000. In a conventional transaction, the $6,000 commission would be divided between the listing broker and the cooperating or selling broker, with each getting 3%.

Now suppose the owner receives an offer from a buyer represented by his own agent. The owner is told that the purchaser will pay his own agent and she accepts an offer of $97,000 for her home. Result: the seller still nets $94,000—after paying $3,000 to the listing broker. The listing broker goes along with the deal because he gets the 3% commission he was likely to earn anyway. The buyer pays $97,000 plus $3,000 to his agent, for a total of $100,000.

In another alternative the buyer offers a higher price to the seller—say, $100,000—and the contract stipulates that the seller will pay both the buyer's agent and his own listing agent, netting perhaps the same $94,000 (6% split between the two brokers) or less, if the listing agent won't accept the split.

## Finding a buyer's broker

Ask for the names of buyer brokers at your local Board of Realtors and large real estate firms in your area. And professors of real estate at local colleges and universities may be able to recommend some.

*The Buyer's Broker Registry,* part of a larger directory entitled *Who's Who in Creative Real Estate, Inc.*, lists about 350 buyer brokers. The directory gives advice, too, on buyer brokerage and how to employ a broker.

All brokers listed in this directory either submitted a completed buyer's brokerage transaction to the company for its review or completed a qualifying course on buyer brokerage. In addition, all listed brokers agree to abide by the publisher's definition of "single agency" and other professional real estate practices.

Copies of the directory are available for $25 from the *Buyer's Broker Registry,* P.O. Box 23275, Ventura, CA 93002. Readers of this book who would like the names of three registered buyer brokers in their state or region can get them by sending $5.00 to the directory, along with a cover letter mentioning this Kiplinger/Changing Times real estate guide; additional names are available for $1.00 each.

## DECODING THE CLASSIFIED ADS

Whatever kind of market you're hunting in, whether with or without an agent's help, you should get acquainted with the classified real estate ads.

They can help you survey a community when you are starting your search with no fixed ideas of where you want to live. A few weeks of discriminating reading can give you an indication of price ranges and neighborhood character. They can also acquaint you with brokerage firms concentrating their efforts in a particular area and, sometimes, an individual agent who sells a particular kind of house. Most particularly, the ads uncover homes being sold by owners and builders, and each weekend they reveal a dazzling array of open houses.

If you're looking for a home in an area far away, subscribe to the local newspapers there and get a detailed map of the vicinity, showing neighborhood names. The two together will begin to give you an arms-length feel for the real estate market there, even before you make your first visit.

The classified section is especially useful in a slow market, even more so if you are conducting your search on your own, without access to a multiple listing service. For example, you can keep current on new offerings and price reductions, as well as probable sales. If you know how long a property has been advertised, what its starting price was, and how many real estate firms have offered it, you have a leg up when you're negotiating an offer. Start a notebook in which you paste in ads that you clip from the paper each day or each weekend.

A successful ad tries to entice you to a property. It tells you only about features that might attract you. It withholds details that might discourage you. Before you start calling agents to inquire about an advertised property, make a standard checklist with your wants and don't-wants listed on a grid. Have it handy when you call, and cut through the smoke screen of the ad with a few key questions at the onset. That way, you'll avoid a long conversation with the agent about how you can buy the property with seller financing, and then realize, after you have hung up, that you don't know how many bedrooms it has, whether it has a garage or when you could move in.

After a while, you get the hang of real-estatese, all those cryptic abbreviations, like "2b, 1ba, lctm, owc, q.pos." You'll decode it as: two bedrooms, one bath, low cash to mortgage, owner will carry mortgage, quick possession.

You'll also get acquainted with all the clever euphemisms that agents use in their ads. "Handyman's special" and "lots of potential" often mean the house is falling in. "Just awaits your loving touch" means a total redecorating is needed. "Charming dollhouse" means the rooms are tiny. "Convenient to everything" can signal a busy corner near the bus route. "Low upkeep" might mean it has no yard at all. And so on, limited only by the agent's gift for prose.

Don't overlook new developments and apartment condominium conversions. You won't be pointed to these properties by most agents, unless they specialize in condos or the builder has promised to compensate agents for bringing buyers in.

Condo and cooperative ads will usually be listed in the same classified section as detached houses, but under their own listings. The new-house market tends to be advertised apart from the classifieds, in large display ads in the newspaper's special real estate section, often on Saturdays.

## HANDLING THE "SALE BY OWNER"

And don't overlook the "sale by owner" ads in the classifieds. They can sometimes result in a sticky, awkward negotiation, but if you're knowledgable about the market and have the advice of a good attorney, a deal can be made—with or without an agent's help.

If you're looking at houses on your own, you and the seller can deal face to face or through an attorney skilled in real estate negotiations and law.

Things get complicated if you've been looking at houses with an agent and you feel indebted to the agent for all the effort and advice you've received in the quest. You have a couple of choices:

1) You can abandon your agent and deal directly with the seller, with no compensation to the agent. After all, the agent knew all along that he or she would get paid only if you bought a house that you first saw with the agent; that's the risk of the business.

2) You could deal directly with the seller but pay the agent some modest fee for the time and trouble that was expended on

you. Keep in mind, however, that you're not under any obligation to do so.

3) You could try to persuade the seller to accept your agent and pay the agent a 3% commission (or any other commission you can all agree on). The agent would provide service to the seller, helping with the negotiation, mortgage arrangements, and getting both parties to settlement without a hitch. The agent will end up getting the same commission (some part of the 3%, shared with the broker's firm) that he or she would have earned from a regular listing.

Why would a seller agree to this? Well, the seller has listed the house himself, performing the duties of advertising it, preparing fact sheets, and holding open houses. For that he has avoided paying someone a full 6% commission. Perhaps he would settle on paying "your" agent 3%, getting some service for the price and avoiding alienating you as a buyer, since you want to stay with your agent and work it out amicably.

This is why many "sale by owner" sellers put the phrase "brokers welcome at 3%" in their ads. They don't want to pay a full 6% commission, but at the same time they don't want agents to boycott their property, refusing to bring clients to see it.

If the seller balks and you really want to be loyal to the agent who's helped you, you could refuse to come see the seller's house without an understanding to protect the agent. In a slow market, that might convince the seller to relent, but if he has other buyers waiting in the wings, you might be hurting your own chances of getting the house.

## TOURING THE HOUSE

If you have the luxury of deliberation, you'll want to make several visits to a house you're considering making on offer on. In a brisk market, however, it's not uncommon for a buyer to make an offer after only one brief visit to a house. Either way, try to get the maximum benefit out of every minute you're in the house. Consider yourself a reporter and detective, there to gather as much information as possible about the house and the sellers.

You probably know your wants and don't-wants list well enough that you won't need to take a check list with you, but by all means take a note pad and tape measure. At most open houses you'll find an information sheet about the house. The most complete sheets have such things as square footage of lot and house, the most recent property taxes, average monthly utility bills, and the age of appliances and major mechanical systems, as well as the basics of number of rooms, etc.

If, at first glance, this looks like a house you'll want to pursue, sketch out floor plans on your first visit; they'll help you envision the house hours or days later. You'll want a professional inspection made if you put a contract in, but you can make some tentative judgments on your own. Take a close look a the furnace, electrical box (fuses or circuit breakers?) and appliances; do they appear to be in good shape, or very tired? How about the roof, gutters and exterior finish? Does the house have storm windows, or will you have to add them at your own cost? If the floor plan doesn't fit the way you live, how easily can rooms be rearranged or new ones added on?

Some buyers who are looking primarily at older houses know in advance that they'll probably have to do substantial remodeling or expanding. As a matter of fact, some buyers would rather buy a slightly shabby but basically sound house and remodel it to their own tastes than pay a premium for a recently completed remodeling that doesn't suit them. These buyers have an architect and/or contractor standing by to accompany them through a house on the second visit, after a preliminary look proves promising. The judgment of these professionals on the ease and probable cost of renovation will play a role in how much the buyer offers for the house.

## ASK QUESTIONS AND MORE QUESTIONS

You should try to find out as much as possible about the sellers, starting with the first visit to a house that you're seriously interested in. Everything you learn will make you a better informed, and therefore more capable, negotiator should you decide to make an offer.

Conversely, don't give away strategic information to the seller or the seller's agent or broker. You are put at a disadvantage, for example, if the seller discovers you have sold your current home and are anxious to find a replacement. The same is true if you have a soon-to-expire lease, or are shopping from out of town.

It's hard for buyers not to be forthcoming in a pleasant conversation with the seller or seller's agent, but if you can resist showing your hand, you'll be way ahead. Put on your best poker face and give noncommittal answers.

Some buyers would rather remain anonymous right up until the presenting of their offer. If that suits your style, then don't give your name to agents at open houses and don't sign their visitor register. And ask the agent who is helping you look to refrain from identifying you to sellers until an offer is submitted.

Here are some things you'll want to know about sellers:

▶ Are they truly "motivated," as the agents say, or are they just trying to find out what the market will pay for their house?

▶ Has the seller purchased another house, with a deadline for settling on it?

▶ Why are they selling . . . a job transfer, retirement, need for more (or less) space, divorce, financial setback, health problem, children off at college, death of spouse, or maybe some dissatisfaction with the house or neighborhood?

▶ How long have they lived here? (You can discover this, and also how much they paid for the house, from public land records.)

▶ When does the seller wish to settle, and do they wish to remain in the house after settlement, in a "lease back" from the new owner?

▶ Will the seller consider assisting you in the purchase, by taking back a second trust?

The degree of motivation will determine how the seller prices the house in the first place, and how receptive to price cutting the seller proves to be later on.

You need to ask questions like these, whether the house is being shown by the seller himself or by an agent. If you have hired an agent to represent you, he or she should learn as much as possible about the seller before you present an offer.

Keep in mind that the seller, and especially the seller's agent, will often be coy or less than candid, because everything told to you will make you a better informed, and therefore tougher, adversary in the negotiation that follows.

However, sellers and their agents are required by law to warn buyers of defects in a property that would not be apparent during a routine inspection by the buyer. For example, a seller must reveal a known structural deficiency or building code violation. An agent can't know everything about a particular property, of course. But honest ones will tell you about problems they're aware of, and agents can be held accountable for giving buyers wrong information on something they should make it their business to know about.

If you can, talk with the seller's neighbors in a non-threatening way that doesn't seem to be invading the seller's privacy. For example, you might ask whether any houses have been sold in the neighborhood recently. Then, try to steer the conversation toward information about the sellers, as well as details of selling prices, type of buyers, and how much houses had appreciated since the last sale.

If you haven't already cased the neighborhood, now is the time—before making an offer—for serious study of the condition of the area and the recent sale prices of comparable houses.

## IF YOU ENCOUNTER DISCRIMINATION

It is not uncommon for members of racial and ethnic minority groups to encounter overt or subtle discrimination when they go looking for a home to buy.

It can take many forms. A real estate agent may try to steer a black family away from an all-white neighborhood, telling them they "wouldn't feel comfortable there." Or a seller may tell the listing agent not to bring any Hispanic families to see the house, or the seller will not seriously consider a bona fide contract from such a buyer. Or an agent will tell a Jewish home buyer that a house is already sold, when in fact it's still available.

All of these kinds of discrimination are illegal. The federal Fair Housing Law (Title VIII of the Civil Rights Act of 1968, as amended by the Housing and Community Development Act of 1974) has broad prohibitions against discrimination in the rental, sale and financing of housing.

In its application to single-family real estate, the law is most sweeping when a professional real estate broker/agent is involved. But the law exempts from its coverage private individuals who own no more than three single-family dwellings, providing that 1) a broker is not involved in the sale or rental; 2) there is no discriminatory advertising; and 3) the owner has not sold more than one house (in which he or she was not the most recent resident) during any two-year period. As you can see, many sale-by-owner situations may be exempted from the provision of the federal Fair Housing Law.

But real estate professionals—who handle the bulk of the nation's housing transactions—are covered by strict sanctions against discrimination. Agents and mortgage lenders may not:

1) Refuse to sell, rent, deal or negotiate with a person because of his or her race, color, religion, sex or national origin.

2) Deny that housing is available for inspection, sale or rent when it really is available.

3) Persuade owners to sell or rent their homes by telling them that minority groups are moving into the neighborhood—a practice called "blockbusting."

4) Set different terms or conditions for mortgage financing based on race, creed, religion, sex or national origin.

If you believe you are being discriminated against by a real estate agent or seller using an agent, you should immediately confront the person and demand an explanation. If the explanation is not satisfactory and your suspicions persist, write a letter about the agent to the agent's employer-broker and send a similar letter to the local Board of Realtors, if the broker is a member. See if there is a fair-housing commission in the city, county or state where you are house hunting, and tell it of the situation in writing.

Also make a complaint to the Housing Discrimination Division, U.S. Department of Housing and Urban Development (HUD) (451 7th St., S.W., Washington, DC 20410-5500), giving all the details. HUD may intervene directly or refer the matter to a state or local agency that administers a law comparable to the federal statute. The state or local agency is required to begin proceedings within 30 days and proceed with "reasonable promptness." Complaints can also be taken directly to a U.S. District Court or state or local court within 180 days of the alleged discriminatory act.

# 8

# Determine Your Price

You know what you can afford to pay. Now decide what you are willing to pay for this particular home. There are several ways to go about this. Some methods are more realistic in slow markets when you have plenty of time to decide, but all require you to gather certain information.

Get an analysis of comparable properties from your assisting agent. There should be several properties on the list. Obviously, no two can be exactly alike, but be sure that those being represented as comparable are similar enough to the property you intend to bid on to be useful in setting an offering price. Look at the date of sale for each case on the list. Under normal market conditions, it should be no more than six months old. Note the location. A similar property in a different neighborhood may not really be comparable at all. The same house on a prime lot in the same block may be worth more because of its location. Examine the physical features of each property. Comparables should be roughly the same age and condition. The size of the lot, the number of rooms and baths, and total square feet of living space should be close.

Finally, the terms and conditions of sale should be scrutinized. A property sold with seller financing does not compare directly with one sold using standard financing. For example, if the seller took back a second mortgage at a below-market interest rate, that's the equivalent of a reduction of the sale price, so you should discount the price of the house when you use it for comparison.

## GETTING AN APPRAISAL

If already you know the neighborhood, if you've obtained good comparables, and if you have an adequate sense of the seller's motivations, you may be prepared to make an offer without additional advice. But, if you're not certain—and if time permits, which is not the case in a hot seller's market—consider paying for an appraisal to determine the value of the property.

An appraisal may cost you a few hundred dollars, but weigh that expense against the consequences of paying thousands too much for a home. If price appreciation doesn't make up the difference between what you pay and what the property is actually worth, it comes out of your pocket when you sell.

You may be from out of town and under pressure to find a home quickly. The property may have a big addition that's unusual for the neighborhood, or it may have been on the market too long. In fact, any circumstance that makes a property or a sale unusual calls for a professional evaluation. You can hire a disinterested real estate broker to give you advice on how much to pay, or you can pay an independent professional appraiser for a report.

If you decide on an appraiser, pick one who specializes in residential appraisals. Check on work experience, education and training. Ask several prominent local mortgage lenders for recommendations from their list of appraisers they hire often. (The appraiser organizations listed in the appendix may be able to supply you with lists of their members in your area.)

You will be required to pay for a lender's appraisal before your mortgage is approved, but if the appraiser you hire before making your offer is on the lender's approved list, you may not have to pay for a second, unnecessary appraisal later.

If you don't get an appraisal, and your purchase offer turns out to be a lot higher than the appraised value, the mortgage lender may reject your application or at least reduce the amount of the loan. This can be avoided by getting an appraisal before you bid.

Appraisals are not infallible, even those commissioned by the mortgage lender itself. In 1985 the Mortgage Guaranty Insurance Corp. studied 300 foreclosed properties throughout the country. The properties were selected for examination because the original appraisal and the appraisal done at foreclosure were more than

20% apart. While MGIC found that in most cases the value differences resulted from a change in the real estate market, in about 40% of the foreclosures, the appraiser's inexperience or incompetence was usually responsible.

Even more common, apparently, was a widespread willingness to fudge the numbers so that the appraised value was the same as the full contract price being offered. Lenders anxious to make loans tended to reward appraisers with repeat business when they overvalued. Appraisal departments found it particularly difficult to resist pressures exerted by the loan production departments of their own institutions.

Since then many lenders have tightened their standards. But the problem for buyers remains. Unless you hire your own appraiser before you submit an offer, your offer may be higher than it needs to be.

If you get your own appraisal and the lender insists on another one by an appraiser of its own choosing, request a copy of the second one, too. You've paid for it, and unless there's some wording to the contrary, you're entitled to have it.

Appraisals vary in complexity. Before you hire an appraiser, tell him or her exactly what purpose the appraisal is to serve, and ask about the fee; both should appear on the final report. One appraisal report commonly used by lenders is written on a standard FNMA form. Depending on where you live, such an appraisal may cost from $150 to $350. It should show how the appraiser arrived at the value and include a list of limiting conditions, pictures of the house and street, a map locating the site and, possibly, a floor plan.

A full narrative report, which may run well over 100 pages, typically would be required as court testimony, or to settle an estate. But it is much more expensive, and it rarely would be needed for routine home purchases.

You cannot use an FNMA report for a VA or FHA purchase, and you cannot use a VA or FHA appraisal for a conventional loan. A seller who is amenable to VA or FHA financing already may have obtained a conditional commitment, or a certificate of reasonable value, from the VA or FHA. The two agencies' appraisals are interchangeable.

## ESTABLISH YOUR PRIORITIES

Price always is important, but it may not be the primary factor. Rank the elements of a deal according to your own wants and needs: price, financing, date of possession, extras. Put your priorities down on paper. They will be an important mental tool to employ in evaluating a counter-offer from the seller. Consider how you might accommodate the seller—at the right price.

For example, if the seller must remain in the house for a period after settlement, what would make that worthwhile to you? Do you need financing help from the seller? Would obtaining a price reduction of several hundred dollars assuage your sense of loss at not having the bedroom curtains included? You probably won't get everything you want, so try to decide in advance what you might be willing to give up in order to complete the purchase, or what you might take in exchange for a feature both you and the seller really want to keep.

## NEED SELLER FINANCING?

If you think that your down payment and first mortgage may not be enough to swing the purchase, you'll probably need seller financing to help swing the deal; whether or not the seller is interested in helping you will depend mostly on the condition of the housing market.

Seller financing was very common in the late 1970s and early '80s, when market mortgage rates were very high and sellers had to help out buyers to make any deal at all. But when interest rates came way down in the mid-'80s, seller financing evaporated; there were enough qualified buyers around that sellers didn't have to take the risks associated with seller financing.

Seller-assisted financing ties the buyer and seller together long past the purchase transaction, so the seller has a strong interest in the buyer's financial resources, job stability and personal life. As a buyer seeking seller financing, don't be surprised if the seller requires of you considerable detail about such matters; as your prospective creditor, he's entitled to know.

Your need for seller financing will greatly reduce your negotiating strength on the purchase price of the house. For the seller to do well financially on these deals, he or she must get a sale price that's enough higher to make up for the below-market interest rate and stretched-out payment; remember, in a time of high inflation (when high interest rates create the climate for creative financing), you the buyer will be paying back the seller's loan with increasingly devalued dollars.

So if you're looking for seller help with the purchase, you can't expect to get a great deal on the sale price, too—unless there are so few qualified buyers in the marketplace that the seller is desperate.

If you think you'll need seller financing, turn right now to the discussion of the various kinds of "creative financing" in Chapter 10. You'll need to bone up on the details before you make an offer on the house. Both the kind of seller financing and the interest rate you're seeking are negotiable and must be written into your contract.

## HIRE YOUR OWN REPRESENTATIVE

This is a good time to get expert help, if you haven't already. A buyer's broker or real estate lawyer you pay will represent your interests, deciphering the contract form, suggesting contingency clauses, and negotiating with the seller or seller's agent.

Get names of experienced lawyers from friends, associates, bankers, title insurance officers and the local bar association. When interviewing, ask for an advance estimate of the fee. Find out what kind of role attorneys typically play in sales for your particular area. What is the charge for reviewing a contract? For being present at settlement? Let the attorney know what you are expecting. Do you want assistance in drawing up a contract? During negotiations? At settlement?

## HONE YOUR NEGOTIATING SKILLS

Buyers often are seriously handicapped by their lack of negotiating experience. Many don't realize they may bargain on every element of the deal, and agents don't always tell them. Keep in mind that, as a buyer, you initiate the bargaining, by making an offer to the seller.

Keep a log of the negotiating process. Make note of repairs and replacements that are needed or soon will be. Write down the negative features of the property.

Remember that good negotiating has more to do with knowing exactly what you want from a deal than it does with playing the role of tough bargainer.

If you're going to be doing your own negotiating, here are two current books that address the art of negotiation from the perspective of the homebuyer:

*The Common Sense Guide to Successful Real Estate Negotiation,* by Peter G. Miller and Douglas M. Bregman (Harper & Row).

*Home Buyers: Lambs to the Slaughter?,* by Sloan Bashinsky (Prentice-Hall).

## THE OPENING BID

Whether you should make your highest bid right away or send up a trial balloon in the form of a lower offer depends on how fair you think the asking price is, and how brisk the market is— particularly the market for the property you want.

Many asking prices have a good bit of padding built into the price, to see if someone will take the bait. Don't feel you have to offer the full asking price, or even something close to it, just because that's what the owner is seeking. Offer what you think the house is worth—both in broad market terms and to you in particular—based on your study of comparables or the appraisal. If the owner is offended by a low bid, so be it. You'll find out in their counter-offer or lack of any response when the time limit expires. Conversely, sometimes a house is listed *lower* than market value, because of owner ignorance or a desire to sell very fast. If you're the only buyer who's spotted this bargain, offering the full asking price is fine; but it might be sold to someone else who offers more than asking price.

If you decide to try for a lower figure first, don't let the seller's agent know that you are willing to go up. If, during the contract presentation, the seller should ask his agent directly whether you might go higher, the agent would be obliged to answer yes; the same goes for an agent who has been assisting you without compensation and who will be compensated out of the sales commission. "Your" agent is going to get paid only if you buy this house and he or she splits the commission with the seller's agent. "Your" agent wants to get the deal closed, and "your" agent is going to be paid by the seller. You can't expect this person to represent your interests aggressively in the negotiations, so you shouldn't tell him or her what your top price will be or any other major detail of your strategy.

## BIDDING ON A SALE-BY-OWNER HOUSE

Theoretically, a given house should cost you less if bought directly from the owner, rather than through an agent's listing. And if the deal is structured right, the seller will do fine, too. What the seller wants is the most net proceeds from the sale, so a lower offer that is not reduced by a 6% sales commission could net as much or more for the seller than a higher offer from which the commission is subtracted.

Some sellers will try for a few weeks to sell the house themselves, before listing it with a broker at a slightly higher price. Even after a listing contract is signed by the seller, some contracts allow the seller to sell the house directly—with no sales commission to the agent—provided the seller found the buyer himself, with no help from the agent. In either of these cases, the buyer should move fast and try to buy the house for a lower price than it will eventually be listed for.

How much lower? Well, it could be a full 6% lower, which presumes that all the savings of the commission will go into the buyer's pocket. More realistically, the sale-by-owner seller will probably want to share in that commission savings, perhaps splitting the 6% evenly with the buyer.

## PUT IT IN WRITING

Do all your negotiating in writing. Don't telegraph your strategy verbally, and don't make any verbal offers.

A purchase offer in writing can become a binding agreement for both you and the seller. Whether it is called a contract-to-purchase, an offer, binder, or earnest money agreement, and even if it spells out only the terms of the sale, you can be held to that offer once it is signed by the seller.

So be sure that your first contract submitted is all-inclusive, with everything of any importance written into it; if it's accepted by the seller and you've forgotten to put something you want in writing, it will be too late to add anything.

Most preprinted purchase contracts used by real estate agents are written to protect the seller, not the buyer. They often lack even the most customary contingency clauses for the buyer's protection, such as a home inspection, review of contract by an attorney, and requirement that the offer be accepted within two or three days or be void. A preprinted form is a good starting point, but you should feel free to amend or modify it in any way that meets your objectives. (If contingencies are typed onto the back of the preprinted form, they should be initialed by the buyer before the contract is submitted to the seller.) Feel free to have your own attorney draw up a contract or make the contract contingent on his review.

A real estate contract-to-purchase generally is assumed to be all-inclusive. Everything of importance should be written into it. A contract should include the sales price, down payment, legal description of the property and any items being sold with the home; the way title is to be conveyed; the fees to be paid and who will pay them; the amount of deposit; the conditions under which the seller and buyer can void the contract; the settlement date; how financing will be arranged; and so on.

Everything in real estate is subject to negotiation. That means the way you choose to negotiate, the contract form and everything that goes into it.

A well-written contract protects the buyer. In it, the buyer promises to pay the seller the purchase price only after the seller has shown that he can convey a good title. The seller, in turn, agrees to deliver the deed when the buyer pays for the property.

## A SMART-BUYER'S CONTRACT

Your purchase contract should make clear every aspect of the transaction. Each clause that makes the whole contract agreement subject to or contingent on its fulfillment is commonly called a "contingency."

Here are some of the major elements and contingencies to be considered for insertion in the contract:

**Earnest money deposit.** With the exception of court-ordered sales, no law requires buyers to make a deposit of a particular size, or any deposit at all. As a practical matter, however, a seller will look to the deposit as an indication of your earnest intentions. If your offer is accepted, and then you fail to follow though on your commitments, the seller may be entitled to keep the money. The amount of deposit varies with local custom. In some areas, it may run as much as 5% or 10% of the sales price. A seller might refuse to consider an offer that is not coupled with a reasonable deposit. Conversely, a large earnest money check can help swing a deal in your favor.

Most real estate agents expect an earnest money check when they present a contract, and will ask that it be made out in the firm's name or to the managing broker and add the words "trustee" or "fiduciary agent" after the name on the check as further protection. Never make out a deposit check to a seller.

If the broker doesn't routinely deposit earnest money in an interest-bearing trust account, or with a neutral third party, such as a title company, escrow service or attorney acting as an escrow agent, insert that requirement in your contract, and also specify that interest earned on your money will be credited to your side of the ledger at settlement. If your contract does not contain a clause requiring all money to be handled in escrow, insert one. Private individuals are not answerable to any regulatory authority on how they handle funds while a deal is pending. If it goes sour, you might have to sue to get your money back.

Don't allow your deposit money to be tied up too long. Unless you have plenty of cash, you will need that money to make a commitment to another property if something goes wrong with this deal.

The check shouldn't be deposited until the contract has been accepted; write this clause into the contract. (On the other hand, if the seller has any qualms about your creditworthiness, you can urge him to have the check deposited as proof that it's good.)

If your offer is accepted by the seller, but the purchase falls through later, through no fault of yours, you should get your money back; a clause in your contract should specify return of the earnest money within a specified number of days if the contract collapses.

**Settlement agent:** It's usually the buyer's privilege to select the attorney or title company who will perform the settlement services; write the name into the offer contract. It should be a skilled neutral party, to ensure that all the contract's requirements are lived up to before any money is disbursed or the title is passed. If you don't have a particular person in mind at the time you submit your contract, specify that the settlement agent will be selected by the buyer.

**Deed and title condition.** The buyer's offer should state what kind of deed and the condition of title he or she is willing to accept from the seller. The contract also should make it clear what actions the seller must take to deliver a good title by settlement, and what recourse you have should that not occur. (Chapter 12 discusses getting a good title at length.)

**Prorating.** This is a method of equitably dividing continuing expenses, such as mortgage interest, property taxes and insurance, equitably between buyer and seller. Suppose that in January the owner pays the annual premium for a homeowner's insurance policy. The owner then sells the property and goes to settlement midway through the year. What happens to the insurance coverage paid for but not used? In many cases, the new buyer "buys" the remaining coverage period from the owner by arrangement with the insurance company, and payment is made at settlement.

**Settlement date and possession.** The date of settlement and the date when you will be entitled to take physical possession of your home are stated in the contract.

The settlement date is usually no sooner than the length of time required by the title search and mortgage approval—typically 45 days to two months. In a very busy market, such as during the refinancing boom of 1986, mortgage lenders get backed up, so make sure you allow yourself enough time before settlement. This is especially important if you are planning to sell your current house and need to take that equity to the settlement table on the next purchase. If the settlement is too soon, you'll have to seek an extension from the seller or get a bridge loan. If you're a first-time buyer without a house to sell, and the seller wants a fast settlement, you can oblige the seller and make your offer a little more attractive than that of another buyer who needs a long delay before settlement.

Possession usually occurs immediately after settlement. When a buyer needs to move in before settlement, or a seller needs to remain after settlement, the preferred procedure is to arrange for a separate rental agreement between the parties. Such agreements can have unexpected legal and tax consequences, so the documents involved should be prepared by an attorney and carefully examined before being accepted. Rent can be set at any agreed-upon level; it's often set at a no-profit "wash" level, with the renter paying exactly the total monthly carrying costs on the house—principal, interest, taxes, utilities, and insurance.

**Loan conditions.** Unless you can swing the purchase without a mortgage loan, your contract should be contingent on getting a written loan commitment within a specified time, and at terms agreeable to you. The terms should state the maximum interest rate and number of discount points you are willing to pay. That way, should you fail to obtain the desired financing, you will be released from the contract, and your deposit will be returned. If your contract is accepted, this clause temporarily takes the property off the market and enables you to shop for a mortgage.

If you went through a prequalifying process, you'll know what size loan and interest rate you will be eligible for, so use those figures on this section of the contract. Don't put down some unrealistic numbers—a below-market interest rate or bigger loan than you'll be able to manage; these might raise the seller's suspicions and make your offer unattractive compared with others.

Discount points, appraisal fee and other items must be paid in order to get a loan. Your contract should state how these charges are to be apportioned between buyer and seller.

Just because an agent tells you it's customary for buyers to pay all points (one point equals 1% of the mortgage), this doesn't mean you must do so in this case. In many areas it is common for the seller to help the buyer with financing by agreeing to pay a point or so, which is the same as reducing the sale price by that amount; an anxious seller in a slow market may agree to pay several points.

Finally, if you're proposing that the seller help you with financing, this is where the terms and interest rate must be spelled out.

**Sale of current residence.** In a slow buyer's market, some people trading up to another home are nervous about committing themselves to the next purchase without confidence that they will be able to sell their current house. So they add a clause in the purchase contract enabling them to back out of the deal if they don't get a viable contract on their current home within a specified period of time.

Sellers are justifiably leery of this kind of contingency, and a contract containing it will be far less desirable than others. Avoid adding this clause unless there are compelling market reasons for doing so.

**Response time limit.** Your contract should require the seller to accept the offer *in writing* (not verbally) within a certain time—such as 48 hours—or the offer will be void. How long depends on general market activity and buyer interest in that home particularly. Failure to state a time limit invites having your contract "shopped." That means that the seller or agent may use your offer to stimulate slower-moving buyers to top your offer.

You are free to withdraw and cancel an offer at any time before the seller has accepted it.

The phrase "time is of the essence" should be included to emphasize the time limit on the offer and the closing date. This does not prevent you or the seller from obtaining a mutually-agreed-upon extension, but it precludes it from being available unilaterally on demand.

**Home inspection.** This contingency clause can be inserted to give you the right to have the property inspected, and to withdraw your offer if the inspection report isn't satisfactory for any reason. The clause may also contain language that will let you negotiate price adjustments to pay for any necessary repairs. (See Chapter 9 for more information on home inspections.) Normally, you will not be granted a lot of time, because sellers and brokers regard this as a gaping loophole. Buyers with second thoughts may use the report to get out of a deal, so don't be surprised if your seller insists that the inspection be done within a week by a recognized professional. The seller also may request a copy of the report, and that request should be granted.

The critical portion of a typical inspection clause reads: "This contract is contingent on a property inspection report which, in the sole judgment of the purchaser, is deemed satisfactory." You can see that a contingency clause with that kind of wording leaves a loophole as big as the house itself.

If necessary, offset the negative impact of this clause with a larger earnest money deposit, or some other bargaining chip that will impress the seller with your interest in the property.

Most real estate contracts allow the seller to determine the period in which the inspection must be completed. Normally this is no fewer than three and no more than ten days from the date of the contract. If you have no inspector lined up or are uncertain about how to find one who is reliable and competent, try to negotiate with the seller for as much time as possible. (See the next chapter for details about the inspection.)

**Termite inspection.** Many contracts today require the seller to order and pay for a termite inspection. The contract should set out the conditions that, if active termites are found, will permit the buyer to void the deal or negotiate with the seller for extermination and repairs.

**What goes with the house.** There could be a clause specifying that certain curtains or special-sized rugs or furnishings be included in the deal. It's customary for the seller to leave all major appliances and all built-in things that would normally be construed as part of the property, such as lighting devices, wall-to-wall carpet, built-in bookcases, and outside landscaping. But custom varies from area to area, so you'd better be specific. The more things spelled out in the offering contract, the fewer the later misunderstandings.

**Condition of house at settlement.** The contract should specify that everything in the house will be in demonstrable working order at the time of settlement, as verified during a walk-through of the premises a day or so before settlement. This means mechanical systems like heat, plumbing, kitchen appliances, etc. Note that this is not a guarantee that these things will continue working after you buy the house—just that they are functioning properly at the moment you take title.

If there are any exceptions, they should be noted in the contract, with the notation that certain appliances are being conveyed "as is," with no guarantee made as to working order. It may be impossible to test the air conditioning during the winter, so it should be noted that the test will be done as soon as temperature permits.

As for cleanliness, the contract should specify that the house will be empty of all stored objects and debris (including things in the attic, basement and garage) and will be handed over in "broom-clean" condition.

**Other conditions.** The list could go on and on, but every condition runs the risk of making your offer a little more complicated and a little less appealing than someone else's cleaner contract.

## PRESENTATION AND COUNTER-OFFER

At this point, your offer—signed and all clauses initialed—is presented to the seller, either by you personally, your attorney, the seller's agent, or the agent who has been assisting you.

It is also common for the buyer to submit with the purchase offer a simple statement of his or her creditworthiness. Equally as important as the terms of the contract—perhaps more so—is the buyer's ability to get a loan and get to settlement. The seller will be asked to take his property off the market while the buyer arranges financing, so the seller's confidence in the buyer's financial strength will play a big role in whether the seller accepts this contract or another rival bid.

The financial statement doesn't have to have a lot of detail, but it should include information about employment, current home-ownership, etc. If you have already prequalified for a mortgage sufficient to swing this deal, that should be noted in the statement, with the name of the prequalifying firm. This information should be checkable by the seller or the seller's agent.

If the seller accepts everything in the contract, initials all clauses and signs the contract within the acceptance date specified, the offer becomes binding on both parties, subject to removal of such contingencies as inspection, financing, etc. Rejection of even the smallest provision of the offer is a rejection of the entire thing. If, however, the seller wishes to negotiate, a counter-offer is made.

The counter-offer typically takes one of three forms: a fresh purchase contract is made out that is identical to the buyer's offer except for the seller's changes; a counter-offer is written on the back of the original, or on a separate sheet of paper, accepting the buyer's terms with certain changes as stated; or the seller marks out on the original offer the unacceptable items and notes the proposed substitution above or below, initialing each change. A time limit to accept is noted, and the counter-offer is then dated and signed by the seller.

This is delivered to the buyer. If it is acceptable it is signed and dated, and the contract is complete. If not you can allow the counter-offer to expire or you can make a second offer. Have a new contract written out. Marking over and initialing extensively on a document can lead to confusion and mistakes.

Sometimes, negotiating goes on for days of offer, counter-offer, offer, counter-offer. More commonly, an agreement is reached on the second or third offer.

If the seller has other contract offers besides yours, he will try to play one against the other, often with verbal messages. Sometimes a seller or seller's agent will not formally counter a contract in writing, but will merely tell the prospective buyer that the offer is "too low," and if it's raised to some amount, it will be accepted. Do not raise your offer in response to such verbal signals; the seller has made no commitment to you, and you have no assurance that you'll get the house *even if* you raise your bid. The seller could change his mind again and keep trying to jack up your bid.

Instead, remind the seller that you have a formal offer on the table and you would appreciate a written counter-proposal, stating whatever higher price or other changes would make your offer acceptable. If the seller responds to your offer in writing, you're still in the ballgame; you can accept the seller's counter offer and nail down the deal; or counter again; or let the response time lapse. Your strategy should be to keep the seller involved with you alone until your negotiaton has run its course. Remember that the seller can only give a counter-offer to one buyer at a time; otherwise, the seller would be offering to sell the same house to more than one party, and he would run a risk that both parties would accept.

How much you bend will depend on how much you want this particular house, which is a function of whether you have to buy quickly, the state of the market, and how unusual this house is. If you have the luxury of time, and houses similar to this one come on the market with some frequency, don't despair if negotiations break down.

Stick to your main objectives, whether price or some other point. If this house gets away, you may have a shot at a similar one later; it's not unheard-of for a house hunter to put in unsuccessful contracts on two or three houses before finally buying. You may even have another chance to buy the first house later on—possibly at a lower price than you originally offered; by the time the seller wises up to his overpricing, the other interested buyers may have bought other houses, leaving you as the only bidder.

If your offer is accepted by the seller, or if you accept the seller's counter offer, the agreement becomes a binding contract. You should be aware that if you change your mind after your contract offer is accepted and signed by the seller, you could legally lose your deposit and even be liable for damages for failure to live up to your contract.

Likewise, if the seller simply backs down, you can sue for damages or try to enforce the contract terms. This is unusual, but it sometimes happens, especially in a hot market, when a much better offer comes along after the seller has accepted yours.

Even if the seller dies before settlement, the contract will be binding on the late seller's estate, which must proceed with the sale of the house to you, but you may need an attorney's help to assert your claim and keep the process on track.

## BRIDGE LOANS: BUY NOW, SELL LATER

If your contract is contingent on getting a bridge loan, don't delay arranging one. While loan approval can come as quickly as a week after you apply, the closing may take another two weeks.

And the process could drag on longer if the lender insists on appraising your present home.

Many lenders consider bridge loans risky propositions because of the uncertainty of whether the old house will sell, the time it might take to sell, and whether you will be able to get a price high enough to cover the bridge loan repayment.

It's much easier to get a bridge loan if your current house is already under contract and you're well along in the application process for permanent mortgage financing on your new home. In this case, you need the bridge loan just to make your original settlement date, if there is a processing delay in the mortgage application.

A bridge loan, also called swing, equity-advance or gap loan, is often structured as a balloon note, with the principal and interest due at the end of the term (six months is typical) or when your old home sells, whichever comes first. Some lenders require monthly or quarterly payments on interest.

The interest rate is often one to two percentage points above the prime rate at the time the loan is closed. Another pricing plan bases the interest on a rate somewhat higher than the prevailing rate charged for regular mortgages. Closing costs usually range from 0.5% to 1.5% of the amount borrowed, depending on whether the lender requires a title search, title insurance, credit report or appraisal.

The three most likely sources of these loans are commercial banks, savings and loan associations, and relocation companies that are hired by firms transfering employees.

Often banks aren't keen about lending this money to any but their preferred customers. If you don't fit that description, your real estate agent may be able to turn up a lender.

If you're moving out of the area, your best hope lies with a bank at your current location. Lenders prefer to do business locally—where they have some knowledge of the real estate market.

You may be able to work out a more attractive bridge loan if you're being transferred by your company. Many companies reimburse employees for the interest paid on bridge loans. A large number act as lenders themselves or contract with a relocation company to do so.

# 9

## Have the Home Inspected

You've made an offer, you've haggled over the contract, and a deal has been struck. Now is the time to let a home inspector give you an objective look at the current condition and potential problems of the house or apartment you're buying.

Remember, a purchase agreement with an inspection contingency clause allows you to void the deal based on the findings of the inspector, and if something very alarming turns up—such as serious structural defects—you may want to forget this property completely. Or you may void the first agreement and submit a new contract with a lower price reflecting the cost of correcting the problems—or one which offers the same price on the condition that the seller will make repairs at his expense.

In a brisk seller's market, the seller might not accept your new lower offer or agree to make the repairs, even if he agrees that the house has problems. Why? Because he may have recently received a much better offer than yours, and he's delighted that you have voided the first agreement. Even if he eventually has to correct the problems as a condition of sale, he'll come out ahead selling to the second bidder.

### FINDING A GOOD INSPECTOR

Ask friends, your attorney, real estate agents and lenders for recommendations. Home inspection services may be listed in the Yellow Pages under "Building Inspection Services," "Engineers

(Inspection or Foundation)" or "Real Estate Inspectors." By any name, the professional you want is one who knows old homes and new, inside and out, who makes a living poking into cellars and attics and crawl spaces looking for structural and equipment flaws, and who then gives clients detailed written reports that take much of the gamble out of home buying.

For more information about the inspection process, look for these books:

▶ *Buy Smart! The Complete Home Buyer's Guide to Residential Evaluation*, by R. Edward Brown (McGraw-Hill); a do-it-yourself manual and workbook.

▶ *Getting Your Money's Worth From Home and Real Estate Professionals*, by Mike McClintock (Crown).

▶ *The Complete Book of Home Inspection*, by Norman Becker (McGraw-Hill).

Satisfy yourself that the inspector you're hiring is professionally independent, not beholden to the real estate agent and not primarily interested in promoting a particular repair or remodeling business. Home inspectors' experience in the building field usually comes from a background in contracting, architecture or engineering.

Inspectors who are members of the American Society of Home Inspectors (ASHI), have agreed to abide by a written code of ethics and by prescribed standards of practice designed to protect prospective buyers. You can get names of ASHI members doing business in your area by writing to ASHI at Suite 630, 1010 Wisconsin Avenue, N.W., Washington, D.C. 20007.

There are also several state associations, among them:

▶ California Real Estate Inspection Association, 1100 N Street, Suite 5D, Sacramento, CA 95814;

▶ Florida Association of Building Inspectors, P.O. Box 1083, Maitland, FL 32751;

▶ Texas Association of Real Estate Inspectors, Inc., P.O. Box 50153, Austin, TX 78763.

## THE COST

Fees for inspecting homes generally vary according to contract price and geographical area, and sometimes with age, size and construction of the house. Assuming the home you are interested in is a fairly typical residential property, you might expect to pay anywhere from $150 to $300. Inspections in large metropolitan areas with more-expensive homes, such as New York and San Francisco, may cost more.

An inspector may charge one fee for all homes under $150,000, for example, and bill for inspecting those over that amount on a sliding scale according to price. Inspecting very new or very old homes may take more time, which is in turn reflected in the charge. And inspections on Sundays, holidays and after-hours also are likely to command premiums, as may those that require long-distance travel.

## THE INSPECTION

A thorough home inspection normally takes three hours or more. Most inspectors encourage buyers to accompany them. Arrange to do so and come prepared to ask questions and to get dirty. If the house has a crawl space, get down with the inspector and see whether routine maintenance chores in that space will be within your capacity.

Let the inspector know whether or not you are handy with a pipe wrench or know something about carpentry so you can get an on-the-spot estimate of repair costs. Provide information about family size and habits. A water heater that is adequate for four people may be inadequate for your foursome if everyone showers in the morning and then again after soccer and jogging in the evening. (A formula used by one inspector when calculating demands on a water heater counts a teenage girl with short hair as one person, a teenage girl with long hair as a person and a half, and a teenage boy as two.)

## THE REPORT

What you are really after is a written report covering the structure from basement to roof. The report should include an assessment of the quality and condition of all the following parts of the house or property:

▶ Grading, drainage, landscaping, fences, paved areas, retaining walls, recreational facilities, garage;

▶ Exterior walls (possibly including insulation), doors, windows (including storm and screen), porches and decks, steps;

▶ Roofing materials and construction, vents, hatches, skylights, gutters, downspouts, chimneys;

▶ Crawl space or basement—construction, structural stability, settlement, water penetration, termite or rot damage;

▶ Attic—access, ventilation, insulation, signs of leakage, fire safety;

▶ Electrical system, including capacity, grounding, fuses or circuit breakers, wires, outlets and switches, safety of all parts of the system;

▶ Plumbing system—pipes, drainage faucets, water heater, laundry appliances, sink traps, water pressure;

▶ Heating and cooling systems—type, capacity and condition, distribution of sources of heat and cooling, controls, humidifiers, fire safety;

▶ Kitchen and bathrooms—fixtures and appliances, plumbing, ventilation, tile, flooring.

If the property has special features you wanted inspected—such as a swimming pool, tennis court, well or septic system—you may need to hire a specialist. If you are having the home inspected in the depths of winter, testing may have to be postponed until a thaw; look to the wording of your contract to ascertain what obligation the seller will have at that time.

An inspector may use checklist-type worksheets covering the structure from basement to roof, adding brief remarks as necessary, or he may present a write-up of the overall condition of the property, along with suggested repairs and improvements.

The report should indicate current problems as well as those that may be impending. For example, the original wiring in homes built before World War II is usually not up to handling today's major electrical appliances. The inspector will make a note of such a shortcoming and give you some idea of what is involved in bringing it up to standard.

Whatever the reporting system used, the report itself should give you a realistic idea of what you have offered to buy. This gives you something to study in detail. It also gives you bargaining leverage.

## NEW HOMES, CONDOS AND CO-OPS

If you're buying in a development before the house is finished, hire an inspector to visit the model and then inspect the house while it's being built to make sure that the contractor is duplicating the specifications of the model. You'll pay extra for trips to the construction site, but the cost could be a bargain if it saves you from taking possession of a home that is destined to give you headaches.

Many states and local jurisdictions have held that a builder or developer selling a new house must honor an "implied" warranty on the basic components and systems of the house. But if the problem is a major one and high cost is involved, don't expect the builder to make good on such an unwritten warranty without a fight. A comprehensive inspection report, signed by a qualified professional inspector, should constitute good evidence of the way things were before you moved in. (See also the HOW program offered by member builders, discussed below.)

Apartment-type condominiums and co-ops require careful going over by inspectors knowledgeable and experienced about the special problems and considerations inherent in this type of ownership. For one, that means assessing the condition of a large-scale heating plant, common roofs, plumbing, halls, stairs, elevators and pools.

The typical inspection of a single apartment unit would leave the prospective owner with little or no information about the condition of the building as a whole. Remember, once you become a co-owner of this building, you will have to pay your share of the cost of a new roof, electrical system, furnace, etc.

When a building is converted to condominium use, the developer-seller must provide tenants (as prospective owners of units) with an engineering report on the condition of the building. Make sure you get a copy and have an inspector go over it before buying a unit. In addition, a tenant association or condo owners' association may commission its own engineering report; get a copy of that, too.

If an earlier report said that major work was required or advisable, find out if the work has been performed already or if it still lies ahead—at your expense; and find out if the work was paid for out of a reserve fund or by special assessment.

If you feel you need additional study of the building's condition, consider hiring the same engineering or inspection firm that did the earlier study, on an hourly basis. The re-inspection might take two or three hours and cost $100 to $200 per hour—a lot of money, but not so much when weighed against your share of the cost of major repairs to a large building.

## BACK TO THE SELLER?

When a seller hears that a qualified inspector has found that the roof needs repair or that the hot water heater has already outlived its normal lifespan, he may agree to make repairs or replacements. If not, perhaps you can knock down the price to cover the cost of having the work done yourself.

What if something catastrophic is discovered? Perhaps the floors are heaving or sagging or the foundation is settling, causing cracks in the interior walls. At this point price may no longer be the object, and you may want out. If the deal is contingent upon a satisfactory inspection, and the contingency is written into the offer to buy the house, you'll be legally off the hook.

## HOW TO AVOID THE NEW-HOME BLUES

If, two or three years after buying a brand-new home, you are faced with major expenditures caused by a faulty foundation, leaking roof or fireplace that's separating from its supporting wall, you may find that your dream house has turned into a nightmare.

Add to your woes the possibility of a lengthy, expensive court battle and you'll see the appeal of buying a home protected by the Home Owners Warranty Corporation or one of it's competitors. Home Owners Warranty Corporation (HOW) is an independent company owned by its member-builders.

HOW provides ten years of protection against major construction defects. If one of its 11,500 member-builders refuses to fix such a mistake, insurance covers the repairs. A built-in dispute-settling process determines the outcome when buyer and builder can't agree, and since 1974, when the program began, some 35,000 buyer-builder disagreements have been resolved out of court.

## What it costs, what it covers

HOW policies can't be purchased on the open market but must be obtained through an active HOW member-builder. A builder pays a one-time premium averaging $1.80 per thousand of a home's selling price. Thus, a builder would pay about $180 for warranty coverage on a $100,000 home.

During the first year, HOW builders warrant their new homes to be free from defects in workmanship and materials, major structural defects and flaws in the electrical, plumbing, heating, cooling, ventilating and mechanical systems.

During the second year, builders continue to warrant major structural components and electrical, plumbing, heating, cooling, ventilating and mechanical systems, but no longer cover defects in materials and workmanship.

If, during the first two years, a builder defaults on the terms of the warranty or goes out of business, claims are paid through the insurance portion of the warranty.

In the remaining eight years of HOW protection, a home is insured against major structural defects. HOW covers the cost of all authorized repairs after the owner pays the first $250. This $250 deductible applies to each claim.

Another important feature of HOW protection is that it stays with the home for a full ten years regardless of how often ownership may change—a factor that may enhance resale value.

## Hashing out disputes

When a buyer and a builder reach a stalemate over warranted items, either may request HOW to appoint an impartial third party to mediate, at no cost to the buyer. Referees for such disputes are supposed to have no affiliation with either HOW or the construction industry and are trained by the independent National Academy of Conciliators.

If a mutually acceptable solution cannot be reached, the neutral party decides on the issue. The decision is binding on the builder but not on the buyer, who remains free to take the matter to court. A builder who fails to comply with the decision is subject to expulsion from HOW ranks.

Most homeowners—some 82%—come away from the program's mediation process accepting the mediation results. Accepting a decision and being satisfied aren't necessarily the same thing, however. According to the National Academy of Conciliators, which provides mediators for the majority of HOW disputes, one source of dissatisfaction comes from not fully understanding what the warranty covers. Owners have the documents but they don't spend sufficient time reading them.

Another problem is that HOW has no authority to get tough on delinquent builders, except by expelling them from the program. An expelled builder is still free to go on constructing homes unless local or state regulatory bodies decide to take action.

HOW is the first and largest home warranty provider and its builders operate in every state except Alaska. Still, a HOW builder is not always easy to find. You can get a list of members by writing to the Public Affairs Manager, HOW, 2000 L St., N.W., Washington, D.C. 20036.

Home Buyers Warranty, HOW's largest competitor, enrolls some 7,000 builders around the country. You can obtain a list of their members by writing to Public Affairs, HBW, Suite 210, 1479 Brockett Road, Tucker, GA 30084.

# 10

## Pick the Right Kind of Mortgage for You

$O$nce the contract has been signed and the inspection contingency has been removed—usually within a week of signing—start shopping for financing as soon as possible (unless you're the rare buyer who doesn't need a mortgage). You must get loan approval in time to go to settlement with your mortgage money, and processing backlogs often force a delay of settlement or the necessity of a bridge loan.

Shopping around for the best mortgage can yield dramatic dividends, both in the short run (in "points" paid or saved) and especially in the long run. A difference of one-half percent in the annual percentage rate on a 30-year mortgage can mean thousands of dollars saved or spent needlessly. Paying 9.25% instead of 9.75% on a 30-year, fixed-rate $90,000 loan will save the prudent buyer about $33 each month. That may not seem so dramatic, but, over 30 years, it amounts to almost $12,000, not counting potential earnings if the monthly savings were invested over the years.

If you went through the prequalifying process before your house hunt, you have a head start on the mortgage hunt, in terms of having all your documents in order and knowing that you'll probably qualify for a certain size and kind of mortgage. If you prequalified with a given lender, you can continue to deal with that firm, but by no means should you stop there.

The message of this chapter is simple: *shop for a loan, not a lender*. Mortgage lending is a very mechanical, impersonal process, and it's highly competitive. You should hunt for the best loan—interest rate, points, processing costs, and in the case of adjustable mortgages, the most favorable adjustment features; you shouldn't pay much attention to what firm lends you the money, the kind of financial institution it is, whether you have a prior relationship with the lender, or even what city or state it's in. You can often deal as easily with an out-of-town lender as one in your community. The odds are very good that your loan will be sold on the secondary market once or several times over the term of the loan, and the firm that services the loan—that is, collects the payments and holds your taxes and homeowners insurance in escrow—may change, too.

The next chapter explains how to shop for a mortgage—what kinds of lenders make mortgage loans and how to use a mortgage reporting or finding service. But before you go into the market, try to decide what kind of loan suits your particular needs best; that's what this chapter is all about.

Learn the pros and cons of fixed-rate and adjustable borrowing. Get acquainted with the jargon of the mortgage business. A check list of the major characteristics of your ideal loan will enable you to do a lot of your shopping by phone. Then you can ask lenders the right questions and intelligently compare the many confusing offers that they'll put forward.

## THE BASICS

In essence, there are two ways that mortgage lenders charge you for the use of their money: through the interest charges you'll pay each month over the life of the loan, and in "points," a one-time sum of money (one "point" equaling 1% of the loan amount) that you'll pay up front.

Compare interest rates by asking for the true annual percentage rate (APR) of the loans you're considering; there are many ways to state interest rates, but APR is now the standard form, and lenders are required by law to give you this figure.

Points are prepaid interest charges that raise the effective yield to the lender without raising the interest rate on the note. Points discount the value of the loan to you. If you pay $1,800 (two points) in order to borrow $90,000, you really have borrowed only

$88,200. But you will have to pay back the full $90,000 face value of the loan, plus interest.

The payment of points to the lender is a standard part of the mortgage business today, and they must be factored into any comparison of annual percentage rates on mortgages. As a general rule, the payment of one point is equivalent to an additional ⅛th of one percent on the stated interest rate of the mortgage, over a 30-year loan. So a 10%, 30-year, fixed-rate mortgage with no points is technically equivalent in total cost to a 9% loan with eight points.

In reality, you'll never find a lender charging eight points, since that amount of prepaid interest would scare off all but a few affluent borrowers who know they'll own their homes for many years. In fact, most homeowners sell or refinance their homes long before their mortgages are repaid fully, so they wouldn't want to prepay that much interest. Consequently, the point differential between a 10% loan and a 9% one is more likely to be about three points.

Points on the buyer's mortgage are often shared between the buyer and the seller, with the seller paying something to help swing the deal. Payment of points by the seller is essentially a reduction of the asking price. The sharing of points, like everything else in a purchase contract, is open to negotiation. Points that can truly be regarded as prepaid interest on one principal residence are tax deductible for the buyer in the year paid.

In addition to points, many lenders charge an "origination fee," often calculated at 1% of the loan amount. Don't confuse the origination fee with the separate loan application fees you'll pay to cover the paperwork and approval of your mortgage; application fees are not tax deductible, but an origination fee, if truly prepaid interest, is.

In some cases, the origination fee is labeled with the somewhat confusing term "prepaid point," because it's a partial prepayment of one of the discount points to be charged at settlement or closing. If, for example, a mortgage calls for a buyer to pay three points (3% of the loan amount) at settlement, a credit will be given for the 1% origination fee the buyer paid when he applied for the loan, and only the remaining 2% will be collected at settlement.

## FIXED OR ADJUSTABLE RATE?

After all the exotic mortgages are laid aside, the big choice for most homebuyers comes down to a fixed- or adjustable-rate mortgage.

The standard fixed-rate, fully amortizing mortgage—with the same principal and interest payment each month over the life of the loan—came into existence during the Great Depression and fueled the enormous expansion of affordable home ownership in the three decades that followed the end of World War II. Its beauty was—and still is—the peace of mind that homeowners get from its predictable monthly payments. While taxes, utilities and other costs of homeownership may rise, the principal and interest payment remains the same. But if interest rates fall, the holder of the fixed-rate mortgage must refinance at a lower rate to get any benefit.

Lenders who made loans at fixed (and generally low) rates took a beating on the value of those loans when inflation and interest rates soared in the late 1970s. If they kept the loans, they had to settle for repayment in ever-devalued dollars. If they tried to sell the loans, they had to discount the value to reflect current and rising interest rates.

The increasing reluctance of lenders to make fixed mortgage loans in a climate of rising interest rates led to the creation of adjustable-rate mortgages (ARMs), under which the rate rises and falls with current interest rates charged throughout the economy. With an ARM, the borrower, not the lender, is assuming the risks of rising rates. But the borrower will benefit from declines in rates, too.

At one point in the early-1980s, when fixed-rate loans carried high interest rates, more than two-thirds of all new mortgages were adjustable-rate loans. As inflation and nominal interest rates declined in the mid-1980s, adjustable borrowers were very happy, and homeowners with high fixed-rate mortgages rushed to refinance; so did lots of homeowners with ARMs, too, because they wanted to lock in low fixed rates, rather than take a chance on a resurgence of inflation.

But when fixed-rate loans dropped down into single-digit territory, most borrowers began to think the big drop in interest rates was behind them, and the adjustable loan began to lose its appeal. By the spring of 1986, ARMs accounted for less than one-quarter of all new mortgages. When home buyers demand fixed-rate mortgages, lenders respond. (Unlike back in the 1970s, however, fixe-rate mortgage lenders aren't shouldering the risk of rising interest rates all by themselves. They're passing the risk on to the investment community, by reselling their mortgages in the secondary market.)

So, what's best for buyers today? Conventional wisdom would have buyers lock in low interest rates with a fixed-rate loan when it looks like interest rates are headed up over the next few years. If it's thought that rates will go down over the short term, or stay about the same, an adjustable-rate mortgage should be considered. Either way, guess wrong and you could lose.

For some buyers, especially those who can't count on rising income in a time of high inflation, a fixed-rate mortgage is safer. For other buyers, a one- or three-year adjustable mortgage with rate caps is worth careful consideration. ARMs are especially attractive if you intend to own your home for less than five years and if the current spread beween fixed-rate mortgages and the starting rate on the ARM is two percentage points or more.

Remember, with an ARM you'll never have to refinance to take advantage of drops in interest rates, as you have to do with a fixed mortgage. Over the long term, interest rates will have their ups and downs, but some forecasters believe that an ARM with good caps will produce a lower average (and therefore total) interest cost over many years than most fixed mortgages.

Don't accept an ARM without annual and lifetime caps on interest rates; typical caps today are no more than a two-percentage-point hike in interest rate from one year to the next and no more than a five- or six-point increase over the starting rate at any time during the term of the loan.

## FIXED-RATE LOANS

Fixed-rate loans offer an interest rate that does not vary during the life of the loan. In the traditional fixed-rate mortgage, the monthly payment remains the same over the life of the loan, but the proportion of principal and interest changes from month to month, with the early payments being almost pure interest and subsequent payments shifting progressively towards more and more principal. So over the life of the loan, your interest payments (and tax deductions) will dwindle, and your equity buildup will accelerate.

## Long-term mortgages

The most customary mortgage is the long-term loan of 20, 25 or 30 years.

**Advantages:** Certainty is the big plus. You know exactly how much you will be paying for interest over the term of the loan. The monthly payment of interest and principal is fixed. Payments in the early years consist primarily of tax-deductible interest.

**Disadvantages:** This stability comes at a price. Interest rates on this type of mortgage usually run higher than starting rates on adjustable loans. And you may have to pay more points to get it.

While amortization costs (payments of principal and interest calculated so as to pay off the entire debt within a fixed period of time) remain level over the loan term, monthly payments can increase over the years as property taxes and insurance costs go up.

Attractive (that is, low-interest) fixed-rate mortgages rarely are assumable by subsequent buyers, since lenders want to take every opportunity to retire a low-rate loan in place of a higher-interest mortgage (and if rates have gone down, the new buyer wouldn't want your old mortgage either).

With the regular 20-to-30-year term, principal balance is reduced relatively slowly compared to loans with shorter terms. The total interest cost is high. For example, an $89,000, 30-year, 9.5% fixed-rate mortgage costs $180,409 in interest over its term. A 15-year, 9.5%, fixed-rate loan, on the other hand, has a total interest cost of $78,285—a savings of more than $100,000.

## 15-year fixed-rate, fixed-payment mortgage

**Advantages:** The 15-year loan permits you to own your home free and clear in half the time, and for less than half the total interest cost of a 30-year fixed-rate loan. Principal balance is reduced relatively rapidly compared to longer-term loans. Interest rates are usually 0.5% to 1.0% less than 30-year, fixed-rate loans. FHA offers low down payment, 15-year, fixed-rate loans, and the VA offers no down payment guaranteed loans.

**Disadvantages:** Higher monthly payments make these loans more difficult to qualify for than longer-term mortgages. Monthly payments are roughly 15% to 25% higher than for comparable 30-year loans; this may limit the number of homes you would be able to afford, as an investor or vacationer. On an $89,000, 9.5% note, monthly payments would be $929 for 15 years and $748 for 30 years—a difference of more than $180.

Lenders may charge more points. The principal balance is paid off relatively rapidly compared to longer-term loans, thus reducing total mortgage interest payments and the tax shelter benefits of homeownership.

### Biweekly fixed-rate mortgage

**Advantages:** The biweekly payment schedule of this kind of loan (still very limited in its availability) speeds up amortization, reduces total interest costs, and shortens the loan term—usually to 18 or 20 years. You make 26 bi-weekly payments—which amounts to 13 annual payments—instead of 12 monthly payments. Conversion to a 30-year fixed-rate is usually permitted without penalty. Payments can be made automatically from savings or checking accounts in cases where an employer has arranged for paychecks to be deposited directly to employee bank accounts.

**Disadvantages:** More frequent payments increase opportunities for lender processing errors. The same objectives—shortened loan term and lower total interest cost—can be accomplished more flexibly with a 30-year mortgage by making an extra payment or two each year or by applying an additional sum to principal repayment when you make a regular monthly payment. As with other kinds of rapid-pay-off mortgages, you trade total interest cost reductions for reduced tax shelter benefits.

### Growing equity mortgages (GEMs)

A fixed-rate GEM features payments that increase each year for a fixed number of years and then level off. The mortgage is calculated using a 25- or 30-year amortization schedule, and the difference between what that monthly payment would be and the actual monthly bill is applied against the principal balance.

Annual increases are figured either by using a preset schedule—say 5% a year for seven years—or by using an index as a base from which to compute the increase. If, for example, the selected index rose by seven percentage points, a GEM might figure the new monthly payment by using 50% of the seven-point rise.

GEMs are not promoted when other mortgages are easily obtained. In 1986, for example, 15-year, fixed-rate, fixed-payment loans dominated the shorter-than-30-year market.

**Advantages:** The borrower saves on total interest costs. Interest rates charged by lender may be lower than for longer-term mortgages. Increases in the monthly payments are applied to principal, and loan term is shortened—possibly to 12 or 17 years. Payment hikes can be determined when the loan contract is drawn up if a set schedule is used.

**Disadvantages:** Buyer's income must be able to keep up with escalating payments. Monthly payments typically are increased annually, but some loan contracts may call for adjustments every six months or two years. While rapid principal repayment lowers total mortgage interest cost, it also lowers the total amount of mortgage interest available as a federal income tax deduction.

## Graduated payment mortgages (GPMs)

Fixed-rate GPMs start out with low payments, which rise gradually (usually over five to ten years) and then level off for the remaining years of the loan.

**Advantages:** Lower initial payments enable buyers to qualify for a larger mortgage loan than they otherwise would.

**Disadvantages:** The big problem is "negative amortization." Because low initial payments are not enough to cover fully the interest due on the loan, the difference is added to the loan balance, and future interest payments are calculated on the new higher loan balance. As a result, later payments must be higher than they otherwise would have been in order to pay off the loan.

If you sell after only a few years, you could wind up owing more on the home than you borrowed in the first place. With a GPM you gamble that appreciation in the value of the house will offset your increased indebtedness. If you hold on to the home for the life of the mortgage, you'll have to pay back the interest you borrowed in the early years—meaning the mortgage will be more expensive in the long run than a fixed-rate loan at the same interest rate without the graduated payment feature.

## ADJUSTABLE-RATE MORTGAGES (ARMS)

ARMs may be called variable-rate loans, adjustable-rate loans or adjustable mortgage loans. Whatever the name, they all have in common an interest rate that can change periodically throughout the term of the loan.

The following are characteristics of ARMs; the first four are universal, and caps—both periodic and lifetime—are featured on all adjustable mortgages sold on the secondary market.

1) *Initial interest rate*: The starting rate is usually one to three percentage points lower than current fixed-rate mortgages. Lenders will offer the lower initial rate because the risk of higher rates in the future is being shared with, and shouldered primarily by, the borrower.

The starting rate of the ARM may be pegged especially low as a promotional gimmick, totaling less than the sum of the index rate and the added margin (see explanation of these terms below). Don't be taken in by this discounted teaser rate; ask the lender to tell you what your new interest rate (and monthly payment) would be at the first adjustment date, even if the index rate doesn't change at all between now and then. You'll probably be told that the payment will be higher. (See "discount ARMs" below.)

2) *Adjustment interval*: The changes in the rate to be charged on an ARM loan occur at the end of each adjustment period. ARM adjustment periods are equal in length and repeat throughout the term of the loan. The adjustment schedule is stated in the mortgage contract. Typically it is one, three or six years, depending on the index used. A loan with an adjustment period of one year is called a "one-year ARM," and the interest rate can change once every year; a "three-year ARM" will have its first adjustment three years after you get the loan.

3) *Index*: For each ARM loan, an index is chosen for calculating the changes in the loan rate at the end of each adjustment period. These indexes usually go up and down with the general movement of interest rates. The calculation is based on where the index rate stands at the time your rate is to be recalculated, which is typically one to two months before the anniversary date of your loan.

Among the most popular indexes are the rates on one-, three-, and five-year Treasury securities. Another common index is the national or regional average cost of funds to savings and loan associations. A few lenders use their own costs of funds, over which—unlike other indexes—they have some control.

Some indexes are more volatile than others. In certain circumstances the index with the most rapid ups and downs will prove to be the least expensive for borrowers over the long haul. While it will go up more quickly, it is less likely to "stick" at the high level when interest rates fall. Thus, the volatile one-year Treasury securities index is ideal for adjustable borrowers when rates are falling. Whether this will prove to be the case in years to come depends on the pattern of long- and short-term interest rate changes.

You should ask what index will be used and how often it changes. Also find out how it has performed in the past and where it is published.

4) *Adjustment margin*: The loan rate and the index rate move up and down together, but they are not going to be the same rate. "Margin" is the additional amount the lender adds to the index rate—the smaller the better. Typically, it is 1 to 3 percentage points, and it usually doesn't vary over the life of the loan. The index rate plus the margin gives you the interest rate on your loan at each adjustment anniversary.

5) *Caps on interest*: Most ARMs today provide for limits or "caps" on rate increases or decreases. When interest rates are rising rapidly, caps protect borrowers from extreme increases in monthly payments.

Ceilings on interest are either periodic or lifetime caps. An ARM may have both. Periodic caps limit the interest rate increase from one adjustment period to the next. Lifetime caps limit the overall interest-rate increase over the term of the loan. For example, your mortgage contract could provide that even if the index increases 3 percentage points in one year, your rate can go up only 2 points that year. If you have a 5% lifetime cap, even if the index continued to rise each year, your rate could not increase more than 5 percentage points over the initial rate. In the secondary market, today, purchasers of mortgages typically will buy loans with lifetime caps of no more than 6 percentage points.

Many ARMs offer the possibility that rates may go down as well as up. In some contracts the lifetime caps apply to both decreases and increases. If no limit is placed on how high the loan rate can go, there may be a provision that also allows your rate to go down along with the index.

6) *Caps on payment*: Less common than rate caps, payment caps limit your monthly payment increase at the time of each adjustment, typically to a percentage of the previous payment. Most of these ARMs do not have periodic interest rate caps.

Payment caps are not desirable, because they can result in "negative amortization" when rising interest rates would require payments higher than the cap permits. (See discussion above.) When the day for the amortizing payment adjustment finally comes, you could find (assuming that rates have kept increasing during the previous adjustment periods) that the new payment required to repay a larger loan over the shortened remaining loan term is very large indeed.

ARMs with caps on payments are not as common as they were in the late '70s and early '80s, when buyers and sellers were experimenting with every kind of new mortgage product. One reason is that the large secondary-market purchasers of mortgages generally will not buy uncapped ARMs, which tend to have higher foreclosure rates if interest rates soar.

Uncapped ARMs are safest when a buyer has unusually strong earnings security, can be sure of adequate increases in income at the time of the final adjustment, and when equity buildup in the value of homes is being fueled by inflation.

There are three other things you should ask about when you are shopping for an ARM. They are:

1) *Assumability*: Will you be able to transfer the mortgage to a prospective buyer with the same terms? By assuming the mortgage, the buyer takes on the primary liability for the unpaid

balance of your existing mortgage or deed of trust against the property. Assumability is quite common with ARMs, because the lender has no interest rate risk.

2) *Convertibility*: Will you be allowed to convert the ARM to a fixed-rate mortgage? Many ARM contracts permit this at predetermined periods—say, after two, three or four years. When you convert, the new rate generally is the current market rate for fixed-rate mortgages. This option means you may be able to lock in a low interest rate in the future. You may have to pay for the opportunity with a somewhat higher initial interest rate or front-end fee when you obtain the loan. In addition you can be charged a special fee at the date of conversion.

3) *Prepayment*: Will you have to pay a fee or penalty if you pay off the ARM early? Prepayment penalties sometimes are negotiable, providing you do so before signing the loan documents. In many cases, however, you will be permitted to pay off the ARM loan at any time, in full or in part, without penalty.

## An ARM that requires caution

"Discount ARMs" are offered at initial rates that are below the sum of the index and the margin. This introductory rate lasts only a short while, say until the first adjustment period. These so-called teaser rates can last three months, six months or longer. Discount ARMs often are combined with large initial loan fees (points), which increases their real cost.

Discount ARMs can cause payment shock. Even if the ARM has periodic rate caps, they might apply to the first adjustment, after the teaser rate expires. This means there is no limit to the size of first payment adjustment. Let's see what happens to payments in such a case:

loan amount: $72,000
index rate: 6.5%
adjustment margin: 2%
regular ARM rate: 8.5% with 2-point annual cap
discount ARM rate: 6.5% with no cap on first annual adjust-
    ment, 2% annual cap thereafter

*Monthly payment*:
1st-year discount ARM: $455
2nd-year discount ARM: $554

Even if the index rate stays the same, your monthly payment will increase almost $100 in the second year.

Suppose the index rate increases 2%. When the annual adjustment is made, the 2% will be added to the original index-plus-margin rate of 8.5%, making the new rate 10.5%. That will mean an increase of about $200 a month.

You can end up paying more on a discount ARM if the full rate (index plus margin) starts off higher than other standard ARM rates. If your discounted 6.5% ARM carries a full rate of 8.5%, compare that rate to other ARMs currently being offered. Remember, the discount period is relatively short and the full rate will apply during most of the term of the loan. Compare the cost of discount ARMs with standard ARMs by using the annual percentage rate (APR) for each.

Discount ARMs sometimes are called "buy-downs" when the seller pays the lender a lump sum at the time the loan is made in exchange for a lower rate to the buyer. The interest rate on a fixed-rate loan also can be bought down. Buy-downs can be permanent or temporary. The cost of a permanent buy-down frequently shows up as a higher price on the property.

## FHA LOANS

The FHA (Federal Housing Authority) insures a wide variety of mortgages, including 30-year and 15-year fixed-rate loans, ARMs, GEMs and GPMs. The maximum loan amount varies somewhat from one geographic area to another. It is calculated using a formula that takes into consideration the average cost of a home in that area. In early 1987, the typical maximum was $67,500, with a $90,000 ceiling in the most expensive areas of the continental United States; the cap was even higher in Alaska and Hawaii. FHA-insured loans often carry an interest rate a bit below the going market rate. The rate no longer is set by the

FHA, however, so borrowers will need to shop around for the lowest rate being offered by lenders. And, unlike VA-guaranteed loans, FHA mortgages do not restrict buyers from paying points.

Down payment requirements are lower—usually 5% or less— than those on conventional mortgages not carrying private mortgage insurance. The insurance premium, calculated as 3.8% of the loan, must be paid at settlement. Most buyers handle this by increasing the size of their mortgage by the amount of the insurance and making slightly larger monthly payments. If you prepay your loan, you are entitled to a refund based on the remaining term of the note.

FHA loans are assumable by new owners. If the loan is less than two years old, the FHA will run a credit check on the assuming home buyer, to verify creditworthiness.

FHA loans carry no prepayment penalty. You can make additional payments at any time during the life of the loan.

FHA loans are available from so-called FHA approved lenders. These include savings institutions, mortgage companies and commercial banks. Mortgage companies, however, carry out the vast majority of FHA originations. Loan applications frequently take longer to process than those for conventional loans.

## VA LOANS

The Veterans Administration "guarantees" lenders against losses on mortgage loans taken out by eligible veterans. VA loans are fixed-rate loans with long repayment periods. This may be as long as 30 years and one month. The interest rate usually is lower than conventional mortgage rates, and it is set by the Veteran's Administration.

No down payment is required by the VA unless the veteran is obtaining a loan with a graduated payment feature or the loan amount requested is more than the VA has determined the property is worth. While the VA sets no limit on the size of mortgage it will guarantee, lenders may limit the size of VA loans they make; the maximum portion that VA will guarantee was $27,500 in early 1987.

VA loans can be paid off in full at any time without penalty. There is no penalty for prepaying principal when you make your regular monthly payment so long as the amount involved is at least one full month's installment (if the payment due is less than $100) or $100 (if the scheduled loan payment is more than $100).

The VA collects a one-time funding fee of 1% of the loan amount at settlement. This pays for the VA guarantee. (There may be an exception to this for certain disabled veterans.) In addition to the 1% funding fee, veteran buyers cannot be required to pay more than a 1% fee to the lender (usually called a "point" or "origination fee").

Conventional loans, by contrast, impose no restrictions on how points are to be divided between buyers and sellers. VA's limitation saves a veteran money, but it also may narrow his or her choice of homes during periods when lenders are charging several points to make VA mortgages. At such times, sellers may refuse to consider VA contracts once they realize that all points beyond the 1% cap will come from their pockets.

The VA sets minimum construction standards for new homes purchased with GI financing and requires the builder to provide each veteran purchaser with a one-year warranty indicating that the home has been built in conformity with VA-approved plans and specifications. A similar warranty also is required on new manufactured (mobile or modular) homes.

Regional VA offices can provide you with information on eligibility and other details. Look in the phone book under U.S. Government for the VA office nearest you.

## OTHER TYPES OF FINANCING

When interest rates are so high that few people can afford a mortgage, how can buyers and sellers of homes still manage to make deals? In the late 1970s and early '80s, they did it with "creative financing"—unorthodox loan arrangements that most homeowners would shun in ordinary times. For the buyer, the seller's interest-rate subsidy provides relief from high market mortgage rates (and perhaps a chance to refinance if rates fall). For the seller, this kind of help to the buyer may make the difference between a sale or no sale. But it entails risks and possible tax consequences to both buyers and sellers not present in traditional mortgages.

Seller-assisted financing ties the buyer and seller together long past the purchase transaction, so the seller has a strong interest in the buyer's financial resources, job stability and personal life. As a buyer seeking seller financing, don't be surprised if the seller requires of you considerable detail about such matters; as your prospective creditor, he's entitled to know.

For the seller to do well financially on these deals, he or she must get a sale price that's enough higher to make up for the stretched-out payment; remember, in a time of high inflation (when high interest rates create the climate for creative financing), you the buyer will be paying back the seller's loan with increasingly devalued dollars. Cutting the interest rate is equivalent to lowering the sale price; so if you're looking for seller help with the purchase, you can't expect to get a great deal on the sale price, too—unless there are so few qualified buyers in the marketplace that the seller is desperate.

## Take-back mortgage

In this form of seller financing, the seller helps the buyer finance the purchase by taking back a mortgage for part of the purchase price. Take-backs often bridge the gap between the price of the property and the combined amounts of the down payment and first mortgage. The interest rate is negotiated between seller and buyer, and it is sometimes less than the rate on the first mortgage, if the seller is eager to make a deal.

They can be attractive to sellers who don't need the entire proceeds from the sale right away and to buyers trying to work out a contract with terms they could handle. The seller often earns a yield that is higher than current money market rates—although in a buyer's market, the seller may have to offer a *lower*-than-market rate. As a second mortgage, the seller's loan is protected by a lien against the property, but the claim is subordinate to the primary lender's. If the buyer defaults and a foreclosure results, the second-mortgage holder will get reimbursed only after the first-mortgage holder's claim is satisfied. If the foreclosure doesn't yield as much as the original sale price, the holder of the second mortgage will lose money.

Though payments on seller take-backs may be figured as though the loan would be paid back over a 25- or 30-year period, the loans often are due in full—with a balloon payment—three to ten years after the sale. This means the buyer will have to refinance by that time.

## Purchase-money second mortgage

In this deal, the seller agrees to finance part of the buyer's down payment though a second mortgage, usually of three to five years. The primary mortgage lender should be told of such an arrangement, since the payments on the second mortgage may affect the buyer's ability to meet payments on the first.

## Wrap-around mortgage

This sort of deal involves an existing mortgage plus additional financing to complete the purchase. Say a house is selling for $100,000. The seller has an assumable mortgage with an outstanding balance of $40,000. A buyer makes a down payment of $20,000. He finds a lender, often the seller, who gives him a new mortgage that covers the old loan balance plus an additional $40,000. The buyer makes payments on the wrap-around mortgage to the lender, who uses part of the money to make payments on the old mortgage. The rate on the wrap-around loan is higher than the rate on the old mortgage, and the lender profits from the differential. Thus, by "blending" the rate on the old $40,000 mortgage with the rate on the new $40,000 mortgage, he can afford to offer a rate on the wraparound that is lower than prevailing rates. However, it may be difficult to find a lender for such an arrangement, since most mortgage contracts forbid it.

## Land contract

Also known as a conditional sales contract or contract for deed, this actually is an installment sale. The buyer doesn't get title to the property right away, but must wait until some point agreed upon in the contract—usually years down the road. The 1986 tax reforms impose penalties and restrictions on installment sales. Many sellers who might have considered such a deal under the old tax rules will find that it no longer provides a financial benefit.

Much can go wrong with land contracts. As part of the deal, the buyer may agree to take over payments on the seller's existing mortgage—an arrangement that many mortgage lenders contend violates the "due on sale" provision of their mortgage contract. Lenders may be able to foreclose on such mortgages, leaving the buyer with nothing to show for his payments except a worthless contract. Neither buyer nor seller should draw up a land contract without expert legal help.

## Shared equity

In a typical shared-equity arrangement, the home buyer is paired with an investor—frequently a parent, relative or friend, but sometimes a stranger—who supplies the down payment, while the home buyer occupies the property and pays either all or some share of the carrying costs.

At some future point, when the property is sold or refinanced, the investor gets back the down payment money plus a share of any appreciation that has taken place. The owner/occupant may buy out the investor and stay in the home, or sell and use the proceeds for a down payment on another home.

Shared-equity arrangements may run into trouble if there is disagreement between the parties over when to sell, how much to sell for and how to treat the value of improvements made by the owner/occupant. There may be disputes over what is a fair price, requiring appraisers to be hired to arbitrate. A shared-equity arrangement should address such issues clearly in the agreement.

Because such deals are complicated, there are companies that specialize in bringing together home buyers and investors. They usually provide some or all of the following services: matching up financially compatible partners, preparing the contract, obtaining mortgages for partners or referring them to lenders, and analyzing tax and other financial concerns.

Here are two firms that specialize in this kind of transaction:

Shared Equity Specialists Inc.
819 Silver Spring Ave.
Silver Spring, MD 20910
(301) 587-0867

Ticket Corporation
233 Brookcliff Trace
Marietta, GA 30067
(404) 973-9474
Enclose a self-addressed, stamped envelope with the inquiry.

For a more in-depth look at this type of ownership, consult a book on the subject by Georgia Anderson and Sandra Lamb: *Equity Sharing, Profiting From Joint Home Buying* (Contemporary Books; Chicago; $6.95).

## MAKING A MORTGAGE CHOICE

Deciding which kind of mortgage is best for you requires a close look at your present circumstances, future earnings, and financial goals—not to mention some clear forecasting of economic conditions a few years down the road.

Do you want to put as little down as possible, carrying a big mortgage? Do you want the tax-sheltering effect of large monthly interest payments? Is getting the most house for the lowest possible monthly payment your primary objective, or is fast equity buildup more important?

For example, a 30-year, three-year ARM with a 2% periodic adjustment cap and a 6% lifetime cap might be a good choice for a couple expecting a job-related move within three to six years. Assuming equal points at settlement, if they can obtain this ARM with an initial interest rate 2 percentage points lower than a 30-year fixed-rate loan, here's how they would fare even with the 2% adjustment at the end of the sixth year:

7.5%, 30-year, three-year ARM
$90,000 mortgage

| Yr. | Interest rate | Payment | Balance |
|---|---|---|---|
| 1 | 7.5% | $629 | $89,170 |
| 2 | 7.5% | 629 | 88,276 |
| 3 | 7.5% | 629 | 87,312 |
| 4 | 9.5% | 749 | 86,583 |
| 5 | 9.5% | 749 | 85,780 |
| 6 | 9.5% | 749 | 84,898 |

9.5%, 30-year, fixed-rate
$90,000

| Yr. | Interest rate | Payment | Balance |
|---|---|---|---|
| 1 | 9.5% | 757 | $89,445 |
| 2 | 9.5 | 757 | 88,835 |
| 3 | 9.5 | 757 | 88,165 |
| 4 | 9.5 | 757 | 87,428 |
| 5 | 9.5 | 757 | 86,618 |
| 6 | 9.5 | 757 | 85,727 |

In this example, monthly payments on the three-year ARM cost about $4,850 less than those on the fixed-rate loan over the six-year period, and our couple has reduced their mortgage balance by $829 more than they would have with the fixed-rate loan. If rates on the ARM increase less than the maximum 2% per adjustment period, savings would be even greater.

Three-year ARMs also can be worthwhile if refinancing calculations show that a lower initial interest rate is needed to justify the transaction costs. For a prospective buyer who finds that interest rates on 30-year, fixed-rate loans have gone up during the loan application period, a three-year ARM may allow the deal to go through without higher monthly payments, at least initially.

## Equity buildup

If reducing the total cost of your home is a goal, and you aren't very concerned with the reduced tax benefit of shrinking interest payments, you should consider 15-year fixed-rate loans.

This type of loan is popular with buyers moving up to more expensive properties and first-time home buyers who can afford the higher monthly payments. Under the Tax Reform Act of 1986, home mortgage interest remains fully deductible, but the value of those deductions is reduced, due to lower marginal tax rates.

Beginning in 1988, there will be only two brackets of 15% and 28% (plus a "phantom" but very real 33% top rate for some high-income taxpayers). Under the old tax law, marginal tax rates ranged as high as 50%. At the marginal rate of 50%, every dollar that could be deducted saved the tax payer 50 cents. Under the new tax law, deductions, including mortgage interest deductions, are worth less. The biggest tax "write-off" available under the new law is generally only 28 cents on the dollar. And for thousands of couples with combined taxable incomes of $29,750 or less, the per-dollar subsidy will amount to just 15 cents.

There is another reason for accelerating the equity buildup in your home: the more equity you have, the more you can borrow against your home for future needs—college costs, starting a business, retirement planning, etc. You can deduct from your gross income the interest on all borrowing secured by one or two personal residences (first mortgage, second mortgage, home equity loan—whatever), so long as the total borrowed doesn't exceed the original purchase price of the house plus the cost of improvements; that is, you can't deduct the interest on loans against the *appreciated* value of your home, except to finance home improvements or educational and medical expenses.

Fueling homeowners' desire to be able to tap home equity is the gradual loss of interest deductions on credit cards, auto loans, student loans or other kinds of consumer interest. In 1987, you'll be able to write off only 65% of consumer interest. In 1988, the limit will be 40%; in 1989, 20%; in 1990, 10%; and in 1991, none of your consumer loan interest will be deductible. (See a fuller discussion of the tax angles of home ownership in Chapter 3.)

You can get faster equity buildup even without a 15-year loan, of course. If your mortgage lender permits, other kinds of mortgages can be paid off early, allowing you to reap at least some of the savings on interest. On most 30-year mortgages, you can pay ahead on the principal as much as you like without penalty. You simply make heftier payments on a voluntary rather than mandatory basis. Once you have made your scheduled payment, anything extra is applied to the principal. Making extra payments doesn't mean you can skip a regular payment down the road, however.

If your loan documents allow the lender to charge a prepayment penalty, and you can't get it removed, chances are you'll do better not prepaying, but investing that extra sum elsewhere.

And before embarking on a major campaign of prepaying principal, give some thought to alternative uses of the money. How fast are houses in your area appreciating in value? Will you need that extra money back again? What kind of return on your money can you get these days in fixed-yield investments, stocks, or other kinds of investments? Remember, once you put that money into repayment of your mortgage, it will earn you no current income at all, and you can get it out only by borrowing it back, through some sort of refinancing.

Table 1

## ADJUSTABLE-RATE MORTGAGES

How payments could go up or down

(Figures in this and subsequent tables supplied by Fannie Mae)

Say you have a $90,000 one-year capped ARM loan at an initial rate of 7½% with an annual cap of two percentage points and a lifetime cap of six percentage points. Here's what the monthly payment would be on a fully amortized loan if interest rates rose 2½% every year and payments are adjusted every year:

| Year(s) | Rate and amortization period | Monthly payment | Principal balance at end of period |
|---|---|---|---|
| 1 | 7½% for 30 yrs. | $ 629.29 | $89,170.35 |
| 2 | 9½% for 29 yrs. | 754.44 | 88,562.16 |
| 3 | 11½% for 28 yrs. | 884.61 | 88,108.03 |
| 4–30 | 13½%* for 27 yrs. | 1,018.36 | –0– |

*Maximum rate due to lifetime cap.

And this is what the monthly payments would be if interest rates dropped ½ of 1% every year for five years:

| Year(s) | Rate and amortization period | Monthly payment | Principal balance at end of period |
|---|---|---|---|
| 1 | 7½% for 30 yrs. | 629.29 | $89,170.35 |
| 2 | 7% for 29 yrs. | 599.34 | 88,189.10 |
| 3 | 6½% for 28 yrs. | 570.60 | 87,040.40 |
| 4 | 6% for 27 yrs. | 543.12 | 85,709.18 |
| 5 | 5½% for 26 yrs. | 516.95 | 84,181.67 |
| 6–30 | 5% for 25 yrs. | 492.12 | –0– |

Table 2

## GRADUATED-PAYMENT MORTGAGES

How they compare with fixed-rate loans

This graduated-payment mortgage for $90,000 at 9½% has a predetermined payment schedule and negative amortization. Monthly payments increase 7.5% every year for five years and then level off for the remaining term of the mortgage. The early payments start lower than a comparable level-payment fixed-rate mortgage, but then gradually catch up to the level necessary to amortize the loan. In this loan the last 25 years would be at a higher payment than a comparable level-payment loan. The monthly payment for a comparable loan on a straight 30-year fixed-rate mortgage (FRM), assuming the same 9½% interest rate, would be $767.77, for a total of $9,081.24 annually. (Lenders typically charge about ½% more for a GPM than a level-payment fixed-rate loan.)

| Years | Payment | Difference from FRM | Total paid annually |
|-------|---------|---------------------|---------------------|
| 1     | $573.47 | $183.30 less        | $6,881.64           |
| 2     | 616.48  | 140.29 less         | 7,397.76            |
| 3     | 662.71  | 94.06 less          | 7,952.52            |
| 4     | 712.42  | 44.35 less          | 8,549.04            |
| 5     | 765.85  | 9.08 more           | 9,190.20            |
| 6–30  | 823.29  | 66.52 more for 25 yrs. | 9,879.48         |

After the fifth year this borrower owes $94,230.37, or $4,230.37 more than he did originally. The payment is adjusted every year until the sixth year, when the final adjustment is made. The payment for years 6 through 30 is roughly 9% greater than it would be with a level-payment 30-year fixed-rate loan ($823.29 vs. $756.77).

The convenience of having smaller payments for the first four years does not come cheap:

| | |
|---|---|
| Total payments on GPM | $286,958.16 |
| Total payments on FRM | 272,437.20 |
| Extra cost of GPM | $ 14,520.96 |

Table 3

## HOW A 15-YEAR LOAN SLASHES INTEREST COSTS

The total interest cost of a 15-year fixed-rate mortgage at 8½% is less than half that of a 30-year fixed-rate loan at 9% on an $80,000 mortgage. (The 15-year mortgage is typically offered at an interest rate about a half-point lower than 30-year loans at any given time.)

| | | 15-year fixed rate | | 30-year fixed rate | |
|---|---|---|---|---|---|
| Year | Payment Number | Payment | Principal Balance | Payment | Principal Balance |
| 1 | 12 | $788 | $77,241 | $644 | $79,453 |
| 3 | 24 | 788 | 70,969 | 644 | 78,202 |
| 5 | 36 | 788 | 63,539 | 644 | 76,704 |
| 7 | 60 | 788 | 54,738 | 644 | 74,912 |
| 10 | 120 | 788 | 38,398 | 644 | 71,544 |
| 15 | 180 | 788 | –0– | 644 | 63,410 |

Total interest paid:          $61,802                    $151,731*

*Total interest paid on 30-year loan by end of year 15: $99,330

Table 4

# WHAT WILL PAYMENTS BE ON A FIXED-RATE LOAN?

This table allows you to calculate your monthly mortgage payment for each $1,000 of mortgage amount at common interest rates over four mortgage terms of varying length, from 15 years to 30 years. Only principal and interest are included; insurance and property taxes would be additional expenses. To calculate your monthly payment for a new mortgage, multiply the amount in the appropriate column by the number of thousands of dollars involved. Example: For a 30-year loan of $90,000 at 8%, multiply 90 by $7.34. The monthly payment of principal and interest would equal $660.60.

| Interest Rate | 15 Years | 20 Years | 25 Years | 30 Years |
|---|---|---|---|---|
| 6% | 8.44 | 7.17 | 6.45 | 6.00 |
| 6¼ | 8.58 | 7.31 | 6.60 | 6.16 |
| 6½ | 8.72 | 7.46 | 6.76 | 6.33 |
| 6¾ | 8.85 | 7.61 | 6.91 | 6.49 |
| 7 | 8.99 | 7.76 | 7.07 | 6.66 |
| 7¼ | 9.13 | 7.91 | 7.23 | 6.83 |
| 7½ | 9.28 | 8.06 | 7.39 | 7.00 |
| 7¾ | 9.42 | 8.21 | 7.56 | 7.17 |
| 8 | 9.56 | 8.37 | 7.72 | 7.34 |
| 8¼ | 9.71 | 8.53 | 7.89 | 7.52 |
| 8½ | 9.85 | 8.68 | 8.06 | 7.69 |
| 8¾ | 10.00 | 8.84 | 8.23 | 7.87 |
| 9 | 10.15 | 9.00 | 8.40 | 8.05 |
| 9¼ | 10.30 | 9.16 | 8.57 | 8.23 |
| 9½ | 10.45 | 9.33 | 8.74 | 8.41 |
| 9 ¾ | 10.60 | 9.49 | 8.92 | 8.60 |
| 10 | 10.75 | 9.66 | 9.09 | 8.78 |
| 10¼ | 10.90 | 9.82 | 9.27 | 8.97 |
| 10½ | 11.06 | 9.99 | 9.45 | 9.15 |
| 10¾ | 11.21 | 10.16 | 9.63 | 9.34 |

## Table 4 Continued

| | | | | |
|---|---|---|---|---|
| 11 | 11.37 | 10.33 | 9.81 | 9.53 |
| 11¼ | 11.53 | 10.50 | 9.99 | 9.72 |
| 11½ | 11.69 | 10.67 | 10.17 | 9.91 |
| 11¾ | 11.85 | 10.84 | 10.35 | 10.10 |
| 12 | 12.01 | 11.02 | 10.54 | 10.29 |
| 12¼ | 12.17 | 11.19 | 10.72 | 10.48 |
| 12½ | 12.33 | 11.37 | 10.91 | 10.68 |
| 12¾ | 12.49 | 11.54 | 11.10 | 10.87 |
| 13 | 12.66 | 11.72 | 11.28 | 11.07 |
| 13¼ | 12.82 | 11.90 | 11.47 | 11.26 |
| 13½ | 12.99 | 12.08 | 11.66 | 11.46 |
| 13¾ | 13.15 | 12.26 | 11.85 | 11.66 |
| 14 | 13.32 | 12.44 | 12.04 | 11.85 |
| 14¼ | 13.49 | 12.62 | 12.23 | 12.05 |
| 14½ | 13.66 | 12.80 | 12.43 | 12.25 |
| 14¾ | 13.83 | 12.99 | 12.62 | 12.45 |
| 15 | 14.00 | 13.17 | 12.81 | 12.65 |
| 15¼ | 14.17 | 13.36 | 13.01 | 12.85 |
| 15½ | 14.34 | 13.54 | 13.20 | 13.05 |
| 15 ¾ | 14.52 | 13.73 | 13.40 | 13.25 |
| 16 | 14.69 | 13.92 | 13.59 | 13.45 |

Table 5

## CHECKLIST FOR COMPARING ADJUSTABLE-RATE MORTGAGE LOANS

Check types and lenders against each other. After you have been prequalified for the amount of money you may borrow, use these forms to compare ARMs. After you have identified the one or two that interest you, compare the terms and costs of several lenders.

### Adjustables Without Ceilings

| | |
|---|---|
| Beginning interest rate | _____% |
| Beginning payment | $_____ |
| Cost in points | $_____ |
| Loan is tied to which index? | |

6-month Treasury bills ☐

1-year Treasury securities ☐

3-year Treasury securities ☐

5-year Treasury securities ☐

Federal Home Loan Bank Board (FHLBB) series

for closed loans on existing homes ☐

other index ☐

Adjustments are made every _____ months

every _____ years

First payment adjustment date _____

### Adjustables With Ceilings

| | |
|---|---|
| Beginning interest rate | _____% |
| Beginning payment | $_____ |
| Cost in points | $_____ |
| Is there a cap on the interest rate? | ☐ yes ☐ no |
| What is the cap? | _____% |
| Is there a cap on the payment? | ☐ yes ☐ no |

What is the cap?  $_____

Loan is tied to which index?

6-month Treasury bills ☐

1-year Treasury securities ☐

3-year Treasury securities ☐

5-year Treasury securities ☐

Federal Home Loan Bank Board (FHLBB) series
for closed loans on existing homes ☐

other index ☐

| | |
|---|---|
| 1st adjustment occurs | _____ months/years |
| 2nd adjustment occurs | _____ months/years |
| 3rd adjustment occurs | _____ months/years |
| 4th adjustment occurs | _____ months/years |
| 5th adjustment occurs | _____ months/years |
| Loan calls for | _____ adjustments |
| Loan provides for negative amortization | ☐ yes  ☐ no |
| Interest rate stabilizes in | _____th year |
| Monthly payment stabilizes in | _____th year |

# 11

## Finding a Lender, Getting a Loan

After you've studied the various kinds of mortgages and picked the one that suits your needs best, you're ready to find a lender who will make you the best deal.

As we said in the previous chapter, the identity and location of the lender is less important than the quality of the deal. Back a decade or so, finding a mortgage didn't require much comparison shopping; everything was fixed-rate financing, and rates didn't vary much, so most people dealt with a local institution they already had a relationship with. But things are more complex in today's competitive market.

Fortunately, shopping for mortgages has been greatly eased by the emergence in recent years of mortgage reporting services—firms that survey the major lenders in a given metropolitan area every week or two weeks and publish information sheets on who is offering what loans on what terms. These easy-to-understand grids make comparison shopping a breeze; use them to narrow your choices to a few lenders, and then call the lenders to confirm that a given deal is still being offered.

You can get the names of mortgage reporting services from real estate professionals. Some real estate agents will show you their fact sheets for nothing, but even if you have to pay $20 or so to buy the current sheets, it's still a bargain in time and trouble saved. (See the fuller discussion below.)

If there isn't a reporting service in your area, you can begin the search with your own bank or savings & loan, and real estate agents usually have extensive contacts in the local lending community. The local Board of Realtors probably has surveyed lenders in the community and provides rate information to member agents. Ask them for names of s&l's, banks, mortgage companies and mortgage brokers, but don't depend on them to find you the best deal. For that, you'll have to rely on your own efforts, lots of telephone calls and possibly some old-fashioned legwork.

If you went through a prequalifying process with a lender, of course you'll want to see if that firm is competitive on the kind of loan you want. If so, you'll save some additional paperwork and time dealing with the same company. But don't feel obliged to use their money, and by all means shop around before deciding.

## SOURCES OF MORTGAGE MONEY

The major kinds of lenders are discussed below. The lender you choose will take your loan application, follow through on credit checks, property appraisal, and other details, and then disburse funds to the seller in exchange for a mortgage or deed of trust on your property.

### Savings institutions

Savings and loan associations and savings banks originate about half of all home mortgages. Most are so-called conventional mortgages—those not guaranteed by the Veterans Administration (VA) or Farmers Home Administration, or insured by the Federal Housing Administration (FHA).

Most of the fixed-rate loans made by savings institutions are sold to investors in the secondary market, through firms like Ginnie Mae and Fannie Mae. So if you want a fixed-rate mortgage, you probably will be expected to meet secondary-market standards covering appraisals, creditworthiness and down payment minimums. Standards for adjustable-rate mortgages may be more flexible, if the institution intends to hold them in its own portfolio.

### Mortgage companies

Mortgage companies make the majority of VA and FHA loans. Mortgage bankers continuously shop for the best available loans by working closely with the secondary market. When you get a loan through a mortgage company, the mortgage banker is the lender of record. The company will make a loan commitment to you once your application is approved. Normally, even though your loan will be sold, you will continue to send your payment to the mortgage company after settlement. It also will set up and collect escrow funds.

### Commercial banks

Though mortgage lending is not their main business, some commercial banks are fairly active in residential lending, making primarily fixed-rate loans. Many are affiliated with mortgage companies or operate their own mortgage banking subsidiaries. Banks also are a major supplier of loans for mobile home buyers. Banks are generally more interested in making a mortgage loan to you if you already do business with the bank.

### Mortgage brokers

If you are having trouble locating a lender, consider using a mortgage broker. You may have to pay a flat fee for the service, although in many cases the lender pays the broker's fee as part of the total points collected at settlement; often the total points you pay will be more working through a broker than directly with a lender, but not always.

A mortgage broker shops the mortgage market and can refer a prospective borrower to a mortgage banker, savings institution, commercial bank or even an individual investor. Many brokers represent local, regional and national lenders, and may be able to locate a loan program that is not available in your area.

A broker is not the lender and does not approve the loan or make the loan commitment to a borrower. State and local boards of Realtors should be able to give you names of brokers active in a community.

### Credit unions

More than one-third of all credit unions now make first mortgage loans. You have to be a member of a credit union to get a mortgage from it, and membership is often based on some criterion of affinity—residency in a given city or state, employment, membership in an association or club, etc. Most mortgage loans are made by large credit unions in Massachusetts, New Hampshire, New Mexico, North Dakota, Rhode Island and Wisconsin. If you are already a member of a credit union, or even if you're just eligible to be a member, check out the rates and terms of its mortgages.

## Public agencies

State and local housing finance agencies make below-market-rate financing available to eligible low- and moderate-income, first-time buyers, through the sale of tax-exempt bonds. If you aren't able to locate the correct agency in your state, contact the Council of State Housing Agencies, Suite 118, 444 North Capitol St., Washington, DC 20001, for assistance.

Buyers who cannot get credit from private providers of mortgage funds, but who meet certain income and rural residency requirements, may be able to buy a home through the Farmers Home Administration's rural housing program. Contact the Administrator, FmHA, U.S. Department of Agriculture, Washington, DC 20250, for information.

## USING A REPORTING SERVICE

Most reporting services provide details on a variety of mortgages, including conventional, FHA and VA loans. Many also include rates on second mortgages and other types of loans. Information provided on each loan indicates the category (adjustable-rate or fixed-rate, for example), the term of the mortgage, interest rate, points, and how long the lender will guarantee the rate you're offered at application time. In the case of adjustable-rate mortgages, information is given on the index base, adjustment margin, and periodic and lifetime caps.

Reports usually are updated weekly, but check before you buy. Prices for a single report range from under $5 to $25, with additional reports or subscriptions costing significantly less. In addition, many metropolitan newspapers publish a list of rates in weekly business or real estate sections. Often the data is supplied by a mortgage reporting service.

Use the reports and other resources to screen the local market. Then, thoroughly interview the most promising lenders before making mortgage application appointments.

Listed below are several firms that cover lenders in more than one state:

HSH Associates
10 Mead Ave.
Riverdale, NJ 07457
(201) 831-0550

HSH surveys more than 2,000 lenders in more than 30 states and many metropolitan areas. For $6, HSH provides a very extensive list of lenders and includes information from each on discount points, down payments, interest rates, terms and maximum mortgage amounts. For $12, HSH sells a ''Homebuyer's Mortgage Kit,'' which includes the list described above and a 32-page booklet, "How to Shop for a Mortgage." The booklet discusses the basics of mortgage financing, the mortgage process from application to closing, how to choose a mortgage and adjustable-rate mortgages.

Gary Myers and Associates
20 W. Hubbard St., Suite 500
Chicago, IL 60610
(312) 670-2440

Myers reports mortgage rates weekly for Boston, Chicago, Cincinnati, Dallas, Detroit, Houston, New York City, Phoenix and all of California. A mortgage report for one city, or for California, costs $20. Myers also provides rate information to some 200 newspapers in more than 44 states.

National Mortgage Weekly
P.O. Box 18081
Cleveland, OH 44118
(216) 371-2767

NMW covers the metropolitan Boston, Cleveland, Columbus and Detroit areas. The company surveys about 60 to 80 lenders in each city. Subscribers pay $2.75 per week for one to 12 weeks, or $29.70 for 13 weeks.

Peeke LoanFax Inc.
101 Chestnut St., Suite 200
Gaithersburg, MD 20877
(301) 840-5752

Peeke provides three separate mortgage reports: one for metropolitan Washington, D.C., including northern Virginia and suburban Maryland; one for Baltimore; and one for Dade, Broward and Palm Beach counties in southern Florida. The Florida report includes Miami and Fort Lauderdale.

For Washington, D.C., Peeke's weekly report lists rates offered by about 115 lenders. In Baltimore, it covers more than 80 lenders, and, in south Florida, about 50. The first issue costs $20; reports for additional weeks are $15. Four consecutive weeks cost $50.

## FINE-TUNING YOUR CHOICE

After you've selected the lenders who appear to have the best deal on the kind of loan you want, talk with them extensively on the phone or in person, before you apply to a particular lender. Make sure that the advertised terms of the loan are truly being offered. These discussions before applying for a loan shouldn't cost you anything.

Use the annual percentage rate (APR) to compare loans. APR is the cost of your mortgage loan expressed as a yearly rate. It reflects the effect of origination fees, points and (if applicable) mortgage insurance, by adding them to the loan rate as though they were spread out over the term of the loan. Lenders often promote a particular mortgage loan by advertising the interest rate or monthly payment. By law, they also must divulge the APR of the loan and indicate whether the rate is fixed. This disclosure is required under federal Truth-in-Lending laws.

Before you apply, find out how long the currently advertised or stated rate of the loan is being guaranteed after application, if it's guaranteed at all. That is, if you apply tomorrow for a loan at that rate, will the lender assure you in writing that you can have that interest rate at settlement, whether that takes 30 days, 45 days, 60 days or longer?

In fact, many rate quotes are not guaranteed beyond a particular period of time, and some are not guaranteed at all, with the lender reserving the right to charge you whatever rate is generally current in the marketplace on settlement day. If the rate at closing is substantially higher, a buyer could be shocked with "disqualification" at the eleventh hour.

One way to lock in a rate is to pay a loan commitment fee—commonly 1% of the loan amount. This locks in the rate you're quoted at time of application as the highest rate you'll have to pay within, say, 60 days. If rates drop during your application period, you'll also be able to take advantage of that.

## THE APPLICATION PROCESS

Now you're ready to apply for a mortgage. The application process costs some money—a charge that can run anywhere from $50 to about $300—and it is usually not refundable. Lenders assess it to cover the costs of credit reports, mortgage insurance applications, property appraisals and the like. Because of this cost, you'll want to avoid multiple applications, if possible. Only if you're shakey about the prospects of approval or speed of approval should you waste the fees on more than one application.

If you have paperwork from the prequalifying process, with this or another lender, take along those forms; lots of the information about your finances will be directly transferrable to this application process.

If not, take all the raw material for the application—income and balance sheet figures, plus copies of your last few income tax returns (which may be required by the lender). You should also take the title to your car, which will show it to be free of liens or encumbered by an auto loan.

Be prepared to give the name and phone number of someone who can verify financial information about you—most likely, your employer's personnel office. If you have substantial non-salary income from investments, you'll be asked to substantiate this through an accountant, stock broker, trust officer, etc. If you are self-employed (a definition that could be triggered by as little as a 5% to 10% ownership stake in a closely held company you work for), you may be asked to submit financial information about the company.

Much of this information will be filled in on application forms during the interview, with the help of a loan officer, but you could also fill it in at home and return the forms.

For conventional loans carrying private mortgage insurance (PMI), check with your lender regarding the necessary documentation.

In addition to the application fee, you may be asked to pay a "loan origination fee" or "prepaid point"—typically 1% of the loan amount—when you apply, before approval is made. This is just another way of charging you prepaid interest, like the additional points you may have to pay at settlement.

Ask what will happen to your origination fee should you decide later to accept a mortgage from another lender. Also, what if the lender decides not to give you the loan—will the 1% origination fee be refunded to you? Get the answers to these questions *in writing* before paying this substantial amount.

Check on if, and how long, the quoted interest rate is guaranteed for, and if you really think that interest rates may rise during the 45 days to two months or so that your application is being processed, consider paying a loan commitment fee, as discussed above.

The federal Real Estate Settlement Procedures Act (RESPA) requires a lender to provide you with a "good faith" estimate of closing costs once you complete a loan application or within three business days. The RESPA Statement reflects the lender's experience in the area where your property is located.

The estimate must include costs for such items as points, appraisal fees, title search, title insurance, survey, recording and attorney's fees. You can ask for a hypothetical calculation of such items as property taxes and hazard insurance, based on your anticipated closing date.

## PRIVATE MORTGAGE INSURANCE

Lenders usually require buyers getting conventional loans with down payments of less than 20% to carry insurance provided by a separate private mortgage insurance company. The insurance is designed to protect a lender from losses in the event a borrower stops paying on a mortgage loan; premiums are paid by the home buyer.

Insured low-down-payment mortgages are more attractive— and less risky—investments than uninsured ones, and lenders who wish to sell such loans into the secondary market are generally required to have them insured. FHA-insured and VA-guaranteed loans also protect lenders against borrower default.

Insurance coverage is available for conventional fixed-rate and adjustable mortgages. Coverage of second mortgages may be difficult to locate, but at least one company, United Guarantee, was writing such policies in 1987.

Private mortgage insurance generally covers the top 20% to 25% of a first mortgage loan. This permits lenders to make loans of up to 90% or 95% of the appraised value of a home while taking about the same amount of risk they would assume in making a loan of about 71% to 72% of value. This so-called loan-to-value ratio (LTV or LV) expresses the relationship between the amount of a loan and the value of the property that will be pledged as security. For example, on a 90% loan-to-value ratio, a borrower makes a 10% down payment and therefore holds the first 10% risk of falling real estate values. The insurer takes 20% of the next 90%, or 18%, and the lender holds the remaining 72%.

Insurance premiums vary from company to company and according to the type of loan being insured. In most cases you will pay an initial premium at settlement and a renewal premium at the beginning of each year. First-year premiums typically range from 0.35% to 1.65% of the mortgage amount depending on, among other things, the loan amount, the size of the down payment, and whether the loan is a fixed-rate or adjustable-rate mortgage. Renewal premiums range from 0.25% to 0.75%.

When the loan is paid down to an acceptable LTV ratio (e.g. 80%), the lender usually has the option to terminate the coverage. However, premium payments are not automatically stopped. Find out at what LTV ratio point your lender will agree to release you from paying premiums and whether or not you will be notified once your loan reaches that level.

## CREDIT LIFE INSURANCE

Your lender may try to talk you into buying some kind of credit life insurance that would pay off the mortgage in the event of your death. Even if your lender doesn't offer this to you, you will probably be deluged with mortgage life insurance solicitations after you buy your house.

Mortgage life insurance is a kind of decreasing-term insurance, in which the premium stays the same, but the amount of coverage declines each year, in lockstep with the declining balance owed on your mortgage. It is often promoted as valuable protection for your spouse and children, to keep them from losing the house if the primary breadwinner dies.

Mortgage life insurance does this, but there may be better and cheaper ways to provide the same protection. One problem with mortgage life insurance is that the beneficiary is the mortgage lender, not your heirs. Perhaps your heirs needn't and *shouldn't* pay off the balance on the mortgage, because the original interest rate is much lower than today's rate and there is sufficient income to keep making the payments. With mortgage life insurance automatically paying off to the lender, your heirs won't have a choice of how to use the insurance money. They would own the house free and clear, but they may have to refinance, possibly at a higher interest rate, to get their equity out for some worthwhile purpose, like college expenses.

Undeniably, any new homeowner with family to protect should boost his or her life insurance coverage, so that the insurance proceeds—if invested conservatively—would yield enough income to continue paying the mortgage and other basic expenses of living. For a young person, some form of term life insurance offers the most coverage for the lowest current cost, even though the premiums will rise each year. Before accepting an offer of mortgage life insurance, shop hard for the best deal in conventional insurance coverage that will pay off to your heirs.

## THE WAIT AND THE TENSION

From the time you submit a completed loan application and the appraisal and credit reports are in hand, a lender has up to 30 days to approve your loan request. If the lender turns you down, or refuses to meet your terms, you must be informed of the decision within 30 days. Moreover, the lender must tell you why your application was rejected.

When homes are selling briskly, the time between completing a loan application and the notification of approval from a lender can be all too long. Appraisers and credit bureaus get swamped. Harried mortgage loan officers slip problem applications back into the pile and move on to less troublesome applicants. It's not uncommon for the whole process to take 60 days.

Make sure you haven't been forgotten or put on a back burner. During the process, remind the loan officer of your settlement date and check on how everything is going.

You should have assessed how long the application process will take back when you submitted your contract, making sure the settlement date was placed far enough into the future. If you goofed—by agreeing to a settlement that's looming before your loan is likely to be approved—you have a few choices now.

You can ask the seller for a new, later settlement date, explaining that processing delays beyond your control have made it necessary. Most sellers will agree to a good-faith postponement of settlement, and this kind of delay is generally not grounds for the seller to try to void the contract.

Or—if you already own a home—you can keep the original settlement date and go to the table without your mortgage money, instead relying on a hastily arranged bridge loan; this option isn't generally available to first-time buyers. If the bridge loan need not be repaid for several months (or longer), you now have the choice of either waiting for your mortgage approval currently underway, or re-shopping the mortgage and applying to another lender. Generally, all you'll lose is the loan application fees you've already paid.

During the tense wait between application and approval, as the settlement clock is ticking, you're generally at the lender's mercy. But in a climate of falling interest rates, you have some alternatives to chewing your fingernails.

If interest rates have come down since you agreed to a certain rate, remind the lender that they could lose money by delaying your settlement. If their slowness forces you to reschedule the settlement or get a bridge loan to keep the original date, you might be inclined to re-shop the mortgage and shift your business to another lender who will offer a new, lower rate or assure you of faster approval. If this is a real possibility (or even just a persuasive bluff), make sure they know you're considering it; it could motivate the lender to get moving.

## THE ROLE OF THE SECONDARY MARKET

Three-fourths of all home mortgages are sold once they are closed. The buyers—organizations with such names as Fannie Mae, Ginnie Mae and Freddie Mac, as well as a growing number of smaller firms—make up what is known as the secondary market.

It acts as a conduit, linking the world of the homebuyer to Wall Street by purchasing mortgages from lenders and reselling them, or securities backed by them, to investors.

Because it is so big, the secondary market affects what loans are available and what buyers have to do to get them.

By selling the loans they originate, savings institutions, mortgage companies and commercial banks get their cash back to reinvest, as well as fees for continuing to service the loans. Buyers, usually government or government-backed agencies or large mortgage bankers, get the right to receive the principal and interest paid by borrowers. They, in turn, package their mortgages and sell securities backed by the pooled loans. Pension funds and other institutional investors are the biggest market for mortgage-backed securities.

The secondary market helps redistribute available mortgage funds by buying mortgages in regions where the demand from homeowners outstrips lenders' deposits and selling them in other markets where available credit exceeds loan demand.

## SERVICING YOUR MORTGAGE LOAN

The servicing of mortgage loans—collecting monthly payments, escrowing and periodic payment of taxes and insurance premiums—has become a big business quite separate from mortgage lending. It has also become a headache for many homeowners.

In early 1987 it was estimated that nearly one-third of all mortgage debt in America was being serviced by companies other than the owners of the loans. And during a wave of mergers and acquisitions in the home finance and loan servicing businesses, many homeowners have had a change in their servicing firm. They receive a new coupon book for monthly payments, with the money to be sent to a different company at a different address.

Lots of bookkeeping problems can arise with a change in servicing firm. The new firm may not send you a new coupon book at all, leaving you in the dark as to where to send your next monthly payment. Or it might mess up the computation of your new adjustable-mortgage payment on the adjustment anniversary. Or it might fail to pay your real estate taxes or property insurance premium on time, causing you trouble with the local government or insurer.

If you suspect a problem, try to call the new servicing firm, if you can find its address and phone number; the previous servicing company or the original lender of your mortgage loan should be able to help with this.

If you can't straighten it out, try to find out from the original lender the name of the secondary-market firm—like Fannie Mae or Freddie Mac—that now owns your loan. These giant companies, several of which are based in the Washington, D.C., area, have a strong interest in the proper servicing of the loans they own; they would appreciate learning of problems you're having with servicing firms that do business with them.

# 12

# Getting a Good Title

If you built a new house and it burned to the ground, you'd still own the land, even if you failed to cover the house with insurance. But if you buy a home with a faulty title—due to fraud, forgery, conflict between long-ago heirs, unpaid liens from contractors, or just a title search error—you could lose everything.

When you buy a home, you are essentially buying the seller's title—his right to own, possess, use, control and dispose of his property. The written legal evidence that his ownership rights have been conveyed to you is a properly executed and recorded deed. Naturally, you want a deed that gives you the most assurances and rights to your new property and promises you a marketable title, one you can in turn convey to someone else. That's why you'll want the protection of title insurance, regardless of the customary practices in the state where you're buying.

The title examination goes on during the period between contract agreement and settlement. So it takes place concurrently with the processing of your mortgage loan application; the work is handled by attorneys or other title specialists, usually selected by the buyer.

If title problems turn up, they can usually be cleared up before settlement, but sometimes they can force a delay of settlement. Clearing a title can require the release of a debt or use of a quitclaim deed. If the problem is the result of recordkeeping neglect, such as the failure to remove a paid-up second mortgage from the record, the task may be simple. But other problems, such as a contested will, can be nightmares. If really severe, title problems can lead a purchaser to seek to void his contract with the seller. Learning your legal rights in such a situation will require the advice of a skilled real estate lawyer. Don't try canceling without legal guidance. Such an action must be carried out exactly as the contract requires, or you could end up on the receiving end of a lawsuit.

Insist on being kept informed and on understanding each step in the title checking process.

If a title problem threatens to delay settlement, be sure to let your lender know how much time may be necessary to clear the title. Loan commitments often expire after 30 or 45 days, sometimes earlier than that. If you don't get a commitment extension in writing, you could lose your loan or at least the interest rate you were promised.

## HAZARDS OF A CLOUDY TITLE

There are circumstances, such as assuming an old loan or using seller financing, in which you may be tempted to save money by forgoing a title search and new owner's title insurance. The amount you save is not worth the risk. Regardless of how great a deal you've found or the customs of the region, you should obtain owner's title insurance.

The wisdom of this should become more clear to you after you take a look at the following kinds of title problems that can arise. They are numerous and varied and not at all far-fetched. Some can be straightened out by the seller, but the buyer should have expert assistance in any event. In some, the problems may become so complicated or take so long to correct that the best solution may be to have your contract legally voided.

▶ You are buying a house from a single man or woman. The title search reveals two names on the ownership record and describes them as married: "John and Jane Clark, husband and wife."

▶ You are buying from a middle-aged brother and sister from out of town. They are selling you a home their parents bought for their retirement. The father died several years ago and the widowed mother passed away just recently. A title search reveals that the property is in her name, but there is no will on file to direct what she wanted done with it.

▶ You are buying from a couple who borrowed $20,000 seven years ago to add a room to their house. They have long since paid back the loan but have forgotten that her parents recorded it as a second mortgage when they made the loan. A title search shows the second mortgage but no evidence of its having been paid.

▶ You are buying a house to which the owner added central air-conditioning two years ago. He had a fight with the air-conditioning contractor over some damage to a ceiling that occurred during installation. When the contractor refused to correct the damage, the seller refused to pay the final installment on his contract. The contractor filed a mechanic's lien on the property, and it's never been removed.

▶ You are buying a house at a great bargain from a man who is in trouble with the Internal Revenue Service. IRS has placed a lien on the property.

▶ You are buying a property that is beautifully landscaped. A title search shows that the landscaper has a lien on the property. The seller explains that several of the trees died and when the landscaper refused to replace them, he refused to make final payment.

▶ You are buying a house from an aged widow. She and her husband bought the property many years ago, and when he died last year, she thought she was the sole owner. Now a title search reveals that the deed by which she and her husband acquired title was defective. The deed says only "Horace and Henrietta Jenkins." It should have shown their relationship and the manner in which they intended to take title.

▶ You are buying a house that has a newly paved driveway. Your seller is proud of having improved the value of his property by converting his joint driveway into a private driveway. He bought his neighbor's half in a friendly deal last year when the neighbor built a new driveway on the opposite side of his house. There is just one problem: The expanded driveway doesn't appear in the public records.

▶ The paving, sidewalks and gutters in front of the house you have under contract are all new. A title search shows that your seller has not paid the city's special assessment for the improvements.

▶ You plan to build a garage on the west end of your lot as

soon as you move in. A title search reveals an easement of eight feet over the length of your future yard. The gas company owns the easement, which was granted by the development company that built your house.

▶ You are planning to get away from it all on a piece of land 50 miles from town on which you are going to build a house. A title search reveals that your property was carved out of a large farm, but it was never legally subdivided. It was one of those down-home "from the apple tree on the southwest corner to the stone marker on the northwest corner" land descriptions.

That sort of inadequate land description and the resulting invalid deeds occur in the city, too, when neighbors get together and swap bits of land. Sometimes an owner with an oversized yard sells off a rear 20 feet to the abutting neighbor with a short yard. Or neighbors buy a vacant lot between them and split it. They erect a fence along the newly created lot line and consider the job finished, never thinking to get a survey and a proper deed for their new half lot and have it recorded.

▶ Sometimes it is the owner's financial manipulations in his business that cloud his title. In the case of a bankruptcy or an unincorporated business or partnership, the owner's personal residence may be attached to satisfy part of his business debt. Another business owner may not be in trouble, just expanding, and has pledged his personal residence as part of the security required to obtain a business loan. Until that lien is paid or he arranges with his creditor to substitute other property as security, he can't deliver a clear title to you.

The examples above show why you should never, never take title to a property—not even as a gift—without full knowledge of its legal and financial condition.

## TITLE SECURITY

At closing time you want to feel sure that the title you're getting is what you expected and what it is represented to be. There are three basic methods of assuring everyone concerned that a title is good.

**Title insurance:** This is the most common and desirable form of protection. Before the insurance is issued, a title report is prepared, based on a search of the public records. The report gives a description of the property and shows the owner, title defects, liens or encumbrances of record.

Following examination of the title report, the company will normally insure the title. If problems are discovered, the company can still insure by requiring that certain conditions be met or by making the insurance coverage subject to certain specified exceptions.

**Abstract plus an attorney's opinion:** Title is usually in the form of an abstract, which is a historical summary of everything affecting ownership of the property. It includes not only the chain of ownership but also recorded easements, mortgages, wills, tax liens, judgments, pending lawsuits, marriages and anything else that affects the title. When a property is sold, the abstract is examined by an attorney, who gives a written opinion as to the title—including who the owner of record is and his judgment on whether anyone else has any right or interest in the property. The opinion is often known as the certificate of title.

**Attorney's record search and opinion:** The attorney searches the public records and issues his certificate of title.

## BUYING TITLE INSURANCE

No matter what state you live in or what the customary title assurance practices are, you can arrange to purchase title insurance for a one-time charge if you wish to do so. (In Iowa you can get lender's title insurance only through insurance companies located outside the state; owner's coverage is not available. But changes in these regulations were under way in early 1987, so check the current situation with lenders and other real estate professionals.)

Title insurance companies are regulated by state law, but in most states, rates can vary enough to make it worthwhile to shop around.

When you're checking the fees charged by different title insurance companies, find out exactly what is covered in each case. Some routinely include the costs of handling the closing as well as the search, title report and insurance premiums. Others include just the report and premiums or, in a few states, only the premiums.

If you are getting a new mortgage, the lender will generally require mortgage (lender's) title insurance. This protects his lien on the property and makes the mortgage more marketable in the secondary mortgage market.

The face amount on the lender's policy is the amount of the loan and will decline gradually as the debt is paid off. The lender's policy does not protect you. To protect yourself, you must buy an optional owner's policy and pay an extra fee, unless you live in an area where the seller customarily provides owner's title insurance for the buyer. You can buy this kind of coverage at any time, but it is usually considerably cheaper to purchase both policies at once.

Unlike the lender's policy, the owner's policy is for the contract price and protects you and your heirs as long as you have an interest in the property. Your policy is the title insurance company's contract with you to make good any covered loss caused by a defect in the title or by any lien or encumbrance that was recorded in the public records and was not revealed to you when the policy was issued. Once you become the owner, the title company will also clear up title problems and pay for a legal defense against an attack on the title in whatever manner is provided for in its policy.

Nearly all title policies follow the same standard format, regardless of the issuing company. Take time to read it, and if possible have someone knowledgeable go over the details with you before closing. Pay close attention to what it covers and to the exceptions and exclusions.

Ordinarily, you can expect an owner's policy to cover you against such things as loss or damage from forgery, failure to comply with the law, impersonation, acts of minors, and marital status and competency questions. Policies are sometimes amended by adding special endorsements or by removing exclusions. For example, the insurer may include a clause that will increase the face amount on the contract as your home appreciates.

One possibility for saving money and still receiving full protection is to find out whether the seller is carrying title insurance and, if so, see whether the company that holds his policy offers a reissue rate. Companies in some areas will give a buyer a cost break when they reissue insurance on a title policy made four, six or possibly even ten years ago. In many cases a reissue can also be obtained from a company other than the original issuer.

## TITLE DOCUMENTS YOU'LL SEE AT CLOSING

You'll be wading through a dizzying number of legal papers at closing, and you'll find yourself signing your name over and over again, sometimes on several copies of the same document. Obviously, that's not the most auspicious time to be asking dozens of questions about deeds, titles and insurance protection—or for getting good answers. The time for that is before making a purchase offer. Get information and answers as you proceed. Here's a brief rundown on some of the common documents relating to title transfer:

**Warranty deed:** This document officially transfers title to the buyer. The seller, not the purchaser, signs it and thereby warrants that the title is free of defects that might come to light after closing. Generally, the closing agent will then have the deed recorded at the local courthouse and send you a copy.

In some states a different type of deed, such as a bargain and sale deed, security deed, grant deed or special warranty deed, is used in lieu of a general warranty deed to transfer title. Be sure you understand what kind of deed you will receive from the seller and what rights will be conveyed to you.

**Quitclaim deed:** This is a device often used to deal with title problems. Anyone with a potential claim against the property can sign it, thereby releasing any rights he or she might have. A seller who conveys a quitclaim deed does not guarantee the title against claims, but merely gives the buyer whatever interest in the property the seller may have.

**Mortgage or deed of trust:** The basic purpose of both documents is to secure the loan. When a debt is secured by a mortgage, the borrower signs a document that gives the lender a lien on the property.

When a debt is secured by a deed of trust, the buyer conveys title to a third party who holds it until the note is paid in full. The lender does not receive title but only the right to request that the property be sold should the borrower default. Both documents should be recorded.

**Owner's affidavit:** The seller swears in this document that there are no unpaid liens, assessments or other encumbrances against the property. The affidavit protects the purchaser, lender and title company. If the seller is lying, he or she can be sued for damages.

**Purchaser's affidavit:** Sometimes the buyer is required by the lender to swear that there are no existing or pending suits, judgments or liens against him or her. If the buyer is lying, that is sufficient grounds for foreclosure.

# 13

## Get Ready
## for Settlement

There is no way to ensure a smooth path from ratified contract to the settlement table, but you've done all the right things so far, and the process seems to be moving along well. Your loan application is in, and you are anticipating a written loan commitment. A title examination is underway. Things seem pretty much in order on your side of the fence.

Things can still go wrong and jeopardize your settlement date, if not the contract itself. Title problems are one of the more common causes of delayed settlements. Others include fairly frequent bureaucratic snags: slow appraisals, lengthy credit reporting requirements, delayed loan commitments and the like. In many cases, there isn't much you or anyone can do but wait.

If problems occur on your side—most commonly, a delay in mortgage approval that may cause you to miss the original closing date—contact the seller immediately and work out an extension, ideally at no penalty to yourself. A seller is unlikely to try to withdraw now, and neither are you.

While you're waiting on the completion of all the processes now in motion, there are a few more things to do, including:

▶ Decide how you want to take title to the house;

▶ Apply for homeowner's insurance on the new resident, so it's in place at settlement;

▶ Review the adequacy of your disability and life insurance;

▶ Contact the utility companies about starting service in your name;

▶ Get an exact accounting of settlement costs, and make sure the money and necessary documents will be there at closing.

▶ Arrange for a walk-through of the house a few days before settlement, and again just before the meeting.

## HOW TO TAKE TITLE

Before you can take title to your new home, you'll have to decide what form of ownership you want.

If you're single, you'll probably buy the house in your name alone, but an increasing number of unrelated singles are buying houses together, using such methods as joint tenancy, tenancy in common, etc. (See below.)

The most common way for husband and wife to own property is through joint ownership, either in the form of joint tenancy with the right of survivorship or tenancy by the entirety.

Under either form, if one spouse dies, the other joint owner becomes sole owner of the property. This happens automatically, bypassing probate, avoiding delays and usually trimming the costs of settling the estate. For federal tax purposes, half the value of all property owned by a married couple as joint tenants is included in the estate of the first spouse to die.

The two kinds of joint ownership differ in some respects, and many states don't recognize tenancies by the entirety. You may want to have your lawyer's advice before deciding how to take title. If you live in a community property state (Arizona, California, Idaho, Louisiana, Nevada, New Mexico, Texas and Washington), state law will determine the form of property ownership you use.

The advice of a good trusts-and-estates attorney could be helpful in deciding if joint ownership is right for you, especially if you are wealthy. For couples whose total wealth exceeds $1.2 million, if they die more or less simultaneously, there can be substantial savings on federal estate taxes if their property had been divided equally between them, so each spouse's estate gets the benefit of the $600,000 starting point for taxation.

So to save on estate taxes someday, you may want to put the new home in the name of one or the other spouse alone. But check that this is alright with your lender, too; it may not want the house owned by one spouse exclusively if all the earnings to pay the mortgage will be derived from the other spouse.

And consider this, too: if the house is put in one spouse's name alone, it could affect the division of property in the event of a divorce.

Other forms of ownership include:

**Tenancy in common:** Each owner has a separate legal title to an undivided interest in the whole property, and each can independently sell, mortgage or give away his interest.

It's wise for owners to have a written agreement setting out their rights to deal with their interest in the property. The agreement also should specify the percentage of ownership interest each person has in the property if, for example, they have not contributed equal amounts. When one of the owners dies, the others do not automatically get the deceased's share unless that person specifically provides for such an arrangement in his will. If the will doesn't cover this, or if he dies without a will, state law determines who gets the deceased owner's share.

**Joint tenancy:** Under this arrangement, each person has an equal interest in the property regardless of the amount contributed at purchase. If one owner dies, that person's share passes automatically to the others without going through probate.

**Partnership:** If title is in the name of a partnership, it is the partnership that owns the property, not the individual partners. This arrangement calls for an agreement that sets forth how each partner will share in the management of the partnership.

The death of a partner does not affect the partnership; that person's heirs would acquire the interest. This form of ownership is useful if one or more of the partners are investors who don't plan to live on the property. Another plus for a partnership arrangement is that you may avoid some problems that can arise with the other two forms discussed above, if one person goes into bankruptcy or has other legal problems that could cloud the title.

## INSURANCE ON YOUR NEW HOME

Your lender will require you to take out a homeowner's insurance policy, something you'd want to do anyway. The lender is interested in coverage only on the amount of its mortgage, so it will get its money back in the event of a total loss; but you'll probably want full-value coverage, perhaps enhanced by an inflation-adjustment mechanism that keeps the coverage rising with home values.

If you already own a home, you can deal with the same agent and company that covers it now, or take the occasion to bone up on what's new in insurance and who's offering competitive rates. If you're moving to a new area, there may be some benefit in dealing with a local agent there.

Most policies are set up along these lines:

**Declarations:** This section gives the personal information you supplied to the agent, such as your name and address, as well as a description of the coverage you have purchased. It spells out how long the policy is to run, the premiums and the deductible amount that applies. (The deductible is the sum you have to pay before the insurance cuts in for a particular loss.) The location of your dwelling is included in this section, along with a rundown on the kinds of coverage you have chosen. The dollar limits for each kind of coverage are also specified.

**Insuring agreement:** To be covered, the event involving loss usually must be listed in this section, which is the company's promise to pay. This promise, however, is very broad, and payments for some mentioned occurrences may be limited by the language in other parts of the policy.

**Exclusions:** Some risks—such as damages or injuries a policy-holder inflicts intentionally—are not covered at all, and they are listed in this section. Other risks are only partially excluded, giving you the right to limited coverage under certain circum-stances. In still other cases, a particular risk is considered to be so out of the ordinary that it is thought best to have it covered by a special endorsement rather than have all policyholders pay for it under a standard contract.

**Conditions:** This section clarifies the rights and obligations of both the policyholder and the company. Some of the provisions tell what you must do following a loss in order to get paid.

**Endorsements:** These attachments are used to tailor the broad policy format to individual needs, perhaps by adding specific protection for jewelry and furs. However, the policy and its endorsements are considered as a unit, the latter having as much heft as the former. Make sure that the endorsements don't unduly limit or reduce the coverage spelled out in general terms elsewhere.

If you cannot get home insurance because your home is in a high-risk area, or is considered a high-risk property, you still may be able to buy coverage under the Fair Access to Insurance Requirements (FAIR) plan. FAIR is in efffect in over 25 states. You can find out whether it is available where you live by calling or writing the Insurance Information Institute, 110 William Street, New York, NY 10038, or by calling toll free 800-221-4954. Or ask your real estate or insurance agent.

## EARTHQUAKE INSURANCE

Ordinary property insurance policies don't cover earthquake damage, although you can fill in the gap with a special earthquake endorsement or a separate policy. In California, for example, earthquake insurance usually runs from $1.50 to $2.50 per $1,000 of coverage on wood-frame houses, equal to the cost of most regular homeowners policies. The deductible can go as high as 10% of the policy's coverage, so the insurance pays off only on big claims.

California isn't the only area at risk. Parts of Arkansas, Colorado, Idaho, Illinois, Indiana, Kentucky, Massachusetts, Mississippi, Missouri, Nevada, New York, South Carolina, Tennessee, Utah, Washington and Wyoming are also considered to be at higher-than-average risk.

While most homeowners don't need earthquake protection, there are three conditions that should make you consider buying protection:

▶ Your home was constructed before World War II, when codes covering a structure's ability to withstand shifts in the earth were weaker; this is particularly important for homes not framed with wood.

▶ Your home is located within 10 miles of a fault.

▶ Your home is on unstable soil, such as a hillside, landfill or flood control plain.

## FLOOD INSURANCE

If you are buying a home in a flood-prone area, consider protecting yourself against a major disaster. Some 19,000 communities participate in the federal government's National Flood Insurance Program. Insurance is available to individual homeowners in such communities through private insurance companies and independent agents. Protection doesn't come cheap; the average homeowner's annual premium is $258, and the standard deduction is $500.

## INSURANCE ON YOUR LIFE

If your new home represents a considerably higher financial burden than you've ever carried before, and if you have a spouse and children to protect in the event of your death or disability, this is a good time to review your needs. Have an accountant, trusts-and-estates attorney, financial planner or trusted insurance professional review your situation on disability and life insurance.

Your best bet may be conventional term life insurance whose proceeds, if invested wisely, will produce enough annual income to pay the new mortgage and other basic living expenses. (See the discussion of mortgage life insurance and its drawbacks in Chapter 11.)

## UTILITIES

Arrange for electricity, gas, oil and water to be turned on the day of settlement and the accounts switched from the seller's to your name. That way there will be no interruption in service. Utility companies often require deposits, credit checks and advance notice, so make your arrangements a few weeks in advance.

## ON TO SETTLEMENT

You are only days away from becoming an owner. The search has been expensive in terms of both time and money. Now it's time for you to pay for the property, and for the seller to deliver the deed.

There is no standard name for this next step. Depending on where you live, it is known as title closing, settlement or closing of escrow. The closing officer in your area may be a title company, an abstract attorney or a regular real estate attorney. Occasionally, it is a broker or lender.

When closing involves an actual meeting, the process commonly is called settlement. If no meeting occurs, it's often known as escrow and is handled by an escrow agent. In escrow cases, the buyer and seller typically sign an agreement requiring each party to deposit certain funds and documents with the agent. When all the papers and monies are in, the escrow is "closed." The agent records the documents and makes the appropriate disbursements.

Settling on a home can be as serene as a treaty signing. Too often, it's as full of static as a debate at the United Nations. Planned closings stand a better chance of being peaceful closings. Each party knows what to expect.

As the buyer, you probably selected the person or firm to perform the settlement, so you can rely on their competence and integrity. If for some reason the seller specified the settlement agent, you might wish to take along your own attorney or have an attorney of your choice review the documents beforehand, at your expense. The cost of a few hundred dollars could give you added peace of mind.

## The costs you face

The key to reducing shock at settlement is to know ahead of time what you'll have to pay. You had ballpark figures to work with when you started looking, and once your purchase offer was accepted, you received detailed estimates from the lender with whom you made an application.

Overall settlement costs are influenced by, among other things, where you live, your settlement date, how you finance your purchase and what the lender requires as an inducement to provide the loan.

It's difficult to say what closing costs run on a national basis, simply because there is no uniformity to how the costs are counted and calculated. But within local markets you generally can get a good estimate. For example, in Atlanta closing costs on conventional loans commonly come to 3.3% of the loan amount. In California, 2% is closer to the mark. Neither of those estimates includes any discount points (equal to 1% of the loan amount) or the brokerage commission (usually paid by the seller)—and these, as you know by now, will make up the largest proportion of your settlement costs.

The federal government's Real Estate Settlement Procedures Act (RESPA) covers most home loans, including VA, FHA, FmHA or other government-backed or government-assisted loans; loans eligible to be purchased by GNMA, FNMA or in other federally related secondary mortgage markets; and loans made by lenders who invest or make more than $1 million in residential loans each year. Assumptions and seller financing are not covered by RESPA.

When you applied for a new loan from a lender covered by RESPA, the law required that you be given a "good faith" estimate of fees when you made a written loan application—or within three business days—and that you be given a pamphlet titled *Settlement Costs and You*, put out by the Department of Housing and Urban Development. This contains a description of how the closing process works and explains terms you will encounter in your transaction.

The day before settlement, you are entitled to see the Uniform Settlement Statement. This is a copy of what you will get at settlement. In places where there is no meeting, the escrow agent is required to give you a copy when escrow is closed.

Use the worksheet at the end of this chapter to check the lender's and agent's estimates against actual amounts as you get them. This may provide you with some advance warning if there are substantial changes before settlement. The worksheet, like HUD's Uniform Settlement Statement, breaks the total settlement charges into broad categories:

1) *Costs associated with getting a loan*: These can include the lender's charge for processing the loan, loan discount points and/or origination fees, appraisal fee, borrower's credit report, mortgage insurance, and if relevant, loan assumption fee.

2) *Items to be prepaid at closing*: Mortgage interest, property

taxes, and mortgage and hazard insurance premiums are frequently paid in advance at closing.

Once you become an owner, you will pay interest on your monthly mortgage loan in arrears; that is, you will pay for the use of the loan at the end of each month. The loan is structured so that payments made on the first of each month cover the interest owed from the previous month. In order to make this work, the lender will collect interest in advance at settlement for the period between closing and the end of that month. For example, if settlement is August 15 and you must make your first regular mortgage payment October 1, the lender will collect interest through the end of August.

In addition, lenders often require payment of as much as the first year's mortgage and hazard insurance premiums at closing. In some cases a buyer can arrange for the seller to transfer the remaining hazard insurance, paying the seller on a prorated basis for the remainder of the policy term.

3) *Reserves for insurance, taxes and assessments*: The borrower may be required to pay an initial amount at closing to set up a reserve fund, and each month a portion of the regular payment will be added to the reserve to assure sufficient sums to pay future taxes and insurance premiums.

4) *Title costs*: These pay for various transaction costs, notably the title search required by the lender. An examination is made of the public records to determine whether the title you receive has any ownership or financial claims and restrictions on the use of the property. Other related charges include title insurance, document preparation, notary fees and the lender's attorney fees.

5) *Recording and transfer charges*: These cover the recording of the loan and property documents at the county courthouse, as well as related transfer taxes.

6) *Additional fees* for attorney and buyer broker services, property survey and pest inspection.

In general, items paid for in advance by the seller, such as property taxes, would be prorated in favor of the seller at closing. Items paid in arrears, for example interest on an assumed loan, would be prorated in favor of the purchaser.

You may want to run through the worksheet and note which items are to be paid in full or in part by you. Local custom usually influences whether the buyer or the seller pays a particular charge. You can do things differently, but to avoid conflicts, make sure your purchase contract states clearly how each item is to be handled. Otherwise, it's not unreasonable for the seller to expect you to abide by the prevailing custom.

In some areas, for example, the buyer pays for a title insurance policy because the buyer's lender requires the protection. In other places, the seller absorbs the charge as one of the selling costs. In some areas, the buyer always pays the local tax for recording the deed; in others, the seller always pays it. (To see what closing costs might be involved in the purchase of a $100,000 home, see the example at the end of this chapter.)

## WHAT TO BRING TO CLOSING

In order for things to go smoothly, each person is responsible for bringing certain documents, and for being prepared to write the necessary checks. Many closing costs can be paid by personal check, but double check with the closing attorney. A certified or cashier's check may be required; find out to whom checks should be made payable—the seller or settlement attorney, for example.

Arrange to pay for discount points and loan origination fees with one check and other closing costs with another, so that all your prepaid interest expenses will be clearly segregated for deduction from your taxable income in the year you pay them.

The seller and his attorney, or the settlement attorney you've both agreed on, are responsible for preparing and bringing the deed and the most recent property tax bill. They also will bring other documents required by the contract. This can include property insurance policy, termite inspection, documents showing the removal of liens, a bill of sale for personal property, loan documents and so on.

Your responsibilities include having adequate funds in your checking account, arranging for your attorney to represent your interests at the meeting, bringing your loan commitment and informing the lender of the meeting's time and place.

If your lender requires payment of the first year's mortgage and hazard insurance premiums at closing, you should be prepared to do so or to bring proof that they have already been paid. Finally, it's a good idea to bring a copy of the purchase contract. You may need to refresh your memory.

## THE FINAL INSPECTION

The house you're buying must be handed over to you in the condition specified in the contract. (See the discussion of condition in Chapters 8 and 9.)

To verify this, schedule a walk-through of the house shortly before settlement; several days in advance is best, to allow time for the seller to correct any last-minute problems.

If the house is vacant, it should be empty of debris and in the "broom-clean" condition you specified in the contract. Take along a simple device for testing all the electrical outlets—a plug-in nightlight, for example. Turn on the furnace and air-conditioning. (If it's winter, you may not be able to turn on the AC, and an expert may have to verify that it's in working condition.) Flush the toilets and turn on faucets. In short, put the house through its paces.

If anything needs fixing or further cleaning (aside from things that were conveyed only in "as-is" condition), tell the seller immediately. Neither you nor the seller wants to postpone the settlement, but make it clear you won't go to closing until a second walk-through is satisfactory.

If the seller is staying on in the house after settlement, by leasing the house back from you the new owner, the seller will soon become your tenant. The contract should have spelled out the terms of this lease-back, including a security deposit (for example, one month's rent). You may want to have a formal lease with the previous owner, now your new tenant.

Under this kind of arrangement, you will have two walk-throughs—one just before settlement (in which you check on all the things above except cleanliness) and another one after the seller moves out. Any difference in condition that occurs between the two inspections will have to be settled just as in a normal landlord-tenant relationship, with responsibility for repair determined accordingly. If everything is okay at the second walk-through, the seller will get back the damage/security deposit.

## SAVE ALL THE DOCUMENTS FOR TAXES

With the completion of settlement proceedings, you're now a homeowner. Congratulations!

The tax benefits of homeownership are considerable, but so too is the paperwork necessary to take advantage of all the breaks.

If you haven't read Chapter 3 ("Home Sweet Tax Shelter") carefully, do so after closing on your new home. Now is the time to begin keeping meticulous records of every cost incurred on your new home—from settlement expenses to improvements that add to the home's value. Some of these expenses can be deducted from taxable income in the year you buy the home; others will merely increase the tax basis, lowering the taxable gain when you someday sell the house, whether next year or 40 years hence. The better your records, the easier those calculations will be later on.

## HYPOTHETICAL SETTLEMENT COSTS

Location: Montgomery County, MD
Sale price: $100,000
Down payment: $20,000

### Buyer's Costs

| | | |
|---|---|---:|
| Credit report | | $35.00 |
| Loan origination fee (1%)* | | 800.00 |
| Interest to Feb. 1# | | 591.78 |
| Six months property tax† | | 640.50 |
| Hazard insurance premium** | | 211.00 |
| Two mos. insurance reserve** | | 35.16 |
| Title examination | | 95.00 |
| Binder | | 12.50 |
| Attorneys fees | | 275.00 |
| Recording fee | | 50.00 |
| Survey | | 125.00 |
| State recordation tax | | 440.00 |
| State transfer tax | | 500.00 |
| County transfer tax | | 1,000.00 |
| Stamps | | 440.00 |
| Title insurance | | 332.50 |
| | TOTAL: | $5,583.44 |

### Seller's Costs

| | | |
|---|---|---:|
| Sales commission (6%) | | $6,000.00 |
| Loan discount point (1%)* | | 800.00 |
| Appraisal fee | | 250.00 |
| Closing fees | | 125.00 |
| Termite inspection | | 35.00 |
| | TOTAL: | $7,210.00 |

*The buyer is paying a 1% loan origination fee, and the seller has agreed to pay one point on the buyer's $80,000 mortgage.

#Because interest is paid in arrears—for the previous month—and because the buyer's first regular monthly payment won't be due until March 1, the lender collects interest for Jan. 2 through Feb. 1 at closing.

†Lenders frequently collect one-twelfth of the annual property taxes each month—along with the principal and interest payment—and hold them in escrow until payment is due. How much is paid at settlement depends on the closing date and when taxes are collected in a given locale.

**The lender is collecting and will be paying a full year's premium on hazard insurance covering at least the value of the mortgage; lender is also starting a reserve fund for future premiums.

In other locales and in other circumstances, the buyer's closing costs may include an assumption fee (if the buyer is taking over the seller's mortgage), mortgage insurance, and various other charges.

Total settlement charges are generally less if the buyer is assuming an existing loan or paying all cash, rather than getting a new mortgage.

(Settlement calculations provided by Weaver Brothers, Chevy Chase, MD.)

## SETTLEMENT OR ESCROW COSTS
## WORKSHEET

|  | Agent's estimate | Lender's estimate | Actual |
|---|---|---|---|
| **Costs related to obtaining a loan** | | | |
| Loan origination fee | _____ | _____ | _____ |
| Loan discount, or points | _____ | _____ | _____ |
| Appraisal fee | _____ | _____ | _____ |
| Credit report | _____ | _____ | _____ |
| Inspection fee | _____ | _____ | _____ |
| Mortgage insurance application | _____ | _____ | _____ |
| Assumption fee | | | |
| _____ | _____ | _____ | _____ |
| _____ | _____ | _____ | _____ |
| **Items to be paid in advance** | | | |
| Interest from _____ to _____ @ $_____ per day | _____ | _____ | _____ |
| Mortgage insurance for _____ to _____ | _____ | _____ | _____ |
| Hazard insurance for _____ years to _____ | _____ | _____ | _____ |
| _____ | | | |
| **Items to be deposited with lender at settlement** | | | |
| Hazard insurance _____ months @ $_____ per month | _____ | _____ | _____ |
| Mortgage insurance _____ months @ $_____ per month | _____ | _____ | _____ |
| City property taxes _____ | _____ | _____ | _____ |
| County property taxes _____ | _____ | _____ | _____ |
| Annual assessments _____ | _____ | _____ | _____ |

**Title costs**
Settlement or escrow fee
Abstract or title search
Title examination or opinion
Title insurance binder
Document preparation
Notary fees
Attorney's fees (including the
   charges listed above)

_____

Title insurance (including the
   charges listed above)

_____

Lender's coverage
Owner's coverage

_____

_____

**Recording and transfer charges**
Recording fees:
   Deed $_____
   Mortgage $_____
   Releases $_____
City/county:
   Deed $____ Mortgage $____
State:
   Deed $____ Mortgage $____

**Other costs**
Attorney's fee
Buyer/broker fee
Pest inspection

_____

_____

**TOTAL SETTLEMENT OR
  ESCROW CHARGES**

# 14

## Buying a Vacation Home

A simple log cabin in the Ozark mountains, or a weathered cottage on Cape Cod. A ski condo in Aspen, Colorado. A secluded mansion tucked into a cove on the Caribbean island of St. Lucia. A one-week timeshare at a resort in the Poconos.

The words "vacation property" may be used by the owners of each of these, although the financial, legal and tax consequences of each can be as different as the beach and the mountains.

There are many reasons people buy a second home, some personal, some financial. Typically, they enjoy a particular vacation spot so much they believe they'll want to keep returning over and over. Rather than rent a different house or hotel room each time, living like nomads, they want to have a place where they'll be truly at home—where they can keep their vacation gear and summer (or winter) clothes, entertain friends, and feel like a part of the community.

If your desire is merely to lock in predictable vacation costs in a community where you like to go each year, a fractional interest or timeshare might make sense. Some kinds of timeshares are not real estate per se, but more like a prepaid right to use a given unit for a certain length of time each year. Keep your expectations of financial gain low or non-existent; it's often difficult to sell a timeshare for even your original investment. (See discussion below.)

Many people buy a vacation home where they think they will want to retire some day; at that point, their second home might become their primary residence.

For other vacation-home buyers, the primary motivation is

financial. If this describes you, make sure you check out all the angles before succumbing to the fast talk of a resort sales person. Buying a vacation home to avoid rising rents might make sense in some communities, but not in others; it often costs the vacationer less to rent the nicest house in a given community for a month than it costs the owners to pay the mortgage, taxes and maintenance on that same house for a month, especially in the early years of the ownership period.

Price appreciation is another matter. Some people buy in a given vacation community because they've witnessed, first hand, a rapid rise in home prices (and probably rents, too) over the previous several years; they want to get in on the action. Carefully selected homes in the most sought-after communities can, in fact, appreciate nicely, making them good investments as well as nice places to visit. But appreciation is highly variable from region to region and resort to resort. Some people who hastily bought timeshares or resort houses from persuasive salesmen have found they can't even recover their original investment in a slender resale market. It takes a lot of study, cool analysis, and good guessing to make a smart decision.

Some people buy a vacation home with a big mortgage to beef up their interest deductions, and the Tax Reform Act of 1986 maintains the deductibility of interest on mortgages secured by one or two residences—so long as they are used primarily for personal purposes, not rental. The loans can total no more than the original purchase price of the house plus the value of improvements; loans against the appreciated value of the house— the inflation value—do not qualify for interest deductibility.

Vacation homes that are rented out for most or all of the year used to be a better tax shelter than they are now, due to restrictions in the Tax Reform Act. (See the full discussion below.)

## STUDY BEFORE YOU BUY

In many ways, buying a vacation property is like buying a principal residence, so the preceding chapters of this book will be useful to you.

There are many special considerations, too. You have to define your needs very carefully, such as deciding how big a residence you need, its style, and how far away from your main residence you want your second home to be—a few hours drive? a long plane trip? Is the house exclusively for your own use, or will you want to rent it out for part or all of the year; if the latter, you have to curb your unusual tastes and buy whatever features the rental market wants most.

You shouldn't buy anywhere you haven't visited several times as a vacationer. Most of all, never buy a home on a first visit to a new resort community or timeshare resort that uses intensive sales pressure to convince people to commit themselves on the spot.

While on a vacation in the community you're considering, devote a few days to a thorough investigation of the market. Look at houses or timeshares for sale. Study the market, using actual sale prices, not advertised asking prices. Talk to the leading real estate brokers in the community. If you're intending to rent the house out, deal with a firm that can manage your property—finding tenants, collecting rent, making repairs—when you're not around. Talk to all the year-round residents you can find, and drop by the offices of the local newspaper to learn what you can about zoning, future developments, and commercial growth in the area.

## VACATION HOME STRATEGIES

Most would-be buyers soon have their choices narrowed by lofty price tags attached to the most attractive vacation properties. Here are various scenarios for personal use, renting out, and combinations of both, showing the kinds of properties that make the most sense in each circumstance.

### Personal use only

The most affluent buyers are often looking for a unique or unusual property. They may want it to reflect their status in life. Such owners are not interested in rental income and intend to use the property for their own and their family's enjoyment. The vacation home may qualify as a second residence and, if so, mortgage interest will be fully deductible. Long-term appreciation and estate building are primary investment objectives.

Good bets for these affluent buyers include the most sought-after (and expensive) categories of vacation property: rural acreage near growing metropolitan areas; waterfront property; apartments or townhouses in cities that are hubs of international travel and cultural and recreational attractions.

## Some rental and business use

Another group of affluent, but more practical, buyers may look at vacation property with a sharper focus on potential medium-term investment return. They may own more than one property, to assure themselves a get-away place in the event one property is rented out. Using professional management, they actively seek rental income. Such owners may restrict personal use of a property in order to maintain deductions and tax shelter, although the new tax law demands rethinking of that strategy, as discussed below. They may use property for business purposes, such as entertaining clients or customers. Appreciation and some tax shelter are financial objectives.

Their choices of vacation property might include condos or townhouses in popular resort areas, or perhaps a condo hotel suite in a sought-after area where weather permits either one long vacation season or two peak seasons.

## Limited personal use, heavy renting

Less affluent vacation home buyers need rental income in order to carry their investment. They may manage the property completely on their own, or try to find a few prospects to supplement the rentals lined up for their property by a manager. Such owners may not use the property themselves, or may do so only out of season. (See the discussion below on the trade-offs between personal and rental use.) Cash-flow, appreciation and tax shelter are financial objectives. Investing in an area that becomes overbuilt—driving down rental rates and slowing appreciation—is a serious threat to their investment objectives.

Their best purchase prospects include resort property in areas with perennial popularity and with either one long rental season and/or two rental seasons (for example, a part of New England with winter skiing and summer camping).

## LESS-THAN-FULL-TIME OWNERSHIP

Yet another segment of the vacation home market may dream of owning a beach cottage or a mountain hideaway, but cannot afford the down payment or the cash outlay an unrented property would drain from their budget. ''You can't spend all your time on vacation, so why own a vacation place all the time?'' they reason.

And, because so many people fall into this group, developers and sales people have spent hours upon hours trying to figure ways to help them own—ways that would not work for a primary residence but may make sense for a vacation home. But you cannot count on them for appreciation or tax breaks.

If you fall into this group, consider fractional interests and timeshares in quality developments. Resort developers in such places as Colorado, New England and the Carolinas offer fractional interests in their properties, thus creating a deal that combines the long-term advantages of undivided ownership with a lower price.

### Fractional interest

Fractional interests may be sold as quarter-shares (13 weeks), fifth-shares (ten weeks) or tenth-shares (five weeks). Essentially, you're buying title to a number of weeks throughout the year. With a quarter-share, for example, you get to use the property every fourth week. Each year, the sequence shifts forward a week, giving you a chance to use all the weeks of the year within a four-year period. A mix of floating and fixed time periods sometimes is used.

Fractional interests are likely to offer better prospects for appreciation than timeshares. Pay attention to marketing costs, which may range from zero to 25%. Buyers paying a 25% premium in sales expenses (commissions, etc.) will have to wait some time before they can start counting paper profits.

The resort developer is the most likely source of funds to finance a fractional interest, and terms vary widely. Prices for ''fractionals'' range from $25,000 to $100,000 or more. Check with a knowledgeable accountant regarding tax consequences and interest deductions.

## Timeshares

This is one of the most popular means of dividing up ownership of a vacation property, and often the cheapest way to buy into a resort. You become one of the owners of a property, typically a condo apartment. Usually, ownership is divided into 52 parts—one for each week of the year—and the parts are sold off one or more at a time. A one-week timeshare rarely sells for more than $10,000.

Timeshare ownership can be in the form of tenancy-in-common (sometimes called time-span ownership) or interval ownership. Tenancy-in-common gives you an undivided interest in a property, pro-rated according to the amount of time you purchase. Interval ownership lasts only for a specified number of years. When those years are up, you and the other interval owners become tenants in common. Under either type of ownership, you don't always get a specified unit for a fixed time period. Instead, you may choose from interchangeable units and floating weeks.

One form of timesharing—known as a vacation license, vacation lease or club membership—carries no ownership rights at all, only the right to use the property each year for a number of years. Ownership stays in the hands of the developer.

Whatever the form of purchase, you normally cannot get a mortgage to buy a timeshare. Financing typically is covered by a personal loan over a 5-to-10-year period with a 10% down payment, and the lender usually is the developer. Check with your accountant and attorney about the tax implications. Don't rely on assurances from a sales person.

If vacationing is your only motivation, then a timeshare may suit you. It locks in the cost of staying at a particular place, yet provides the flexibility to vacation elsewhere, too. For an annual fee, usually about $50 or $60, you can use a timeshare exchange that works out vacation-place swaps with other timeshare owners around the world.

But a timeshare doesn't make much sense if you're counting on reselling at a profit in the near future, especially if the unit is new and the developer still is selling others. Heavy marketing costs, which may include free airfare and lodging to lure potential buyers to the resort, push up the price charged for the units. Some buyers of newly built timeshare apartments sadly discover they paid twice as much as the resale market will bear.

### Condo hotel suites

Buying a hotel suite is one way to get a vacation place that has a chance to pay for itself. The suite is yours when you want it, but is rented out on a daily basis like any other hotel room the rest of the time. You get a share of rental receipts and revenues generated by retail shops, restaurants, vending machines, long-distance phone calls and other operations. Check with your accountant and lawyer for tax and investment consequences.

## BUYING WITH PARTNERS

Not infrequently friends will get together to buy a vacation home together, either as tenants in common or in a legally constituted partnership.

Owning as tenants in common, friendly as it sounds, can cause everyone a lot of headaches. Setting up a general partnership to own the place can head off many of those problems by anticipating and dealing with them in the partnership agreement. Use your real estate lawyer to draw up the agreement, but ask an attorney in the vacation area to check relevant regulations.

Make sure the contract addresses the following points:

▶ How ownership will be divided, which in turn determines who pays how much of the down payment, monthly payment, maintenance and repairs. The contract should also describe how any profits or losses from rent or sale of the place will be divided and how tax benefits will be distributed.

▶ Who gets to use the property when.

▶ What constitutes a deciding vote and under what circumstances such a vote is considered necessary.

▶ Which owner will act as managing partner and thus be responsible for signing checks and paying routine expenses.

▶ How much advance notice a withdrawing partner must give and how the buyout price will be set.

A partnership may also protect the existing mortgage when a new owner enters the picture if the lender agrees that it is an interest in the partnership—not an interest in the property—that is being transferred.

Ideally, a general partnership should try to find a lender who is willing to limit each partner's liability on the loan to his or her respective percentage of ownership, even though such agreements are unusual. Otherwise, each partner is responsible for 100% of the loan, so a lender could single out any partner to sue for the money if there's a default, instead of going through complicated foreclosure proceedings.

## TAXES TAKE NO HOLIDAY

One thing you can't get away from at your get-away-from-it-all vacation home is taxes. In fact, Uncle Sam has created an especially intricate web of rules just for vacation home owners. And the Tax Reform Act of 1986 has woven in new complications.

On the plus side, despite threats, Congress decided to preserve the deductibility of mortgage interest paid on second homes. Property taxes remain deductible, too, so the government stands by to help you pay for the place by refunding part of your carrying costs via a reduced tax bill. Of course, as tax rates fall, this subsidy will be worth less than in the past. For that reason the after-tax cost of buying a vacation home will increase.

The two-edged sword of tax reform also hikes the cost of selling a second home by eliminating the capital gains exclusion. In the past, any profit on the deal was a long-term gain, meaning 60% of it was tax free. Now, 100% is taxable and, unlike the rollover provision that lets you delay the tax bill when you sell a personal residence (see Chapter 17), there's no reprieve when you sell a vacation residence. Other changes affect owners who rent out their Shangri La part of the time to help pay the bill with rental income and additional tax benefits generated by deductions for depreciation and other expenses. Tax reform both crimps and further complicates those deductions.

The declining tax subsidy may convince some owners that now's the time to sell. At the same time, the enduring tax benefits are sure to attract new buyers. If you're in the market, be sure you understand how the IRS tags along to your vacation property.

## For personal use only

Things are easy if your home-away-from-home is just that: a second residence that's not rented out. You can deduct all the interest you pay on a mortgage on a second home, whether it's a chalet in the mountains, a condo on the beach or a yacht docked at the marina, as long as your debt on the place doesn't exceed the original cost of the property plus the cost of any improvements you've made.

If you own a third house, you're out of luck. Congress apparently figures that anyone who can afford more than two homes probably can handle the mortgage interest without the help of a tax deduction. Interest on any extra homes—and on debt on the second home that exceeds its cost-plus-improvement value—falls into the category of "consumer interest," with the write-off phased out between 1987 and 1991.

Property taxes you pay are also deductible, just as they are on your principal residence, regardless of how many homes you own. When you buy a vacation home, points paid to get a mortgage are *not* deductible in the year they are paid, unlike the rule that applies when you buy a principal residence. Instead, points on a vacation home are deducted proportionally over the life of the loan.

## Mixed personal and rental use

If you rent the vacation home, things get tricky. First of all, if you rent it out for 14 or fewer days, you can pocket the rent tax-free. This nugget in the tax law has prompted some homeowners who find themselves in a temporarily hot rental market—one recent example was in the Los Angeles area during the 1984 Olympics—to rent their homes briefly when they can command especially high rents. There is no limit to how much you charge for the use of your home, so long as your temporary tenants stay no more than two weeks during the year.

Rent it for more than 14 days and you become a landlord in the eyes of the IRS. You have to report the rental income, and you qualify to deduct rental expenses. The amount of time tenants use the property and the time you spend enjoying it yourself control what you get to deduct.

The amount of personal use—which includes whenever you let family or friends use it without paying fair market rent, as well as the time you use it yourself—determines whether the place is considered a residence or a business property.

Basically, if your personal use is more than 14 days or more than 10% of the number of days it is rented to others (20 personal days for 200 rental days, for example), it is considered a personal residence. But if you use the place less than that, the IRS says you may treat the property as a business. The tax ramifications are vastly different, and tax reform has changed the rules of the game significantly.

Before tax reform, many owners went out of their way to pass the 14 day/10% test so the property qualified as a business. If rental expenses—including operating costs, repairs and depreciation, as well as a share of the mortgage interest and property taxes—exceeded rental income (as it usually did), the owners could claim a loss on their tax returns. When personal use exceeded 14 days/10%, rental deductions were limited to the amount of rental income. Any excess expenses were of no tax value. In many cases, that effectively ruled out depreciation write-offs.

With tax reform, Congress seems to be encouraging owners to spend more time taking it easy at their vacation get-aways, and some advisers are saying it now makes tax sense to flunk the 14 day/10% test.

Why? Because the new law slaps a limit on the tax losses that can be claimed on a rental property, and because being classified as a business rather than a personal residence means forfeiting the right to write off part of the mortgage interest.

As part of the crackdown on tax shelters, Congress decided to eliminate the deduction of "passive" losses, a new category in the tax lexicon that includes any losses on rental property. There is an important exception, though, for taxpayers with adjusted gross incomes under $100,000. They can still deduct up to $25,000 in rental losses a year. To qualify you have to "actively" manage the property, and you can probably pass that test so long as you're involved in decisions such as approving new tenants, rental terms and repairs. As adjusted gross income moves between $100,000 and $150,000, that $25,000 exception is gradually phased out. Any losses that can't be deducted because of the passive-loss rule are carried over to future years and can be used to offset any profit you make when you sell the vacation home.

To ease the pain of this rule change, it is being phased in for taxpayers who had rental property in service as of October 22, 1986. For them, 65% of otherwise nondeductible passive losses can be deducted in 1987, 40% in 1988, 20% in 1989 and 10% in 1990. Properties purchased after that date are hit with the full force of the new rules beginning in 1987.

Even if the $25,000 exception seems plenty high to you, there is a catch. Holding down personal use to get your property designated a business property probably means giving up the right to some mortgage interest deductions. Tax reform permits the continued deduction of mortgage interest only for loans secured by your first and second *residence*. If your vacation place is a business property, the mortgage on it isn't covered. Part of the interest would still be deductible—the portion attributable to the business use of the property—and the rest would be considered "consumer interest." Only 65% of such interest is deductible in 1987, 40% in 1988, 20% in 1989 and 10% in 1990. Starting in 1991, there will be no deduction for consumer interest.

Alternatively, if you use the place more than 14 days or 10% of the number of days it will be rented, you preserve the full interest write-off. Although part of the mortgage interest will be deductible to offset rental income and part as a personal itemized deduction, you'll still get to write off 100%. If the mortgage interest and property taxes allocated to the rental use don't offset all the rental income, you'll get to deduct enough of your operating expenses and depreciation to wipe out the remaining income. What you give up is the opportunity of claiming a tax loss.

If you hold personal use under the 14 day/10% test, interest and taxes allocated to rental use are deducted from rental income and, if there is any rental income remaining, other rental expenses and depreciation can offset it.

Any excess expenses—including depreciation—are subject to

the passive-loss rules. Any amount not deductible under the $25,000 exception would be held over until future years, when there is income against which to offset it. Mortgage interest not allocable to the rental use of the property would be subject to the phase-out of the deduction for consumer interest. The property taxes allocable to personal use would still be deductible as a personal expense.

With the phase-in of the passive-loss rules and the phase-out of the deductibility of consumer interest, the after-tax costs of owning a vacation home may change substantially over the next few years. If you are in a situation to choose whether to pass or flunk the personal-use test, you'll have to work out the figures both ways to see which produces the best tax result.

As you work through various scenarios, remember that tax reform also stretched out the depreciation period for rental real estate, from 19 years under the old rules to 27.5 years for properties purchased after January 1, 1987. This will significantly reduce depreciation write-offs.

### Retirement plans?

What if you want to buy a second home now with the idea of renting it out completely for several years and then possibly retiring to it? It would be classified as a business property and you could deduct your expenses—including mortgage interest, property taxes, operating costs and depreciation—up to the amount of your rental income. Any excess expenses would be subject to the passive loss rules.

If you do sell your current home and retire to the rental unit after several years, you would not be able to roll over the profit from your old home. To qualify for the rollover, you must buy and move into the replacement residence within two years of the time you sell the old one. However, if you are age 55 or older when you sell your old home, and have owned and lived in it for at least three of the five years leading up to the sale, you could qualify for the special provision that permits taxpayers to exclude from income up to $125,000 of profit on the sale of a home. (See discussion in Chapter 17.)

## FOR MORE INFORMATION

### Books

*Maximize Your Resort Property Investment,* by Christopher S. Cain (P.O. Box 2669, Columbia, MD 21045; $22.95 including postage and handling).

*Investing in Residential Income Property,* by Douglas M. Temple (Contemporary Books).

*Equity Sharing, Profiting From Joint Home Buying,* by Georgia Anderson and Sandra Lamb (Contemporary Books).

### Periodicals and newsletters

(These are mostly sales listings of vacation properties in upper price ranges; call or write for price and frequency information.)

*Previews Guide to Fine Real Estate* (230 Park Avenue, New York, NY 10169; 212-557-4466); annual catalog of exclusive homes.

*Homes International* (411 Putnam Ave., Greenwich, CT 06830; 800-243-4006). Magazine published six times a year.

*Island Properties Report* (P.O. Box 58, Woodstock, VT 05091; 802-457-3734). Monthly newsletter on the Caribbean; eight islands are covered in depth each year, along with four quarterly reports covering the region generally. Thirty to 40 properties are featured in each letter, along with a list of real estate brokers.

*Hideaways Guide* (P.O. Box 1464, Middleton, MA 01460; 800-843-4433). Directory of vacation homes for rent and for sale worldwide; published twice a year; newsletter is quarterly.

*Timeshare Quarterly* (6555 N. Powerline Rd. Suite 205, Fort Lauderdale, FL 33309; 800-874-6722); quarterly magazine lists about 1,200 timeshares for resale or rent in the U.S., Mexico, Europe and the Caribbean. Free to prospective buyers.

*Resort Development* (The CHB Company, Inc., P.O. Drawer 730, Los Altos, CA 94023; 415-941-4431). Published eight times annually for developers and other professionals involved in resort real estate development and marketing.

*John T. Reed's Real Estate Investor's Monthly* (Reed Publishing; order from PBS, P.O. Box 643, Cambridge, MA 02139). Plain talk and cautionary counsel about real estate investment from an expert in the field.

*Directory of Partial Ownership Properties* (Holiday Condominiums, 7701 Pacific St., Suite 300, Omaha, NE 68114; 800-447-1414); annual directory listing resort properties by state, including existing properties, those under construction and some still in the planning stage.

## Brokers and clearinghouses

Sotheby's International Realty (1334 New York Ave., New York, NY 10021; 212-606-7070.

Chestertons USA (630 5th Avenue, Suite 3170, New York, NY 10111; 212-765-1540).

Atwater Timeshare Resales (1499 Old Bayshore Hwy., Suite 130, Burlingame, CA 94010).

Holiday Condominiums Inc. (7701 Pacific St., Suite 300, Omaha, NE 68114; 800-447-1414).

## Other sources of information

Fractional Interest Council (Gordon McMahon, president, Tahoe Leisure Homes, P.O. Box 8187, Truckee, CA 95737; 916-562-0667).

American Society of Real Estate Counselors (430 N. Michigan Ave., Chicago, IL 60611;312-329-8427).

# 15

# Investing in
# Residential Real Estate

$S$ome people become landlords almost by accident, when
they decide to keep and rent out a former residence rather than
sell it—either because they can't sell it for a fair price or it makes
sense as an investment.

Others are part-time landlords of a vacation property, which
they rent to vacationers and also use personally.

Still other people are enthusiastic, deliberate investors in
residential properties, whether single-family residences, condominium units or small multi-unit apartment houses.

The reason for the popularity of small-scale real estate investing is simple, and it's rooted in the track record of home prices
since World War II. A well-chosen residence in an economically
stable area has long been a pretty good investment, by at least
holding its value and often appreciating at more than the rate of
inflation.

In picking a good property for investment, you should be
guided by many of the same criteria that affect value in a
residence you would occupy yourself, especially the importance
of a good location and a property that is in keeping with its
surroundings.

Your rental property should be typical, not overly special. It
should appeal broadly to the most renters in a given price range.
You want nothing that will disqualify major segments of the
market. For example, it should be near public transportation, so
its enjoyment is not dependent on owning a car; it should not have

too hilly an approach or too many steps inside, which would turn away many elderly renters. Even that swimming pool that you're crazy about might not be appealing to a family with young, non-swimming kids, or people who don't want to tackle the maintenance.

## Equity sharing

For those who want minimal personal involvement in a real estate investment, there is equity sharing, in which the investor puts up part or all of the down payment for a home, while the partners—the occupants of the home—pay most or all of the carrying expenses, including monthly mortgage, taxes, utilities, etc. The investor participates in the appreciation on the home, eventually receiving the original investment and (ideally) a gain when the property is sold.

This is one way that parents and other relatives can help young families buy their first home, but equity-sharing plans also involve investors who don't know the homebuyers but who find them through a firm that arranges equity-sharing deals.

For a fuller discussion of equity-sharing plans, see Chapter 10.

## Rental vacation homes

The tax treatment of second residences used for both rental income and the personal enjoyment of the owner has always been tricky. It's even more so now, under the 1986 Tax Reform Act.

For a full discussion of vacation real estate—selecting, managing, renting out, and tax accounting, see Chapter 14.

## Risks and rewards

This chapter is a guide for the small-scale, beginning investor in residential real estate, but the principles discussed are the same ones that the biggest investors are guided by, too.

Note that we call this "investing." Some purchasers of real estate are really speculators, and the distinction is largely one of risk. The speculator buys low-priced properties in decaying neighborhoods that he believes are poised for a rebound. The speculator buys foreclosed houses at auctions in cities suffering from economic distress, believing that when things get better, he'll make a killing on appreciation. Most investors won't touch situations like this. As in every kind of financial challenge, the rewards are commensurate with risks. The speculator who gambles correctly will make a lot of money, and he's willing to accept the possibility of losing a lot, too.

Before deciding to buy a property, you should consider not only the investment fundamentals, but also how such a choice compares with other possible investments. How does it fit with your long-range financial goals? And do you want to make the time commitment required to manage even a small holding? If you want to invest in real estate without active involvement, have you considered buying shares in a well-managed real estate investment trust, which buys and manages many properties for current income and appreciation, passing the gains on to its stockholders?

Whether residential real estate turns out to be lucrative for you—or just a costly ordeal—depends on when you buy, what you pay, where the property is located, how long you plan to hold it, and how diligently you study this business, among other factors.

## THE RECENT EXPERIENCE

From the mid-'70s through 1981, when governmental policies and rising world commodity prices sent the inflation rate soaring, money fled from financial assets into hard assets like real estate, antiques and gold. Real estate was the star performer. Adjusted for high inflation, interest rates were exceptionally low (and sometimes even "negative" after taxes), so borrowing was easy. A top marginal tax rate of 70%—coupled with the full deductibility of mortgage interest and real estate taxes—enabled many homeowners to pass more than a half of their housing expenses on to Uncle Sam.

Not surprisingly, a lot of homeowners decided to become landlords, investing their money in small down payments on single-family houses and condominiums. Rents tended to lag rising home prices, but it hardly mattered to these investors. High depreciation losses were fully deductible against other income, and appreciation in the home prices made them a winner in the end.

The Reagan tax cut lowered marginal rates, decreasing the value of deductions, but at the same time it sweetened the deal for real estate investors by accelerating depreciation. Then things began to sour. Recession in '81–'82, coupled with declining inflation, cooled off the meteoric rise of home prices in most areas. Regions hard hit by falling energy prices suffered actual declines in both home prices and rents. Then came the Tax Reform Act of 1986, with an avowed goal of trimming the over-generous tax treatment of real estate.

## A NEW BALL GAME FOR TAXES

The new tax law—with its stretched-out depreciation, lower marginal tax rates, limited deductions of passive losses, and higher taxes on capital gains—stacked the deck against the casual investor hoping for easy profits.

January 1, 1987, was a milestone for real estate investors. Suddenly the game had a whole new set of rules. But contrary to popular myth, the new tax law doesn't ruin real estate as an attractive investment vehicle. Positive cash flow and appreciation potential have replaced tax losses and capital gains as the important criteria in the equation.

Most importantly, the real estate market is still controlled by supply and demand, and in some high-growth areas of America—like Washington, D.C., and the Boston area—home prices and rents have been rising at far more than the rate of inflation. Some analysts even believe that tax reform will cool off new construction, help work down the oversupply of residential and commercial real estate in most regions, and set the stage for a stronger landlord's market a few years from now.

But right now, people considering real estate must carefully calculate their real rate of return, to see whether it's higher than they can get in, say, the stock market—and whether it's worth the considerable time and trouble of real estate investing.

## THE ABC'S OF INVESTING

Start your inquiry by familiarizing yourself with some of the analytical tools needed to evaluate the economics of owning and renting a property.

Despite the complications, there are several relatively simple methods you can use to compute real estate gains and losses. Once you have developed your own predictions of inflation and real estate appreciation, the calculations require only straightforward arithmetic applied to the data normally used to prepare an income tax return.

Return on an investment property involves the interaction of four elements: on the positive side, there is rental income and appreciation, and on the debit side (in addition to maintenance expenses) there are the expenses of interest payments and depreciation, which can be used to offset income from the property—and may be used to "shelter" other income as well.

## Loan payments

Each mortgage payment consists of interest and principal amortization. The entire payment reduces the cash flow of earnings from a rental property, but only the interest is deductible for tax purposes. The amortization reduces the mortgage loan principal, thereby increasing your equity—your stake in the property.

During the first year of a loan, monthly payments consist almost entirely of interest. The proportion steadily declines thereafter. As a result, the tax break you get on mortgage interest drops off year by year until it disappears. Most investors sell or refinance their mortgages before that happens. By obtaining a new loan, you can draw money out of the property without selling it.

## Depreciation

Structures owned as a business qualify for an annual deduction for depreciation, which is the theoretical "using up" of an asset, even if the asset is actually increasing in value. Depreciation is a noncash business expense and consequently does not reduce the property's cash flow. It doesn't matter that your rental house or condo is increasing in value; you still claim depreciation on your tax return—in fact the law says you must claim it.

The new law established the fourth new depreciation schedule in five years, and it's stingy. Previous law let owners write off the cost of a building over the course of 19 years, under an accelerated schedule that bunched bigger chunks of income-offsetting depreciation into the earlier years.

Under the new tax code, the write-off span stretches to 27.5 years for residential buildings placed in service after Dec. 31, 1986, and 31.5 years for commercial property. Furthermore, the new law mandates straight-line depreciation: an equal percentage of the cost must be deducted each year.

The effect of that change alone is dramatic. Under a 19-year depreciation schedule, for example, the buyer of an apartment house could deduct as much as 8.8% of the cost the first year. Under the new schedule, the buyer gets only a 3.48% deduction in the initial year.

To figure how much your property is worth for depreciation purposes, start with the purchase price, including such settlement costs as legal fees, title search and title insurance costs, and similar expenses not taken as deductions elsewhere. Loan origination fees and points cannot be deducted in full the first year, but must be amortized over the life of the loan.

Next, subtract the value of the land (land can't be "used up," so it isn't depreciable), allocating to it a reasonable proportion of closing costs. Typically, land accounts for 20% to 25% of the total value of a residential, single-family property. If you own a condominium, the land may be as little as 5% of the unit's total value.

If you are converting your home to a rental property, you'll have to figure what the land was worth when you bought it. Your tax assessment may be helpful in determining the breakdown, but local practices vary and the assessment sheet may overvalue the land portion. Alternatively, you could use a fire insurance agent's generous estimate of the building-replacement costs. The most conservative route, however, is to hire an appraiser to do the job.

Finally, add the cost of any permanent improvements made since you bought the property. This gives you the depreciable value, or tax basis. To calculate your annual depreciation deduction, divide your basis by 27.5.

While depreciation can be pivotal in changing red ink to black, the stretched-out depreciation timetable makes it a less potent force than before.

## Cash flow from rent

With the reduced benefits of tax losses under the new tax code, most investors are trying to get a positive cash flow from their properties.

The rent you can charge is a function of supply and demand in your area in general, and rents on comparable properties in particular. One rule of thumb for estimating potential receipts holds that the annual rent should amount to about 9% of the market value of the property. That translates into $7,200 a year on an $80,000 home, or $600 a month.

Look for a property that, when rented, will produce a positive annual cash flow, however slight. That means the rental income will have to come close to covering mortgage payments, maintenance, taxes and insurance.

John T. Reed, editor of *John T. Reed's Real Estate Investor's Monthly* (PBS, P.O. Box 643, Cambridge, MA 02139) recommends buying investment homes at the low end of the price spectrum. "The guys who have the positive cash flow buy at gross rent multipliers (GRM) of 90 to 110 times monthly rent. For example, a house that rents for $750 a month and sells for $80,000 has a gross rent multiplier of $80,000/$750, or 107. In general, the cheaper the house, the lower the gross rent multiplier."

As a buyer of a principal residence for you and your family, you might be willing to pay a premium for a very unusual house in a fancy neighborhood, carrying a high price relative to its square footage and number of bedrooms. But as a cash-flow-conscious investor, you should be wary of that kind of house. While it might appreciate more rapidly than the more modest house (the finest examples of every kind of asset tend to out-gain the average-quality items), it will probably not generate enough rent in the early years, relative to its high price, to generate a positive cash flow.

## Appreciation prospects

Single-family detached homes and condominiums often are overpriced relative to the rent they generate. This is because their market prices are influenced by the value buyers place on them as *homes*—including future appreciation. On the other hand, when the property is rented, tenants typically pay only for current *shelter* value, which is a function of space, number of bedrooms, etc.

Because the rent collected often does not cover the cost of holding the property, investors experience a negative cash flow—an operating loss. Not only must they dig into their pockets every month, but they must rely on a substantial increase in property value to offset that loss and to provide a good return on investment. And that means having a pool of prospective buyers seeking to purchase a home at the appropriate time (and willing to pay a price higher than would be justified by rents alone), as well as timing the sale to occur when mortgages are readily available and reasonably affordable.

Homes probably will remain a good long-term hedge against inflation, as they have been for decades. Nevertheless, counting on appreciation to turn a negative return into a positive one will be, on the whole, riskier than it was during the 1970s, when prices were going up by leaps and bounds almost everywhere.

## FIGURING RATES OF RETURN

There are various standard methods of figuring rate of return on investments in small residential properties.

In all the methods described below, we'll examine two different properties, one costing $120,000 and the other $80,000. Each is bought with a 30-year, fixed-rate mortgage at 9.5% covering 80% of purchase price.

We'll presume that each property was sold after five years of ownership, and we'll assume each appreciated at a compounded rate of about 4% a year. However, we'll assume that rents, property taxes and maintenance costs did not increase during the five years; they probably will, but they could be considered self-canceling factors, and leaving them constant simplifies the equation considerably.

We'll see, by the end of our calculations and the sale of the properties, that the less expensive property—bought for $80,000 and sold for about $97,000—generated an average annual return of about 10% over five years of ownership—a healthy return but nothing spectacular; many stock market investors get at least that return with much less work than is involved in real estate investing.

The more expensive property—costing $120,000 and later sold for $145,000—showed an annualized return of about 5.5%—not much better than money-market funds have been paying in recent years.

A note of caution: there are many variables that will affect your rate of return. For example, you'll do much better if your properties are in high-growth regions where home prices (and possibly rents) might appreciate at 7% or 10% a year. Our examples presume agent-assisted sales with a 6% commission; a sale by owner with no commission would improve the return.

On the other hand, our scenarios assume full rental of the homes for 12 months a year, with no rent lost to the transition between tenants; that's not always the case. Likewise, we assumed full owner management of the properties and rather modest maintenance costs. The bottom line would be worse if you hired a professional property manager or if maintenance costs were particularly high.

Our examples also assume a 20% down payment on each property—the standard amount that most mortgage lenders require. A smaller down payment—say, 10% or even 5%—and a larger mortgage would probably increase monthly out-of-pocket loss, but it might also improve your eventual return on a modest cash investment.

Several best-selling books have been written on techniques for buying investment properties with little or no money down. To be successful, these methods—which worked for many small investors in the high-inflation late '70s—tend to require very intensive investor involvement, seller financing of distressed properties, and—most importantly—a gamble on a high rate of appreciation to offset large operating losses. Some people have done very well with this approach, but it's definitely not for everyone, especially under the new tax laws and in a climate of lower inflation.

## CASH FLOW BEFORE TAX

This tells you how much spendable cash the property yields for the year. Essentially, you match the anticipated gross income against overall cash outlay. Expenses typically include such things as taxes, insurance, maintenance and management fees.

The mortgage payment figure used for both properties in the illustration represents the first year's payments on a $96,000, 9.5%, 30-year mortgage for property A, and a $64,000 loan with the same terms for property B. It is assumed in both cases that the tenant pays the utility bills, so they are not included as operating expenses.

Because you are measuring cash income and expenditures, include as an expense the part of the mortgage payment that reduces the loan principal, even though that item is not tax-deductible, and exclude depreciation, which is deductible but requires no cash outlay.

Cash Flow Before Tax

|  | Property A | Property B |
|---|---|---|
| Purchase price: | $120,000 | $80,000 |
| Plus settlement costs | 3,600 | 2,400 |
| Cost | 123,600 | 82,400 |
| Minus mortgage balance | 96,000 | 64,000 |
| Cash invested: |  |  |
| Downpayment + settlement costs | 27,600 | 18,400 |

*Gross income: Property A*

| Rent of $850 x 12 months: | | 10,200 |
|---|---|---|

Minus expenses:
Mortgage payment (interest + principal
 on $96,000 at 9.5% for 30 years)

| 807.22 x 12 = | 9,686.64 | |
|---|---|---|
| Taxes: | 1,000.00 | |
| Insurance: | 600.00 | |
| Maintenance: | 500.00 | |
| TOTAL | 11,786.64 | (11,786.64) |

*Cash flow before tax* (negative): ($ 1,586.64)

*Gross income: Property B*
Rent of $700 x 12:                                                8,400
Minus expenses:
  Mortgage payment (interest + principal
    on $64,000 at 9.5% for 30 years)
  538.15 x 12 =    $6,457.80
  Taxes:              800.00
  Insurance:          500.00
  Maintenance:        500.00
  TOTAL            $8,257.80                        (8,257.80)
*Cash flow before tax:*                             $  142.20

Return on cash flow, before tax:

*Property A:*
$$\frac{\text{Cash flow before tax}}{\text{Cash invested}} = \frac{(1,586.64)}{27,600} = (.057) \times 100 = -5.7\%$$

*Property B:*
$$\frac{\text{Cash flow before tax}}{\text{Cash invested}} = \frac{142}{18,400} = .0077 \times 100 = .77\%$$

## CASH FLOW AFTER TAX

Here, you measure current return after taking depreciation and taxes into account. Because loan payments that reduce principal are not tax deductible, adding the principal payment on the mortgage back into the cash flow before tax is a mechanical device for removing that item. It was subtracted from gross income to arrive at cash flow before tax, and adding it back merely cancels out the subtraction.

In the example, annual depreciation is computed by taking the depreciable tax basis and dividing it by 27.5. That figure is then divided by 12 to arrive at a monthly figure, and then multiplied by the number of months and half-months you held the property during the tax year. Regardless of the day of the month you buy, the law considers the property to be "placed in service" at mid-month. It makes no difference whether you become owner of a rental home on January 1, or January 31—you claim depreciation for 11.5 months of that year.

For the tax calculation, a 1987 marginal 35% income tax rate was assumed. If your analysis indicates that investing in a property will increase your income for federal income tax purposes, estimate the tax liability and subtract it from the cash flow before tax. It is likely, however, that you will come out with a negative figure.

In the past, real estate purchases often were arranged to produce just such a loss, which was then used to offset income the investor earned from other sources. An investor in the 50% marginal bracket paid $50 less in tax for every $100 removed from taxable income.

But beginning in 1987, the law breaks all taxpayer income or loss into active, passive and portfolio categories, and then severely limits the taxpayer's ability to offset gains or losses in one category against gains or losses in another. Your salary or the income you earn while actively involved in a business or trade on a regular and continuing basis is classified as active income. Money received from investing in a trade or business usually is passive income. Dividends on stock, interest from bank certificates of deposit, bonds and annuities are examples of portfolio income.

Rental activity (other than very short-term activity such as would occur in operating a hotel, motel or country inn) is "passive," and most individual taxpayers no longer will be able to use "passive losses" to offset taxable income from such things as wages and investment income.

The exception: individuals with less than $100,000 of adjusted gross income may use up to $25,000 in losses from their real estate activities to offset active and portfolio income, *providing* the investor "actively participates" in the business. (More on what constitutes "active participation" later.)

The adjusted gross income amount is figured before adjusting for passive losses, IRA contributions and any taxable social security benefits. The $25,000 allowance is reduced by 50 cents for every dollar of adjusted gross income over $100,000, and is completely eliminated at $150,000. Married couples filing separate returns are subject to special rules.

There are phase-in rules for passive activities begun or purchased under contract before the law was enacted. For 1987, 65%

of losses outside the $25,000 exception still can be deducted from other income; 40% in 1988; 20% in 1989; and 10% in 1990.

Cash Flow After Tax

*Property A*

| | |
|---|---:|
| Cash flow before tax: | (1,586.64) |
| Add back principal payment: | 591.98 |
| | NET: ( 994.66) |
| Minus depreciation: | |
| ($121,000- 30,250 = 92,750; 90,750/27.5 = 3,300; 3,300/12 = 275; 275 x 11.5 = 3,162.50) = | (3,162.50) |
| Taxable income (loss) | (4,157.16) |

*Property B*

| | |
|---|---:|
| Cash flow before tax: | 142.00 |
| Add back principal payment: | 394.69 |
| | 536.69 |
| Minus depreciation: | |
| ($81,000−20,250 = 60,750; 60,750/27.5 = 2,209.09; 2,209.09/12 = 184.09; 184.09 x 11.5 = 2,117.04) | (2,117.04) |
| Taxable income (loss) | (1,580.35) |

*Tax liability or saving*

taxable income x tax rate = tax liability
or
tax loss x tax rate = tax saving

*Property A*

| | |
|---|---:|
| Cash flow before tax: | (1,586.64) |
| Plus tax saving (4,157.16 x 35%): | 1,455.00 |
| *Cash flow after tax:* | ( 131.64) |

*Property B*

| | |
|---|---:|
| Cash flow before tax: | 142.00 |
| Plus tax saving (1,580.35 x 35%): | 553.12 |
| *Cash flow after tax:* | 695.35 |

## TOTAL RETURN AFTER SALE

In this calculation, you compute the overall return, after tax, from selling the property. In the example, the sale takes place after five years. Accumulated passive losses (those carried forward in any given year because they could not be used to offset passive income in that same year) are used in full to offset gain when the property is sold.

The 1986 Tax Reform Act eliminated the special tax treatment of capital gains, which are profits from the sale of such assets as stocks and real estate owned more than six months. Prior law excluded 60% of those profits from taxation. Since only 40% was taxed, the top effective rate on profits ranged from 4.4% to 20%. In 1987, 100% of capital gains are taxed at rates from 11% to 28%. In 1988, 15% to 33% rates kick in.

In the example, it was assumed for simplicity that gross income and costs—except for the interest deduction and annual income tax—did not change during the five-year period. The selling price, though, rose about 4% a year compounded—enough to produce a profit. In practice, your costs and income will change to some extent each year.

*Property A:*

| | |
|---|---:|
| Sales price: | $145,000 |
| Minus sales expenses: | − 8,700 |
| *Gross sales proceeds:* | 136,300 |
| | |
| Gross sales proceeds | 136,300 |
| Minus mortgage balance: | − 92,391 |
| *Net sales proceeds:* | $ 43,909 |
| | |
| Cost: | $123,600 |
| Minus total depreciation: | − 15,813 |
| *Adjusted cost:* | 107,787 |
| | |
| Gross sales proceeds: | 136,300 |
| Minus adjusted cost: | − 107,787 |
| *Taxable gain:* | 28,513 |

*Taxable gain × marginal tax rate = tax*

$28,513 x .28 =                 $ 7,984
(Although 1987 rates can exceed 28%, special rules prevent capital gains from being taxed above 28%)

| Net sales proceeds: | 43,909 |
|---|---|
| Minus tax: | − 7,984 |
| *Net sales proceeds after tax:* | $35,925 |

| Net sales proceeds after tax: | 35,925 |
|---|---|
| Plus annual cash flows after tax: | ( 658) |
| | 35,267 |
| Minus cash invested: | − 27,600 |
| Total return: | 7,667 |

*Total % return:*

$$\frac{\text{Total return}}{\text{Cash invested}} \times 100 = \% \text{ return}$$

$$\frac{7,667}{27,600} \times 100 = 27.78\%$$

*Annual average return:*

$$\frac{\text{Total \% return}}{\text{Years property held}} = \text{Annual average return, or}$$

$$\frac{27.78}{5} = 5.56\%$$

*Property B*

| Sale price: | $97,000 |
|---|---|
| Minus sales expenses: | − 5,820 |
| *Gross sales proceeds:* | 91,180 |

| Gross sales proceeds: | 91,180 |
|---|---|
| Minus mortgage balance: | − 61,594 |
| *Net sales proceeds:* | 29,586 |

| Cost: | 82,400 |
|---|---|
| Minus depreciation for all years: | − 10,585 |
| *Adjusted cost:* | 71,815 |

| Gross sales proceeds: | 91,180 |
|---|---|
| Minus adjusted cost: | − 71,815 |
| *Taxable gain:* | 19,365 |

*Taxable gain × marginal tax rate = tax*

19,365 × .28 = 5,422.20

| | |
|---|---:|
| Net sales proceeds: | 29,586 |
| Minus tax: | − 5,422 |
| *Net sales proceeds after tax:* | 24,164 |

| | |
|---|---:|
| Net sales proceeds after tax: | 24,164 |
| Plus annual cash flows after tax: | + 3,477 |
| | 27,641 |

| | |
|---|---:|
| Minus cash invested: | − 18,400 |
| *Total return:* | 9,241 |

*Total % return:*

$$\frac{\text{Total return}}{\text{Cash invested}} \times 100 = \% \text{ return}$$

$$\frac{9,241}{18,400} \times 100 = 50.22\%$$

*Annual average return:*

$$\frac{\text{Total \% return}}{\text{Number of years property held}} = \text{Annual average return}$$

$$\frac{50.22\%}{5} = 10.04\%$$

## OVERALL RETURN ON TOTAL CAPITAL

This measures operating income as a percentage of a property's worth and is calculated by dividing net operating income by current market value. Calculate net operating income by subtracting annual operating expenses, such as taxes, insurance and maintenance, from the total income from the property, which, in this example, comes entirely from rents. Do not include annual mortgage payments in operating expenses.

$$\frac{\text{Net operating income}}{\text{Market value}} = \text{Overall return on capital}$$

*Property A:* $\quad 10,200 - 2,100 = \dfrac{8,100}{120,000} = .0675 \times 100 = 6.75\%$

*Property B:* $\quad 8,400 - 1.800 = \dfrac{6,600}{80,000} = .0825 \times 100 = 8.25\%$

Overall return on capital, however, doesn't give you any perspective on whether the money you will keep tied up in the property each year (the down payment, settlement costs, repayment of principal and appreciation) could be earning a higher return elsewhere. Looking at return on equity will give you a better measure for making those kinds of comparisions.

## THE RIGHT STUFF: RETURN ON EQUITY

Most investors, especially less sophisticated ones, tend to judge how well they are doing by their return on investment. By "investment" they typically mean the down payment they made when they bought the property in the first place. When you calculate it that way, return on investment usually goes up every year. As a result, the investor thinks he or she is flourishing, when in fact, actual investment performance probably is deteriorating a little bit every year that the property is held. Why? Because the value of the property may be increasing faster than the income.

The down payment you made on the property when you bought it is irrelevant after the purchase. What matters is your equity in the property—the difference between what the property is worth and the balance owed on the mortgage. The equity represents your stake in the property, because it is money you could realize—and use for some other investment—by selling the property. Return on equity provides a more valid measure of investment performance than return on original investment.

$$\frac{\text{Cash flow before taxes}}{\text{Current equity}} = \text{Return on equity before taxes}$$

The table below shows how the two return figures differ. Say you buy a rental property for $100,000. After covering the mortgage payments and operating expenses, you have $1,000 left over at the end of the year—the before-tax cash flow. Your down payment was $20,000. Assume that the before-tax cash flow and the value of the property both increase 10% per year, and that you pay off $400 on the mortgage each year. The table demonstrates what your return on the $100,000 investment would look like, before taking selling costs into account.

Return on investment

| Before-tax cash flow: | $1,000 | 1,100 | 1,210 | 1,331 | 1,464 |
|---|---|---|---|---|---|
| Investment: | 20,000 | 20,000 | 20,000 | 20,000 | 20,000 |
| Return on investment: | 5% | 5.5% | 6.05% | 6.7% | 7.3% |

Return on equity
Assuming 10% price and income growth each year

| Before-tax cash flow: | $1,000 | 1,100 | 1,210 | 1,331 | 1,464 |
|---|---|---|---|---|---|
| Property value: | 100,000 | 110,000 | 121,000 | 133,000 | 146,400 |
| Loan balance: | 80,000 | 79,600 | 79,200 | 78,800 | 78,400 |
| Equity: | 20,000 | 30,400 | 41,800 | 54,200 | 68,000 |
| Return on equity: | 5% | 3.6% | 2.9% | 2.5% | 2.2% |

Notice that the return on investment increases each year. But look at return on equity. As you can see, it goes down, not up. In a rising real estate market, where equity in the property increases as fast or faster than the income, returns will fall.

Even if property values increase only modestly and the demand for rental homes permits rents to rise substantially, returns on equity still fall, but more gradually. In the example below, cash flow is increasing at the same 10% each year, but the market value of the property is going up by only 4% a year.

Return on equity
Assuming income up 10% a year, value up 4%

| Before-tax cash flow: | $ 1,000 | 1,100 | 1,210 | 1,331 | 1,464 |
|---|---|---|---|---|---|
| Property value: | 100,000 | 104,000 | 108,160 | 112,486 | 116,986 |
| Loan balance: | 80,000 | 79,600 | 79,200 | 78,800 | 78,400 |
| Equity: | 20,000 | 24,400 | 28,960 | 33,686 | 38,586 |
| Return on equity: | 5% | 4.5% | 4.18% | 3.95% | 3.79% |

## THE BENEFITS OF IMPROVING A RENTAL PROPERTY

One way to improve the return on equity is to renovate or otherwise improve the property, boosting both the rental income it can generate and the market value for resale.

Keep in mind, however, that the same warning applies to improving a rental property as a principal residence: don't over-improve it relative to comparable homes in the same neighborhood, or you'll get neither higher rent nor appreciation sufficient to offset your additional investment.

Landlords, even more than homeowners, must investigate what kinds of improvements and additions yield the best return on investment and stick to those guidelines. For a landlord, for example, adding two bedrooms or finishing the basement into another rental unit will immediately enhance rental income, while building a garage might not.

Return on equity
Refinancing for improvements and to hike rent

| | | | | | |
|---|---|---|---|---|---|
| Before-tax cash flow | $700 | 700 | 2,000 | 2,200 | 2,420 |
| Property value | 100,000 | 104,000 | 150,000 | 156,000 | 162,000 |
| Loan balance | 80,000 | 79,600 | 120,000 | 119,600 | 119,200 |
| Equity | 20,000 | 24,400 | 30,000 | 36,400 | 42,800 |
| Return on equity | 3.5% | 2.86% | 6.66% | 6.04% | 5.67% |

## PULL OUT EQUITY, PUT IT TO BETTER USE

One sure way to deal with the decline in the return on equity is to pull some of it out of the property, with a full or partial refinancing. The proceeds of the loan can be used for other investments—either additional down payments on more real estate or financial investments likes stocks and bonds. This is how many small-scale real estate investors used inflation and leverage (borrowed money) to snowball their wealth in the 1970s. It's harder to do in a low-inflation environment, but the techniques are the same.

Most investors realize that their return can be magnified by borrowing a large portion of the purchase price when they invest in real estate. But the same investors who are eager to use leverage when they buy a property often forget about it after the purchase.

Most investors hate to make a down payment of more than 20% or 25%. But those same investors too often let their equity grow well beyond that level. (In the first return-on-equity example above, the investor's equity rose from 20% to 46% of the property's value, and the return plummeted.)

The reasons for using leverage when you buy a property apply equally to the period when you hold the property. Some investors make it a practice to set and maintain an equity target—say 20% or 25% of the property's value. Theoretically, you could achieve this by refinancing periodically with a second mortgage or a new first mortgage.

The decline in return on equity and the difficulties and expense that may be encountered in refinancing create, in effect, a penalty for retaining property for long periods. However, the loss of special capital gains tax treatment and the effect of lowered marginal tax rates from tax reform may counter the pressure to sell—at least for properties producing income on a before-tax basis.

Returning to Properties A and B above, let's calculate the return on equity at the end of the first year, using before-tax and after-tax cash flows. We'll assume that each property appreciated 3% over its total cost of $123,600 and $82,400, respectively.

Return on equity before tax:

|  | Property A | Property B |
|---|---|---|
| Before-tax cash flow | (1,587) | 142 |
| Property value | 127,308 | 84,872 |
| Loan balance | 95,408 | 63,605 |
| Equity | 31,900 | 21,267 |
| Return on equity | (4.97%) | .67% |

## EQUITY DIVIDEND AFTER TAX

This recognizes the tax savings resulting from the mortgage interest and depreciation deductions of real estate investments.

Remember, though, that these figures are projections, not results. Use them to assist you in making investment decisions, and then at least once each year, to see where you stand.

*Return on equity after tax:*

|  | Property A | Property B |
|---|---|---|
| After tax cash flow | (132) | 695 |
| Equity | 31,900 | 21,267 |
| Return on equity after tax | (.41%) | 3.27% |

## BEYOND BASICS: INTERNAL RATE OF RETURN (IRR)

Most small-scale investors in single-family houses will find the calculations above to be adequate, but if you want to figure an even truer rate of return, use one of two calculations relied upon by the most savvy investors in multi-family housing and commercial properties: the internal rate of return (IRR) or the adjusted rate of return (ARR). You'll need a financial calculator and computer spreadsheet . . . plus lots of patience. Daniel Bolar, a partner in the accounting firm of Deloitte, Haskins and Sells, suggests that investors use the ARR instead of the IRR. The IRR assumes that cash flows are reinvested at the IRR rate, whereas the ARR allows you to choose a reinvestment rate—typically an after-tax rate. In general, he notes, the ARR will be lower than the IRR on any given property.

Using an IRR or ARR allows you to interject the time value of money into your analysis. It is a sophisticated measure of return that takes into account the fact that the money made on the sale is earned not in equal annual amounts (as an annual return assumes) but in a lump sum at the end of the holding period. The calculation factors in expenses, income, beginning equity, tax savings from interest and depreciation deductions, appreciation, income taxes, and the timing of payments and receipts.

This time-value factor is significant. It's not hard to grasp that the after-tax cash flow you earned three years ago counts more than the same amount earned one year ago. That's because the money, if invested, could earn more interest for you in three years than it could in one. By the same token, the reverse is true of cash you won't receive until next year: the same amount would be worth more to you today because you could put it to work earning interest. Both the IRR and ARR take these differences into account.

IRR/ARR also properly values appreciation. Unlike the measures of profitability used on the preceding pages, it doesn't assume that money made on the sale is earned in equal annual amounts. Instead, the IRR/ARR assigns the after-tax sales proceeds to the after-tax cash flow in the year of the sale, thus crediting earnings when they are actually received.

What the IRR or ARR tells you is the percentage rate of return it would take to make your initial cash investment equal to the present value of all the benefits associated with the property, accounting for the time value of all costs incurred and income received along the way. A respectable IRR on major residential and commercial properties is thought to be at least 15% or 18%.

If you're boggled by the complexity of the IRR or ARR, an accountant probably can run the numbers for you. Members of the American Society of Real Estate Counselors, an affiliate of the National Association of Realtors, will advise investors on all aspects of a deal, including IRR. You can get a free directory of members by writing the society at 430 N. Michigan Ave., Chicago, IL 60611.

## PROPERTY MANAGEMENT: MORE IMPORTANT NOW

In its crackdown on shelters of all kinds, Congress severely limited the ability of investors in "passive activities"—the definition includes real estate rentals and limited partnerships—to deduct losses from those investments.

Under the old law, you could deduct the mortgage interest, depreciation, property taxes and other expenses of rental property, whatever their total. Under current law, deductions are limited to the amount of rental income you receive. Any excess deductions are considered a passive loss and—with some exceptions—can be used only to offset income from a similar activity, such as another rental house.

The exceptions are designed to protect small real estate investors. If you "actively manage" the property, and your adjusted gross income is under $100,000, you may deduct as much as $25,000 of rental losses against other income, including your salary. The loss allowance is phased out between $100,000 and $150,000 of income.

Although the full $25,000 allowance starts in 1987, the disallowance rules are being phased in for passive activities begun, or purchased under contract, before the law was enacted. For 1987, 65% of losses outside the $25,000 exception still can be deducted from other income; 40% in 1988; 20% in 1989; and 10% in 1990.

### Stay active

If your property generates a loss, and your income is less than $150,000, be sure you qualify as an "active" manager to protect the loss allowance.

You don't have to cut the grass and unplug drains to qualify. You'll probably pass the tests, even if you pay a management firm to handle day-to-day matters, as long as you're involved in approving tenants, setting rents and okaying repairs and capital improvements.

Managing a rental home, duplex or triplex takes a lot of time, and novice investors nearly always underestimate how much—at least initially. Too often, they also discover that collecting rents and getting repairs done at reasonable costs can be a big headache. This scenario is played out often enough that professional managers consider such "self-managers" a good source of business.

What can you do to avoid taking on a commitment you will end up despising? Carol Stone King, vice president of King Associates in Denver and co-author of *The Successful On-Site Manager* (Institute of Real Estate Management), believes that an investor/owner shouldn't try to manage a property located more than 20 minutes away.

Even if time will not be a pressing factor, ask yourself whether you have the skills, toughness and perseverance to handle the job in a business-like manner. Can you do a thorough job of screening prospective tenants? Can you handle phone calls? Respond calmly to emergencies? What kind of liability insurance will you need? Where will you get good contracts?

In addition to answering these questions, you will need to be prepared to tackle the following:

**Setting an attractive rent,** one that is not too high or too low.

**Advertising:** A well-placed sign and classified newspaper advertising are effective ways to advertise your property.

**Showing prospects:** You can't rent a home without showing it to prospective tenants. Be prepared not only to take them through, but also to have the property cleaned, painted and in good repair. As you take tenants through, you may need to help them visualize what it will look like once they have moved in.

**Screening:** Rejecting a potentially troublesome tenant can save you endless grief. Finding a tenant who will use the property as if he owned it is your goal. Use an application form that gives you all the information you need to check out the prospect thoroughly. Be sure to obtain written permission to check an applicant's credit history with the local credit bureau. Then follow through: Check all references, talk with former landlords, obtain new credit reports, and verify income and job history with employers.

**Lease negotiations and renewals.**

**Collecting security deposits:** You will need to know what the law requires of landlords in your state and community.

**Move-out and move-in inspections:** A major source of conflict between owners and tenants centers around property condition and what constitutes ordinary wear and tear.

**Maintenance and repairs:** You will have to do them yourself or hire someone else to do them. Finding reliable, honest repair people willing to do small jobs on short notice is not easy.

**Problem tenants:** Remain a landlord for long, and, at some point, you will encounter a tenant who does not pay the rent. If you become too friendly with your tenants or sympathetic to their personal problems, you will have a harder time collecting rent and periodically raising the rent.

**Record-keeping:** You may have an accountant, but you nevertheless will need to keep good records and detailed accounts.

Many individual investors successfully manage their own properties. Many also get themselves leg-tied in legal squabbles or hobbled with horrible tenants.

Professional property manager Ralph Tutor urges investor/ owners to consult with their insurance agents about liability protection. In many situations, owners can purchase substantial protection with a rider on their homeowner's policy. This coverage should be reviewed annually and increased in tandem with net worth.

Another problem area, Tutor notes, is failing to screen tenants adequately. Landlords may ask for all the pertinent information on an application form. They frequently get the necessary written permission needed to verify creditworthiness and employment. But then they don't check, relying instead on intuition. One solution is to hire a firm that will find you a qualified tenant. Such outfits, often called "lease only" companies, take on the job of advertising and screening tenants for a fee, commonly 50% of the first month's rent.

Tutor also suggests that landlords develop an inventory and condition report, which should be filled out in detail when the first tenant moves in. This report establishes a baseline against which future property inspection reports can be compared. Give a copy of this report to the first tenant when he moves in. Allow 48 hours for changes or additions. Then repeat this inspection process when the tenant moves out, using the report records as a basis for determining whether all or part of the security deposit will be returned. Repeat with each move-in and move-out.

## For more information

In addition to sources cited elsewhere in this chapter, see the following materials for information on investing and managing residential real estate:

▶ *Investing in Residential Income Property*, by Douglas M. Temple (Contemporary Books, Chicago).

▶ Articles on single-family property management published by the Institute of Real Estate Management, in its *Journal of Property Management*. You can get single copies free by writing to the institute at 430 N. Michigan Avenue, Chicago, IL 60611. Also inquire about their new book on managing single-family rental properties, by management professional Barbara Holland.

▶ *How to Make Big Money Managing Small Properties*, by Ralph Tutor (Real Estate Software Company, 10622 Montwood, Suite D, El Paso, TX, 79935). It covers all the important aspects of property management, including leases, credit investigation, tenant/manager relationships, property maintenance, rent collection, cost control and choosing a computer system. It also has an excellent selection of model contracts and forms that can be reproduced or adapted for use by individual owner/managers.

▶ *Equity Sharing, Profiting From Joint Home Buying*, by

Georgia Anderson and Sandra Lamb (Contemporary Books, Chicago).

▶ *Real Estate Investing: The Tax Reform Act of 1986;* available from Century 21 offices.

## USING A PROFESSIONAL MANAGER

Good professional management can be a boon to an investor. For example, if you will be living overseas, or if you own rental property in a distant resort area, trying to do without hands-on local management is just plain risky. Even investors with local properties decide they don't want the hassle of dealing with tenants. So weigh your options and be realistic about your capabilities. If you decide to go with professional management, select carefully.

You will pay anywhere from 8% to 14% of your monthly rental income for the services of a property manager. On top of that, each time the property is leased or the lease is renewed, there will be a leasing fee of 20% to 50% of the first month's rent. On a home that brings in $900 a month in rent, that amounts to $1,350 each year, assuming a 10% monthly management fee and a 25% leasing fee. And, if you want the manager to handle mortgage or insurance payments, you also could pay a one-time set-up fee.

What should you expect in return? For starters, a property manager should be more than a rent collector. A good one will see that your property is rented and cared for in a way that maximizes income and enhances value. That means selecting good tenants and keeping turnover low. It means maintaining the property and charging the right amount of rent.

### Questions to ask

Before you hire a property manager, get answers to the following questions:

1) What kind of experience does he or she have? Look for a manager with at least five years of full-time property management experience. Look for experience with properties similar to yours. Ask about educational background and professional affiliations. The Institute of Real Estate Management, for example, desig-

nates qualified individuals as Certified Property Managers (CPMs) and Accredited Resident Managers (ARMs).

2) What kind of properties does he manage? To whom do they belong? Can you look at them? Can you speak with the owners?

3) How many properties does she manage? What kind and how many support staff does she have? A property manager may be able to handle a large residential apartment building with very little help. That is not the case when managing dozens of single-family dwellings scattered over a metropolitan area. (What's a good ratio of support staff to properties? Ideally, a manager should have one support staffer for every 50 to 75 properties under management.)

4) Are his record-keeping and bookkeeping handled on a computer? You wouldn't automatically reject a manager for not having this in place, but, these days, it is a sign of efficiency and service capability. And better to have the system up and running before you come on board than to be involved in a "transition," with its inevitable glitches and gaps.

5) What kind of reports will you the owner get, and how often? Monthly accounting statements and an annual property condition report are minimal service. Look for routine property reports every six months and then again each time the lease changes. How often will drive-by inspections occur?

6) How will repairs and maintenance be handled? Does the firm have repair people under contract? On retainer? Are they licensed and bonded?

7) How does she handle vacancies? Advertising? Tenant screening and credit checks?

8) What kind of insurance does he carry?

9) How does the fee structure work?

10) Under what circumstances can you be released from your contract? Under what circumstances would she terminate your contract with you? Will the contract be automatically renewed? If so, what action must you take to terminate the agreement?

11) May you have references?

### The management contract

Ultimately, everything should be laid out clearly in a management contract. You are appointing the property manager as your attorney-in-fact and giving him the authority to negotiate leases, collect rents, hold security deposits and, if necessary, evict tenants, on your behalf.

On-the-ball property management firms already have modified the language in their contracts to ensure that investors will be treated as "active" managers for tax purposes. But don't take it for granted. Discuss the matter with prospective managers and double check the contract wording. Remember, too, that should you be audited, the IRS will be look beyond the contract for evidence of correspondence, telephone calls, and the like to verify your involvement.

Many management contracts commit you to using the property manager as broker should you decide to sell your property. That may suit you fine if you are satisfied with your property manager. The manager even may be willing to charge you a lower-than-market commission if it appears that you may be able to sell to your tenant or to another investor with properties under the same management.

But where do you stand if you believe your investment has been badly managed and has been allowed to run down? You don't want that manager handling the sale. You can cancel your contract and manage the property yourself for the next three months, then put it on the market. Suppose, though, that the current tenants are uncooperative or destructive? Then, you'll have to decide which is worse: paying a sales commission to a broker you think did you wrong or taking the risk that the property will be worth considerably less by the time you can sell it. And, if you don't sell it yourself, you'll wind up paying a sales commission anyway.

PART TWO

# FOR SELLERS

# 16

## Do You Really Need to Sell?

There are as many reasons for selling a home as there are for buying. Some people sell because they are being relocated in their jobs, and they believe they must sell their current house to get back equity they'll need to buy a home in their new area. Some people sell because they need more space for a growing family—or less space because the children are grown.

Others sell because they need the capital tied up in their home for living expenses, due to retirement, ill health or a reduction in income. They are thinking about giving up homeownership to become renters.

Whatever the reason you're thinking about selling your home, consider the alternatives first; there is frequently a way that your objectives can be met without selling. But you won't hear about these from a real estate agent. The real estate business is fueled by commissions paid by sellers, so it's a rare agent who will advise you not to sell. Nor *should* they advise you on something that is really a financial-planning decision, in which you'll need the advice of a skilled planner, accountant or lawyer. But once you set the sales process in motion with a real estate broker, you may make a decision you're not ready to make—or one that may not be in your best financial interest.

This chapter examines various alternatives to accomplish various ends. For example, if your present house is too small, consider remodeling or adding on. If you have to move for a job change, examine the strengths of the markets in your current and future areas. If houses are appreciating in value rapidly where you live now, but less so where you're moving, you might want to refinance your current home, rent it out as an investment, and either rent or buy in the new community.

If you want to stay in your current home but you need cash— for college expenses, retirement, medical bills, whatever—consider the various ways of tapping the equity in your home.

## BUY ANOTHER OR BECOME A RENTER?

If you definitely want to sell your current home, the gain in its value can be rolled over into your next house without any tax to be paid, provided the next house is your principal residence, you bought it within 24 months of (before or after) the sale of your last residence, and its cost (price plus improvements made within two years of purchase) is at least as much as your last home.

But if you don't roll the gain over, choosing instead to give up homeownership at last, you'll have to pay tax on the gain, and that's a powerful reason not to leave the ranks of homeowners, especially if you're under 55 years old. For sellers 55 or older, the first $125,000 of your gain may be exempted from tax, if you meet certain conditions, and that eases the tax pain a lot. (See the next chapter for a fuller discussion.)

### Disadvantages of renting

Homeowners who become renters often find the transition a difficult one, after they've been the kings and queens of their own castle. A bigger problem: Rental space that affords the amenities of a well-appointed home can be very expensive and, in some areas, hard to find at any price.

While homeownership is still the best tax shelter there is, renting offers no tax advantages whatsoever. And rents, unlike fixed-rate mortgage payments, can—and usually do—keep going up. A number of real estate experts predicted that rents would rise more rapidly as a result of the Tax Reform Act of 1986. Why? Because a reduction of tax incentives for new construction will slow overbuilding, and owners of existing current buildings will try to make up for lost tax breaks by getting more revenue from tenants.

The rate of rent increases has been highly variable around America, depending on the local economy. In some cities that have faced hard times or gotten very overbuilt, like Houston, Denver and Oklahoma City and parts of Florida, vacancy rates have been high and rents soft. But in cities like Boston, New York, Philadelphia, Detroit, Washington, Los Angeles, San Francisco and Chicago, the rental market has been tight.

## HOW ABOUT EXPANDING YOUR HOUSE?

If what you need most is more space, consider improving your present home. Moving to another home is usually the most expensive solution to the tight-space problem. With sales commission costs of 6%, financing fees on your new mortgage, moving expenses, and decorating costs, picking up and relocating your household is a formidable effort both financially and emotionally.

Think about whether your present home lends itself to remodeling or an addition. Do you like the neighborhood enough to want to stay a long time? Is your lot big enough for an addition, or will the expanded house be too big for the lot? Would your improved house be too big or fancy for the neighborhood, making it difficult to recover the cost of your improvements if you have to move? If there is little possibility you will ever move, you don't need to be so careful about "over-improving" your house; otherwise, keep your total investment in line with current property values in your immediate vicinity.

Adding on to a house you like, without over-improving it relative to its setting, is usually cheaper than buying a larger house, especially if you bought it years ago at a much lower price. Even though you may get a seemingly high price for the sale of your current home, someone else is going to charge you a comparably high price for your *next* home.

### Paying for home improvements

There are many ways to pay for remodeling, ranging from personal loans to home equity loans. Look into the economics of paying for an addition by withdrawing some or all of the equity in your home, through a total refinancing—with a new first mortgage—or a partial refinancing with a fixed-rate second mortgage or variable-rate home equity loan. Partial refinancings tend to cost less. (See discussion below.)

If you need to borrow a relatively small sum, look for a lender offering FHA Title I home improvement loans; maximum loan amount is $17,500. FHA loans of less than $2,500 are treated as unsecured personal loans. For larger amounts, a lien is placed on your home as security for the loan. The loan can be foreclosed if you default. Title I loan terms run from 6 months to 15 years.

Many remodelers will offer to finance a job, just like car dealers. While the convenience may be tempting, you can probably find a lower rate and a longer term elsewhere. There's another reason to be careful. Although the annual percentage rate (APR) must be disclosed before you sign a loan agreement, remodelers sometimes express their rates initially as add-on interest. The APR on such a loan will be nearly twice as much as the add-on rate quoted.

Lenders typically offer second mortgages of up to 15 years for remodeling. The stated interest rates on such loans usually are one to two percentage points above those on conventional first mortgages. Adjustable-rate versions start a little lower. Discount points make comparisons difficult. However, on a 10-year, fixed-rate remodeling loan at 11.5% to 12%, one discount point adds about one quarter of a percent to the rate. You generally can borrow up to 75% or 80% of a home's appraised value; if you can find a lender willing to count the value remodeling will add to the property, you may be able to borrow more.

## TAPPING YOUR HOME EQUITY

If you're thinking about selling your home because you need major funds for some good purpose—sending the kids to college, paying large medical bills for a parent, starting a new business of your own, etc.—explore the various ways to use your home's value without selling it.

Americans have more than three trillion dollars in equity tied up in their homes. Lenders are eager to help them tap it, and this motivation—coupled with changes in the tax law that penalize borrowing not secured by a principal residence—has brought a boom in second mortgages and so-called home equity loans.

## Home equity loans

These are typically variable-rate second mortgages that are attached to your checking account (or even bank credit card) as a line of credit, easy to draw on and easy to repay. Lenders prefer equity loans over unsecured personal loans, because when a homeowner takes out a home equity loan, the equity in the property serves as collateral for a line of credit; and lenders like the low risk to them of an interest rate that rises and falls with the market. Borrowers like home equity loans for their flexibility of use and low, tax-deductible interest costs when the prime lending rate is low. These kinds of loans are very convenient, but remember that irresponsible use could lead to the draining of your home equity—or at worst, the loss of your home.

Here's how a typical equity line works. The lender agrees to extend a line of credit based on what is called the loan-to-value ratio. The formula subtracts the amount owed from the appraised value (one set by a lender-approved appraiser) and then multiplies the remainder by 70%, 80% or even 90%. For example, using an 80% multiplier, if your $100,000 home is paid off in full and nothing eliminates you as an acceptable credit risk, you are eligible for an $80,000 line of credit. If you still had $40,000 left to pay on your mortgage, the most you would qualify for is $48,000.

A credit line may be available for five or ten years. Once it is on the books, you can take out an advance simply by writing a check, up to the maximum. This type of loan does not amortize like a fixed- or adjustable-rate mortgage, so you can tap and repay that same money whenever you want. As you make payments on the outstanding loan balance, you pump up the available credit. There may be a minimum withdrawal amount and there is usually an annual maintenance fee.

Credit lines usually are not fixed-rate loans; interest rates are figured by adding one to three points to a floating rate, commonly the prime rate. The rate can vary as often as monthly. Unlike most adjustable-rate first mortgages, home equity loans generally carry no lifetime or annual caps on interest rate increases;

however, as competition among home equity lenders heated up in early 1987, caps were beginning to appear.

You pay interest on the amount borrowed, not on the amount of credit available. In most cases, you will be required to make at least a minimum monthly payment on the outstanding loan amount, say 2%. Some equity loans may allow interest-only minimum monthly payments for a fixed term. At the end of the agreed-on period, the loan must be paid in full or rescheduled at the then current rate.

Soon after the new tax law passed in 1986, lenders began competing hard for home equity loan business. Temporary low teaser rates were being dangled before homeowners, and many lenders were reducing application and closing charges to "cost." Some were even offering to set up equity lines free of all closing costs.

But more often, appraisals, title searches, credit reports and the like are added to the cost of the loan. In the past lenders have calculated closing costs as a percentage of the credit line, or have charged a flat fee plus actual costs. As a rule, the larger the line of credit, the more you pay. That is so because the amount charged is based on the maximum loan available, not on what you actually borrow. Generally, you pay these costs when you open the credit line, although, in certain cases, you may be able to roll them into the first loan advance.

Tax laws impose limits on the deductibility of interest paid on home equity loans, second mortgages and all other residence-secured loans. Basically, interest is fully deductible on equity loans up to the original price of the home plus improvements. If you go beyond that point—borrowing against the appreciated value of your home—the interest is not deductible unless the loan is used to pay for certain medical and educational expenses or for home improvements.

Here's an example of the practical effect of the limitation. Assume you bought your house a few years back for $100,000 and added a sunroom that cost $10,000. Thanks to appreciation, the place is now worth $180,000. Say your current mortgage amount is $70,000. The new law will permit you to borrow another $40,000 against the home—for whatever purpose—and still deduct the interest. (That $40,000 plus the $70,000 left on the first mortgage equals the $110,000 price-plus-improvement amount.) But if you borrow more, interest on the excess will be classified as consumer interest and will be subject to the phaseout rules on deductibility.

## Second mortgages

Unlike home equity loans, second mortgages—or second trusts—are usually fixed-rate loans. Loan terms are set, commonly for five, 10 or 15 years. Interest rates are usually one or two points higher than on conventional first mortgages; that's because the second-trust holder would get paid off after the first mortgage owner in the event of foreclosure, so there is more risk to the lender.

The application process for a second mortgage is similar to that for a first. You won't get approval until your home is appraised, your credit checked and title insurance written. Turnaround time for approval can be fairly short; you could close within two or three weeks of applying.

You'll also have to pay closing costs, which typically amount to 2% or 3% of the loan. For second mortgages of less than $15,000, lenders are often satisfied with a drive-by appraisal and verification of existing title insurance and an in-file credit report. As with home equity loans, lenders may allow you to finance the closing costs as part of the loan.

Even with a higher interest rate, adding a second trust on top of a first mortgage usually costs far less, over the whole term of your homeownership, than refinancing with a new first.

Say, for example, you're faced with college expenses of nearly $10,000 a year for the next four years, and you realize your budget just isn't going to stretch for monthly payments of over $800. You paid $70,000 when you bought your home and took out an 8%, 30-year loan for $63,000. The loan balance is just over $55,000 today. Your home has appreciated $60,000 over the last decade and is now worth $130,000. You decide to tap $40,000 of the equity.

Compare how you'd fare if you refinanced with a 30-year, fixed-rate, 9.5%, $95,000 loan, compared with taking on a 10-year, 11% fixed-rate second mortgage on top of your old loan:

|  | *New loan* | *Combined first and second loan* |
|---|---|---|
| *Principal*: | $95,000 | $55,000 old first mortgage balance<br>$40,000 new second mortgage |
| *Interest*: | 9.5% | 8% first mortgage<br>11% new second mortgage |
| *Term*: | 30 years | 20 years remaining = 240 payments |
|  | 360 payments | 10 years new mortgage = 120 payments |
| *Monthly payment*: | $798.81 | $    462.27 old<br>$    551.00 new<br>$ 1,013.27 |
| *Total cost*: | $287,571.60 | $166,417.20 old<br>$ 66,120.00 new<br>$232,537.20 |
| *Interest*: | $192,571.60 | $103,417.20 old<br>$ 26,120.00 new<br>$129,537.20 |

So taking on the second mortgage, rather than refinancing, would save you about $63,000 in interest. While your monthly payments would be $214 a month higher, you would pay off the debts against your home ten years earlier.

## FULL REFINANCING

You can refinance your home in order to reduce monthly mortgage payments. You can refinance to free cash tied up as equity.

Refinancing means getting a new first mortgage. It means paying origination, appraisal and credit check fees and points. It also means making monthly interest and principal payments for the entire term of the new loan.

Should you consider refinancing as an option to selling? Yes, if you can get a new fixed-rate loan for at least two percentage points below the rate you are now paying on your current mortgage, and you plan to remain in the home for at least five years. It's harder to figure the break point on an ARM, in which interest rate forecasts come into play.

Getting a good grasp on whether refinancing could work in your favor will take some number crunching and close analysis, as shown by the above comparison of refinancing with a first-and-second-trust combination.

Whether it is worthwhile hinges on how many points you pay and the break-even point—the point at which the savings on a lower-rate mortgage equal what you paid for refinancing. You can calculate this yourself or ask an accountant for comparative calculations. *Home Refinancing*, by Don DeBat (Contemporary Books), provides a thorough discussion of the subject and extensive worksheets to help you make your own decision.

Should you consider refinancing instead of moving? The economic argument for refinancing improves if the alternative is to sell your current home and buy another of comparable value. Say you need another bedroom and bath, but you aren't in a financial position to "move up" to a larger home. You probably could find a house in roughly the same price range as the one you now occupy—one with three bedrooms instead of two, and two baths instead of one—but it's probable you would have to make compromises in other areas of the house or in location. You might be better off refinancing and adding a bedroom and bath to your current home. True, you'd have to pay points and other refinancing costs, but they probably would be less than those you would incur in selling your home and acquiring a new one.

The case for refinancing in order to free up equity is weaker. Instead, consider getting a second mortgage, a home equity loan or a home improvement loan. If you have an older mortgage, most of your monthly payment may be going towards principal repayment; refinancing puts you back on square one, with most of your payment going to pay interest for years to come.

Up until May 1986, points paid for a mortgage to buy or improve a principal residence were deductible in the year paid, so long as a couple of conditions were met. The points had to be paid for with a separate check rather than included in the amount financed, and they had to be for the use of the money, rather than a charge for services connected with making the mortgage.

But in 1986, the IRS said refinancing points—unlike points paid in an original financing of a principal residence—are not deductible all at once in the year you pay them. Instead, this expense is considered prepaid interest to be written off over the life of the loan. But if the lender holding your original mortgage slaps on a prepayment penalty, that fee is considered interest and is fully deductible in the year you pay.

Assume that you pay 2.5 points on a $150,000, 30-year mortgage to refinance your home. With each point equaling 1% of the mortgage amount, your out-of-pocket cost comes to $3,750. Someone in the 28% tax bracket who deducted the full amount would save $1,050 in taxes. But the IRS says that you must deduct refinancing points over the life of the loan: one-thirtieth each year, for an annual deduction of $125—and an annual tax savings of a paltry $35 for someone in the 28% bracket. And you have to prorate it for the year; if you refinanced in July, you could deduct just one-half of the first one-thirtieth of the interest.

That's just the beginning of the complications. If you refinance for more than the balance of your mortgage and use the extra cash for home improvement, you have to split the points for tax purposes. If 15% of the new mortgage goes for improvements, for example, 15% of the points can be deducted in the year of the refinancing, with the other 85% deducted in little chunks over the life of the loan.

It's unlikely that anyone who refinances for lower rates will find it unprofitable because of the limited deduction. However, there's generally a correlation between the interest rate and the number of points charged: Lower rates usually mean higher points, and vice versa. The loss of immediate deductibility will require you to take a second look at the advantage of putting up extra cash in points to capture a lower rate.

Consider refinancing with an assumable mortgage such as VA or FHA. Then, if you end up selling sooner than anticipated, such a loan may make the property attractive to buyers, especially if interest rates have risen in the interim.

This issue bears watching by all homeowners. In the spring of 1987, legislation was pending in Congress to reverse the IRS position and permit the full deduction of points on refinancing in the same way the write-off is allowed for points on original-purchase mortgages. Also, there may be taxpayer court challenges to the IRS position.

## TURN YOUR HOME INTO A RENTAL PROPERTY?

Maybe there are plenty of good reasons why you can't—or don't wish to—continue living in your present home. Maybe you've been transferred to another city; maybe the house is too big for your needs, or too small; maybe you want to retire to an exotic spot far away.

But don't immediately assume that you should sell your home, just because you're moving to another one. You may not have to sell, and it may be financially advantageous to keep your present home and rent it out.

A standard piece of advice to investors in search of rental real estate is to buy a place you wouldn't mind living in yourself. So what could be better than the very home you have lived in? What you'd be doing, in tax parlance, is converting your primary residence into rental property. Refinancing your current home and renting it out could be a good investment; whether the cash flow is positive or negative for the first few years, if the house has had a long record of strong appreciation, you might do very well on its future increases in value.

But before you jump at this option, you'll have to take a hard look at many factors—the economy, taxes, your interest in managing the property, whether hands-on or from afar, etc. The 1986 Tax Reform Act threw a number of wrenches into the mechanisms of real estate investing, generally reducing the financial attractiveness of rental properties. Read carefully Chapter 15, on investing in residential real estate, before proceeding with a plan to rent out your former residence.

Take into account the same things you'd consider if you were going out and buying a property to rent that hadn't served as your residence. Will the location, floor plan and other features of this property appeal to a wide range of prospective tenants as much as they appealed to you when you bought it as your home? Will the rent you collect and the tax deductions that make real estate investments attractive be enough to offset the headaches, time and effort of being a landlord?

In addition to these questions, a decision to convert your own residence to a rental property requires weighing some unique considerations that aren't present when you're buying a rental property right from the start. For starters, you'll be giving up the opportunity to defer taxes on the home when you sell it, because the rollover feature on real estate profits applies only to a primary residence that is replaced with another primary residence. (It is possible, however, to regain that privilege—or some of it—if someday you convert the rental property back into your residence.) In contrast, when rental property is sold, you'll owe tax that year on any profits you make on the sale.

## SPECIAL HELP FOR THE ELDERLY

Many elderly homeowners are in the awkward position of having too little income for comfortable living, but plenty of value in their paid-up homes. In 1985 the National Association of Home Builders estimated that 72% of all couples 65 years and older owned their own homes, and of that group, an estimated 84% had no mortgage debt at all. Total home equity held by America's elderly may be as much as $2 *trillion.*

But many of these elderly people have only modest incomes; they wouldn't benefit from conventional means of tapping home equity, because they couldn't handle the monthly repayment schedule for a new mortgage or home equity loan. These people may want to look into ways to unlock that equity and convert it into monthly income.

### Sale to children and lease-back

One way is by selling their home to their children and investing the proceeds for maximum income—whether in a lifetime monthly annuity or some kind of fixed-yield investments like CDs, tax-free mutual funds or unit trusts, etc. The elderly couple remains in their home by leasing it back from their children. The parents get guaranteed lifetime tenancy and regular income, and the home stays in the family while reducing the size of the estate. The children help their parents stay in the home, receive rental income and possible appreciation on the home, and they get the tax benefits of a rental property. There are sometimes tricky tax and estate-planning angles to this kind of deal, so an attorney's counsel is essential.

## Reverse mortgages

Another equity-tapping method for the elderly is the "reverse mortgage," under which the equity they borrow doesn't have to be repaid, so long as they own their home. The principal and interest repayment will come out of the sale proceeds of the home, when they sell it or when their estate sells after their deaths.

A few years ago there were expectations that these would become very popular, but they haven't really caught on in a big way yet. Only about 1,500 of these transactions have taken place over the past seven years.

Some have been arranged through state and local government agencies, including programs in Rhode Island, Connecticut, Buffalo, NY, and Little Rock, AR. Some of these are so-called life estate arrangements, in which ownership of the home reverts to the non-profit agency upon the death of the homeowner.

Private-sector reverse mortgage loans have been made in Arizona, California, Connecticut, Maryland, Massachusetts, New Jersey, New York, Pennsylvania, Ohio, and Wisconsin.

The most active lender has been American Homestead Mortgage Corp. (305 Fellowship Rd., Mt. Laurel, NJ 08054), whose Individual Reverse Mortgage Account is available to qualified homeowners in Connecticut, New Jersey, Pennsylvania, Maryland and Ohio. It provides regular monthly payments to single or married elderly homeowners as long as they remain in their home. The owner or owners retain title to the home and can receive up to $700 per month, with the actual amount varying according to life expectancy and the amount of home equity. AHMC is repaid from the eventual sale of the house, and the lender receives no more than 94% of the sale price, even if that amount does not fully equal the accumulated mortgage debt.

Here are two sources of information on how the elderly can tap their home equity for daily living expenses:

▶ Home Equity Information Center, American Association of Retired Persons (1909 K St., N.W., Washington, DC, 20049);

▶ National Center for Home Equity Conversion (110 East Main St., Madison, WI 53703).

# 17

# Tax Angles of Selling a Home

$S$o you weighed all the alternatives to selling your home, and you decided it's the right thing for you to do. Take a close look at the tax ramifications of selling.

You don't have to file any forms with the IRS when you buy your home or to report improvements that hike your basis. But when you sell, the government wants to know the details. After all, there might be a tax to be collected, although there is a good chance—if you re-invest the sale proceeds in another home of comparable or greater value (see below)—the transaction won't add a dime to your current tax bill.

When you sell your home, you will realize how clever you've been to keep meticulous records of every improvement to your home over the years of your ownership. To determine the tax consequences of the sale, you have to know the adjusted basis of your home, a value you can compute easily with the information in your files. Every capital improvement to the house (as opposed to repairs, which merely maintain value, rather than increase it) gets added to the original purchase price of your home to arrive at the adjusted basis.

## Compute your gain

Your profit or loss is the difference between the adjusted basis and the amount you realize on the eventual sale. Since nothing involved with taxes is easy, the amount realized is not simply the selling price. That's the beginning point, from which you subtract costs connected with the sale such as real estate commissions, advertising and legal fees. (In some cases, certain selling expenses may be deducted as moving expenses, an advantageous alternative discussed later.)

If your bottom line shows a loss, it is not deductible. In the more likely event that your home sale produces a profit, your gain may be taxable in the year of the sale, in a later year, or perhaps never.

The chance to put off or completely avoid tax on the profit has long been one of the most valuable tax benefits enjoyed by homeowners. These days it's more important than ever, since Congress abolished the capital gains tax break, effective January 1, 1987.

In the past, the law permitted taxpayers to exclude from taxation 60% of capital gains, which are the profits from the sale of any asset—stocks, real estate, whatever—owned more than six months. Because only 40% was taxed, the effective rate on profits ranged from 4.4% to a top of only 20%, compared to a 50% marginal rate on regular income.

But beginning in 1987, 100% of capital gains is taxed at ordinary income rates from 11% to 28%; in 1988, 15% to 33% rates kick in. So it's easy to see that the effective tax bite on capital gains has been hiked substantially by tax reform.

## Deferring the tax bill

Fortunately for homeowners, it's easy to defer the tax bill on your gain almost indefinitely, if you put it into your next principal residence. To qualify, you must buy and occupy another principal residence within a specified replacement period, which encompasses the two years before and the two years after the sale of your house. (If you are in the armed forces or living outside of the United States, you may qualify for a longer replacement period allowing you up to four years after the sale of one home to buy and occupy a replacement.)

Basically, if the new house costs at least as much as the one you sold, you get a reprieve on paying tax on the profit from the sale. The profit is considered to be reinvested, or rolled over, into the new home.

Assume, for example, that you sell a house for $100,000, an amount that includes a $30,000 profit. And, within the replacement period, you buy a new home for $125,000. Rather than pay tax on the $30,000 profit, you reduce the basis of the new home by that amount. Its adjusted basis thus becomes $95,000. If you later sell that home for $150,000 ($25,000 more than you paid), you would actually have a profit of $65,000—the $30,000 gain on the first sale plus the $25,000 profit on the second. Of course, you could put off the tax bill again by buying a replacement home that costs $150,000 or more.

If you choose a replacement home that costs less than the one you sell—after the kids are grown, say, or when you retire—you will owe tax on the built-up profit to the tune that the *adjusted sales price* of the old home exceeds the cost of the new one.

The adjusted sales price is usually the same as the amount realized on the sale, but it can be less if prior to the sale you incurred qualifying fix-up expenses, such as the cost of painting or repairs to make the home more attractive to buyers. These expenses come into play for tax purposes only if your replacement home costs less than the one you sold. In such cases, the expenses—which must be for work done during the 90 days before you signed a contract to sell and paid for within 30 days afterward—are subtracted from the amount realized to arrive at the adjusted sales price. That, in turn, can boost the amount of profit on which tax is deferred.

Consider this example: You sell for $100,000 a home with an adjusted basis of $70,000 and you buy a replacement home for $90,000. Of the $30,000 profit on the sale, $20,000 would be rolled into the new home, giving it a $70,000 basis. The other $10,000 would be taxable in the year of the sale. If you had $1,000 of qualifying fix-up expenses, though, you could defer the tax on an extra $1,000 of the profit on the sale and have to pay tax on just $9,000. The basis of the new home would drop to $69,000.

What if you plan to buy a replacement home but haven't closed the deal by the time your tax return for the year of the sale is due? You still postpone the tax on the gain. Simply fill out the first part of the tax form used to report the sale of a home (Form 2119, "Sale or Exchange of Principal Residence") and note that you intend to buy a new home during the replacement period. If the house you ultimately buy costs enough so you defer the entire gain, all you have to do is notify the IRS of that fact and file a completed Form 2119.

If you don't buy in time to take advantage of the deferral, or if the house you buy costs less than the one you sold, you have to file an amended tax return (Form 1040X) for the year of the home sale. On that form, you would report the profit to be taxed, and you would be charged interest on the tax due from the time the original return was due until you paid the bill.

There is no limit on the number of times you can use the deferral technique to put off tax on the profit that builds up while you own a house. The fact that profits can be rolled over from one home to the next means the basis of your first home can affect the basis of your last—a point that reemphasizes the importance of detailed record keeping.

There is a restriction, however, that generally prevents you from using the rollover provision more than once every two years. Assume, for example, that you sold one house in January 1986 and deferred tax on the gain by buying another home the same month. Then in August 1986 you sell that home and buy another one. The rules prohibit postponing tax on the gain from the sale of the intermediate house. However, because in this example the third home was purchased within two years of the time the first one was sold, the profit from the first house is considered to be reinvested in the third. You would have to pay tax only on the profit that built up during the months you owned the second house. Note, however, that even this restriction is waived if the home sale is connected with a job-related move that qualifies you to deduct moving expenses.

## The $125,000 exclusion

But what happens when you finally decide to cash in on all that profit that has built up tax-deferred? When you retire or for some other reason decide not to buy another house, is the IRS going to swoop down and demand a healthy share of your nest egg? Not if you qualify for the icing on the cake for older homeowners: the right to escape tax completely on up to $125,000 of profit.

You can qualify if you are at least 55 years old when you sell your home and have owned and lived in the house for at least three of the five years leading up to the sale. If you are married and the house is jointly owned, you can qualify as long as either you or your spouse meets the age, ownership and residency tests.

This tax break is a once-in-a-lifetime opportunity and the exclusion can be applied to only one home sale. You can't use part of the exclusion to shelter $50,000 profit on one home, for example, and later use the rest of the exclusion to avoid tax on the sale of another home. If you use any part of the exclusion, you use it all up.

Married couples are limited to a single $125,000 exclusion, and if one spouse used the exclusion before marriage, that scotches the other spouse's right to it as long as they are married. Although available only once, the exclusion can serve to exempt the tax on the profit on several houses, thanks to the deferral of gain from one house to another. When you decide to use the exclusion, the profit built up in any number of homes over the years—up to $125,000 worth—can be sheltered.

You report the sale of your home on Form 2119 and attach it to your tax return for the year of the sale. The form shows how much profit you made on sale, whether any of it was rolled over into a new home, whether any of it was excluded under the 55-and-older tax break and whether any of it is taxable.

If you helped finance the sale, your tax picture gets more complicated. In addition to filing Form 2119, you have to deal with the tax consequences of the payments you receive from the buyer. If you are either deferring the tax on the profit or excluding it, payments you receive on the note may be a combination of return of your basis (nontaxable), a return of your gain (either deferred or excluded) and interest on the loan (taxable as ordinary income).

The exact tax treatment of the payments you receive depends on the specific arrangement. If you are receiving interest-only payments on a note that calls for a balloon payment of the principal at a later date, for example, all that interest is taxable as you receive it.

As you can see, owning a home can be a great tax shelter and selling one can call for some tax planning. Even if you normally handle your own tax return, it would be well worth your while to consult a tax attorney or accountant before filing for a year that involves a home sale. Just as you work hard to get the best possible price for your home, you should invest some effort to get the best possible tax deal.

## House-hunting and moving expenses, too

Buying a new house is often part of a move to take a new job. If your purchase is connected with a job switch, you can rack up additional benefits; some of the cost of selling your old place and buying the new house may be deductible. To qualify to write off moving expenses, your new job must be at least 35 miles farther from your old home than your old job was. If your former job was 10 mile away from your old home, for example, the new job has to be at least 45 miles away from that old home. It doesn't matter how far the new home is away from your new job. (If you are moving to take your first job, the 35 mile test applies to the distance from your old home to your new job location.)

In addition to the distance test, to be eligible to deduct moving expenses you must work full time for at least 39 weeks during the 12 months after the move (or at least 78 weeks out of the first 24 months if you are self-employed). If you qualify, here's what you can deduct.

▶ The cost of trips to the area of the new job to look for a new house. There's no requirement that the house-hunting expedition be successful for the cost to be deductible.

▶ The cost of having your furniture and other household goods shipped, including the cost of packing, insurance and storage for up to 30 days.

▶ The cost of getting yourself and your family to the new hometown, including the cost of food and lodging on the trip.

▶ The cost of food and lodging for up to 30 days in the new hometown if these temporary living expenses are necessary because you have not yet found a new home or it is not ready when you arrive.

▶ Certain costs associated with the sale of your old house and purchase of the new one. These expenses—including real estate commissions, legal fees, state transfer taxes, and appraisal and title fees—are the same costs discussed earlier as potential additions to the basis of the house you buy or reductions in the amount realized on the home you sold. If you qualify to write off moving expenses, you can choose whether to deduct these costs or use them as adjustments to your basis. It's almost always beneficial to count them as deductible expenses.

There is a dollar limit on the amount you can deduct for certain expenses. The cap for house-hunting trips and temporary living expenses is $1,500, and those costs plus buying and selling expenses can't exceed $3,000. There is no limit on how much you can deduct for the cost of shipping household goods or travel expenses. Any reasonable amount you pay can be deducted.

If your employer reimburses you for moving expenses, the amount should show up on your W-2 form for the year. You include the amount with your income and offset it by claiming your moving expense deductions. Until 1987, the write off was an adjustment to income claimed on the front of Form 1040. The Tax Reform Act of 1986, however, converted moving expenses to itemized deductions to be included with other miscellaneous deductions on Schedule A. Although other miscellaneous expenses are deducted only to the extent they exceed 2% of your adjusted gross income, that restriction does not apply to moving expenses. You may deduct your qualifying expenses in full, without regard to the 2% threshold.

# 18

## Polishing the Merchandise

Before you make any decision on how to sell your home—through an agent or by yourself—or even what price to ask for it, put your property in the finest possible condition to impress buyers, agents, appraisers and inspectors.

How your house looks and functions will have a lot of impact on your bargaining power as a seller. Nothing can help a sale more than a thorough spit-and-polish campaign, so now is the time for cleaning, touch-ups and postponed maintenance. Repair the torn screen in the basement window, reset the loose tile in the bathroom, fix leaking faucets, and repaint the scratched front door.

Real estate agents have a phrase for a well-maintained, nicely decorated home: they say it "shows well." Other things being equal, this kind of home will sell faster and for a higher price than a comparable house that isn't as attractive.

Do not, however, undertake a major redecorating or remodeling of your house just to prepare it for selling. Why? Because your tastes may not coincide with the tastes of the buyer, and the work will just have to be redone anyway—at the buyer's expense. Rather than crediting you with work already done, the buyer is going to factor the cost of the redone work into his offering price.

So stay away from such things as fancy new curtains, wallpaper, and wall-to-wall carpeting over otherwise good floors (plank hardwood, parquet, etc.).

As for the decorating that you deem necessary for making your home look good—new paint, replacement of worn linoleum or wall-to-wall over unfinished flooring, etc.—choose neutral colors and simple patterns that are likely to harmonize with the tastes of most prospective buyers; they'll view these improvements as savings to them in both money and time.

## FIRST IMPRESSIONS COUNT

Make your home look as spacious as possible. Get rid of everything extraneous, admit as much daylight as possible, and keep things shipshape. Inventory what you want to sell, give away or throw away when you move. Then do it now, *before* you begin showing your home. Clutter turns buyers off, so empty out crammed closets, pack away extra books and rarely-used china and sort out attic and basement storage spaces to avoid the flea-market look.

Depersonalize your space. Reduce distractions, and help would-be buyers visualize making themselves at home. Tuck away the family pictures covering your bedroom wall. The display of family roots may fascinate some shoppers and embarrass others. A home that appears to be stamped indelibly with your personality and style can be harder to sell.

Neutralize it ideologically. Remove obvious clues to your political, religious and social sentiments. Store away banners, bumper stickers and partisan literature, including magazines.

*Packaging Your Home for Profit*, by Bruce Percelay and Peter Arnold (Little, Brown and Company), provides comprehensive advice on what you can do, both inside and outside your home, to enhance its value and make it easier to sell. It includes tips on using color and smell, and suggests which improvements will yield the highest returns on your money.

## GET THE PLACE IN SHAPE

Walk through your home making a list of everything that needs to be done. During your inspection, jot down the problems and what can be done to make each room attractive. Taking down dark curtains and opening a room to sunlight may change its character completely. So can repainting.

You can't anticipate what will catch the attention of a prospective buyer. Plaster walls and a new furnace may get only passing notice, while the cracked toilet tank top elicits several questions. Or hours may be spent evaluating the heating and plumbing, while fresh paint, refinished floors and brand-new windows are overlooked.

Use this inspection guide to see your home as buyers might:

## INSIDE

### Attic

Check underside of roof for leaks, stains or dampness.
Look around chimney for condensation or signs of water.
Clean and clear ventilation openings if necessary.
Clean out stored junk.

### Walls and ceilings

Check condition of paint and wallpaper.
Repair cracks, holes or damage to plaster or wallboard.

### Windows and doors

Check for smooth operation.
Replace broken or cracked panes.
Repair glazing.
Check condition of weather stripping and caulking.
Examine condition of paint.
Test doorbell, chimes, burglar alarms.
Wash windows and woodwork, if necessary.

### Floors

Inspect for creaking boards, loose or missing tiles, worn areas.
Check baseboards and moldings.
Test staircases for loose handrails, posts, treads.

### Bathrooms

Check tile joints, grouting and caulking.
Remove mildew.
Repair dripping faucets and shower heads.

Check condition of painted or papered walls.
Test operation of toilet.

### Kitchen

Wash all appliances.
Clean ventilator or exhaust fan.
Remove accumulation of grease or dust from tiles, walls, floors.

### Basement

Remove clutter.
Check for signs of dampness, cracked walls or damaged floors.
Inspect structural beams.
Check pipes for leaks.

### Electrical system

Check exposed wiring and outlets for signs of wear or damage.
Repair broken switches and outlets.
Label each circuit or fuse.

### Plumbing system

Look for leaks at faucets and sink traps.
Clear slow-running or clogged drains.
Bleed air off radiators if needed, and check for leaking valves.

### Heating and cooling systems

Change or clean furnace and air-conditioning filters.
Have equipment serviced if needed.
Clear and clean area around heating and cooling equipment.

## OUTSIDE

### Roof and gutters

Repair or replace loose, damaged or blistered shingles.
Clean gutters and downspout strainers.
Check gutters for leaks and proper alignment.
Inspect flashings around roof stacks, vents, skylights and chimneys.
Clear obstructions from vents, louvers and chimneys.

Check fascias and soffits for decay and peeling paint.
Inspect chimney for loose or missing mortar.

### Exterior walls

Renail loose siding and check for warping or decay.
Paint siding if necessary.
Check masonry walls for cracks or other damage.
Replace loose or missing caulking.

### Driveway

Repair concrete or blacktop if necessary.

### Garage

Lubricate garage door hinges and hardware.
Inspect doors and windows for peeling paint.
Check condition of glazing around windows.
Test electrical outlets.

### Foundation

Check walls, steps, retaining walls, walks and patios for cracks,
heaving or crumbling.

### Yard

Mow lawn, reseed or sod if necessary. Trim hedges, prune trees
and shrubs.
Weed and mulch flowerbeds.

# 19

## Sell Through an Agent or Go It Alone?

The vast majority of homes are sold through a listing contract with a real estate agent, with the seller paying the typical 6% commission on the sale price. In 1985, for example, four out of every five homes were sold that way.

But that other one-fifth of sellers apparently asked themselves, "Why pay someone thousands of dollars for doing something I can do myself, with the help of a few professionals I'll compensate on a flat-fee or hourly basis?"

Saving $9,000 on a $150,000 home sale is plenty of motivation for a "fizzbo," or FSBO (For Sale by Owner)—a term real estate agents use somewhat disdainfully. The urge to try selling one's own home is especially strong in a seller's market, when qualified buyers are plentiful, listings are relatively few, and everything that's fairly priced gets snapped up fast.

Agents can reel off a dozen or more arguments against trying to sell your own home, among them that you could set the wrong price, accept an unqualified buyer, and lose out on the cooperation of agents, who won't bring their clients by to see your home. Sure, all of those things can happen—but some of them might happen even if you list your home with an agent.

### AN AGENT'S STRENGTHS

The fact that most people do use an agent to sell their homes suggests that a lot of homeowners believe they get good value for the 6% commission. Selling a house by oneself is hard work, and it requires time, savvy, and a knack for selling. For a no-holds-barred look at what homeowners are up against when they go to sell their homes, read *Selling Your Home Sweet Home,* by Sloan Bashinsky (Simon and Schuster, 1985).

The benefits of good sales agents are many. They are experienced at the proper pricing of a property and writing of effective ads. They'll advise you on sprucing up your home for an easy sale. In a slow market, they will beat the bushes for buyers. They can help screen buyers on financial qualifications. They'll review the buyers' offers and negotiate the best deal they can get for you. They'll help locate financing for your buyer and shepherd both parties through the twisted maze toward settlement.

Another important benefit of selling through an agent is getting your home listed in a multiple listing service—the computerized clearinghouse of properties listed with professional brokers. You can't use the agent's MLS on your own, and you'll have to make up for this with your own advertising efforts.

Finally, if the agent can get you a sale price that is at least 6% higher than you could get selling your home yourself without paying a commission, then the agent's skills cost your nothing, theoretically. That's a big "if," however. (See Chapter 21.)

## A MIDDLE GROUND

Some sellers don't begrudge the real estate agent a piece of the action, but they believe the full 6% or 7% commission is too high, considering how much work the seller has to do even with an agent's help (preparing the house for sale, cleaning up for showings, etc.).

These people look for a discount agent who, in exchange for a reduced list of duties, will charge a lower commission than a "full-service" agent will. (See the next chapter, "Picking a Broker.")

Other sellers will, in a sense, list the house themselves, doing the pricing, advertising and showing themselves, but they agree to pay a small commission—say, 2% or 3%—to any agent who brings in the eventual buyer. They do this so their home won't get a cold shoulder from the agents.

Many house hunters these days do their searching with an agent, and the agent will get compensated for those efforts only by sharing in the sales commission. So agents will try to steer their clients away from FSBO listings, and a FSBO who refuses to pay any commission will, in effect, be trying to split house hunters away from the agents who may have given them considerable help in the search.

Offering to pay a broker and his agent 3% for bringing in the buyer will guarantee the cooperation of the real estate pros, because that's as much as they're usually going to make on most home purchases—a split of the 6% commission with the listing broker and broker's agent. In this case, you the FSBO are the lister.

If you decide to try this partial FSBO method, make sure you put the words "sale by owner; brokers welcome at 3%" in your ad. That's the signal that you're willing to deal with the real estate profession.

## GOING IT ALONE

Without denying the real estate agent his or her due, all the tasks of selling a house can be accomplished by an energetic, imaginative seller aided by a few professionals—appraiser, inspector and real estate attorney—who will charge on an hourly or flat-fee basis, rather than commission.

You don't need a license or any kind of official permission to sell your own property. But you will need these resources:

**Time:** Finding a buyer can take time, even in a feverish market. A house or condominium unit may not move quickly if it is unusual in some way, in disrepair, in a deteriorating neighborhood or equipped with extras not every buyer wants, such as a swimming pool or tennis court.

Going it alone is risky if you must sell in a hurry. You might speed things up by telling prospects that you will cut the price by a pecentage of the amount of a sales commission. Still, the odds are an agent with access to a multiple listing service and other contacts would get faster action.

**Flexibility:** You will need plenty of time to show your home during the day, as well as at night and on weekends. You can decide to show it by appointment only, but you probably can't afford to be too rigid about that either. If you can't be at home, arrange for a responsible, interested adult to be there. It's not enough to make your home accessible by having a painter, babysitter or child open the door. That may be okay if an agent is coming to show it, but it's not good enough for a FSBO. You have to *show* your home to prospects, not just allow them to wander about.

**Patience:** Unless you are used to dealing with the public, it is easy to underestimate the amount of patience you'll need to handle telephone calls, answer questions, give directions and show the property—again and again.

**Information:** You will need to know all about your neighborhood, your property, your appliances, furnace, roof, plumbing and electrical systems. You must be willing to get the facts you need to assist prospects with financing. You should be thoroughly familiar with all comparable properties in your area.

**Knack for selling:** If the prospect of displaying the merchandise, fielding questions, overcoming objections and solving problems in order to make the sale impresses you as indelicate or undignified, reconsider handling this project without a real estate agent.

**Intuition:** Will you be able to sniff out a genuine candidate from a window-shopper? Time spent with individuals or couples who haven't really decided to buy is time not spent with those who have—and who only need to be sold on your home.

**A little money:** You will need to pay upfront for advertising, the copying of fact sheets, and hiring a lawyer to draw up a contract and buyer qualification forms. An appraisal isn't required but could be well worth the $150 to $350.

**Elbow grease:** Make your place gleam, even if it means hiring a cleaning crew. Use a paint brush and make other improvements. Everything said in Chapter 18 about getting your home ready goes double if you are selling it yourself. A glib agent can talk a client past a plaster crack or dirty wallpaper, but it will be much harder for you to do so.

Keep track of what you spend in getting the place in shape. If you buy a replacement home that costs less than the one you sell, fixing-up expenses incurred in the 90 days before the sale can be used to shave the tax on any profit.

## STEPS TO SUCCESS FOR THE FSBO

### Price it right

The single most important task in the selling of a house is the proper pricing of it—right at the market value, neither too low nor too high. This requires either your own careful study of comparable transactions in your neighborhood, or the services of a professional appraiser, who will do the same thing for you.

The FSBO must decide whether to price the house right at full market value and try to pocket the commission savings himself, or share these savings with the buyer, settling for a little less than the full asking price but more than would result from an agent sale at asking price minus commission. For a full discussion of pricing, see Chapter 21.

### Prepare fact sheets

Prospects seldom take notes as they are being shown around. They may be reluctant to appear too interested, or they may find writing distracts them from looking. But they rarely refuse to accept a printed fact sheet.

These fact sheets are important; they tell at a glance what you're selling, highlight the best points, and later on can refresh the memories of lookers who may have seen a dozen other offerings. For added impact, attach a snapshot of the place—one that shows it to advantage in its best season of the year.

The sheet should include all relevant facts about the property— age, construction, square footage, room dimensions, mechanical systems (heat, air conditioning, etc.), appliances that go with the home, amenities, lot size, and proximity to schools, public transportation, shopping and such. Add to that the price, taxes, maintenance and utility costs, and any relevant information about the current mortgage (if assumable) and seller financing help, if any. You may want to include the appraised value and a drawing of the layout.

Arrange all this in logical order and type it up, preferably on a single page. Add a statement that the "information is not guaranteed but deemed accurate to the best of my knowledge." Make copies to give to each prospect.

Inform potential buyers about known problems or defects. You're legally obliged to, and failing to do so could cause you to lose a sale or become entangled in a lawsuit.

### Get contract and buyer qualification forms

Preprinted contract forms, which vary from state to state, generally are available from office supply stores, stationers, real estate boards and lawyers. Alternatively, arrange for the attorney who will represent you to draw up a contract to meet your requirements and protect your interests. Some real estate lawyers may help clients negotiate a deal and assess the creditworthiness and financial abilities of prospective purchasers.

Qualification forms, which you can draw up yourself or with your attorney's assistance, will help you decide whether a prospective buyer is financially able to follow through on his or her offer. When an offer is submitted, have the person fill out the form, listing annual income, debts, assets, place and length of employment, credit references and such.

### Gather documents you may need

Questions may come up that could be answered by a site plan or surveyor's report. If you're selling a condominium unit, have handy the declaration or plan of condominium ownership (also called the declaration of covenants or the master deed), the bylaws of the owners' association and the rules governing property use. Have handy your actual stubs or photocopies of utility bills and recent tax bills.

### Bone up on mortgage financing

Offers usually are made contingent on the buyer's ability to get financing. It is in your interest to be helpful to buyers who find the prospect of getting a mortgage more intimidating than finding a home. Remember, this is the sort of service that a real estate agent provides to prospective buyers, and you must do the same if you're serious about selling your house yourself.

Draw up a list of lenders and check weekly on financing rates and terms. Your local newspaper may publish such information, or you can subscribe to a mortgage reporting service. (See Chapter 11 for names and addresses of some of the larger services.) You might even keep an interest-rate table and calculator handy so a prospect could calculate on the spot what the monthly principal and interest payments would be.

Be prepared to answer questions on VA and FHA loans if your home is likely to attract veterans and first-time buyers. Albert Santi's *Questions & Answers for FHA, VA & Conventional Loans* provides extensive coverage. The book is available from Mortgage Techniques, P.O. Box 17214, Memphis, TN 38187-0214.

You're going to be asked by some prospective buyers whether you are willing to assist them by taking back a second trust on your house. Before the issue arises, study the various kinds of "creative financing" discussed in Chapter 10 and decide whether you want to offer anything like this, and see Chapter 22 for mistakes to avoid when offering seller financing.

Generally, in an economy where interest rates are not unreasonably high and there are many qualified buyers, you don't have to help the purchaser with financing, and most sellers would rather not bother with it. If possible, go for a sale that will give you the total cash value of your property, for you to invest as you wish, either in your next house or some other kind of investment.

## Put up an attractive sign

Create a good impression by putting up a bright new sign in the front. Look in a hardware or sign shop for a "For Sale by Owner" sign that has a place below the main message for an add-on sign (or have one made professionally). During the week, you can hang out a phone number. And, should you decide to have an open house, you can remove it and hang an "Open" sign.

Signs are effective sources of clients for both amateur sellers and real estate firms. A response to a sign is a more valuable inquiry than a response to a newspaper ad. The sign caller is already in the neighborhood. He or she probably knows and likes the area and obviously likes the look of your home well enough to want to see the inside. You are two selling steps ahead of a classified ad caller. That person is responding to general information, and may or may not like your area or the external appearance of your home when and if a viewing appointment is made and the prospect arrives.

## Study effective real estate ads

Read the Sunday paper and study the ads written by the professionals. The best ads have very full descriptions of the house, not sketchy write-ups with so much abbreviation that they're hard to decipher. The strong points are played up, the weak points are omitted or put in the best possible light. (A small house becomes "cozy" in a good ad.) Avoid exaggeration and overly cute writing. Always put in the price. List the address (with some general directions) if it's an ad for an open house. Otherwise, you may wish to list only your phone number, to get calls for an appointment. Run the ad in the Sunday paper; to ensure the most accurate ad, deliver ad copy to the newspaper, rather than calling it in by phone.

## Give good directions

All the good advertising money can buy won't get people into your home if they get lost trying to get there. Prepare maps and directions. Anticipate where prospects will be coming from, and route them along the simplest, most direct and most attractive route you can devise.

Put up a large map by the telephone to answer questions and redirect turned-about buyers who care enough to call.

## Hold an open house

Sunday open houses are a ritual among house hunters. You'll get a lot of serious buyers, a lot of curiosity lookers, and a few neighbors who like to keep abreast of the local market. Any of these could lead to a successful contract, sooner or later.

Have a vistor register handy—a simple pad of paper will suffice—so you can get names and phone numbers. Some people will gladly sign it, while others will decline, preferring anonymity; don't press the point.

Most buyers like to go through a house by themselves, so they can discuss its strengths and weaknesses without embarrassing the owner. Station yourself in the front hall or dining room, greet visitors warmly, and hand them a fact sheet to take through the house with them. But don't escort them until they ask you to. (If you're worried about security, make sure small objects of value are stashed out of sight.) Before they leave, ask them if they have any additional questions. Remember that you're a salesman for your house; try to engage visitors in conversation so you can make your best points.

If both spouses of a couple feel comfortable showing the house together, it's a good idea. If one gets into a deep discussion (or even an unexpected negotiation) with a serious prospect—in a private place, out of earshot of other visitors—the spouse can continue to greet new visitors.

## Be ready to negotiate

Some interested buyers will want to sleep on their first impressions and return to your house one or more times, ideally getting more and more comfortable with it each time.

But the highly prepared buyer—who knows just what he wants and thinks he has found it in your property—may want to get right into a negotiation, especially if the market is tight and he's afraid your house will go fast.

It isn't unheard of for a visitor to an open house to take one of your prepared contract forms, go home and fill it out, and return to submit it before the day is out.

If you have a "live wire" buyer in your midst, be ready to deal. There are some questions about your acceptable contract terms that you would be happy to discuss verbally, such as an ideal settlement date, occupancy date (if different from settlement), your willingness to finance part of the deal yourself, etc.

But the most important element—price—should not be negotiated verbally, nor your intentions telegraphed. While still in your home, some buyers will ask questions like, "Is your price firm?" or "What are you really willing to accept?".

Don't answer directly, but try to deflect these questions in a courteous, noncommittal way that keeps the buyer interested, with an answer like, "The house is fairly priced for the market right now, but all offers will be considered," or "The price, like other aspects of your offer, can be negotiated; please make us your best offer."

For a fuller discussion of seller negotiating strategies, see Chapter 22.

## DEALING WITH AGENTS

As soon as you start advertising or hold your first open house, you'll get calls from agents asking for a listing. They will often tell you that your home is priced way too low, and if they help you sell it, they'll get you enough more to more than cover the commission and net you more than you'll get selling by yourself.

Of course, they might be right, but then, their judgment isn't exactly objective. If you've proceeded on your course with care and have priced your house according to comparable values in the market, stand your ground—at least for a while. Tell inquiring agents you intend to try it yourself first.

Be wary of anyone who attempts to get a sales listing on your house by claiming to have a hot prospect who is looking for a home just like yours. If the agent's prospect is truly motivated, he or she probably checks out the Sunday real estate ads and will see your ad; at that point, you will get a direct inquiry from the buyer. (The main exception to this assumption, which makes the agent's claim more valid, is the out-of-town buyer who is relying totally on the agent to find houses.)

While you're holding firm to your own sales effort, don't allow agents on your property with prospects. If you allow the agent to bring a prospect without a written agreement, you may have—in effect—granted an open listing to the agent. And, if the prospect buys, you may end up paying a commission, even without a written agreement. (But some states have tried to avoid misunderstandings—and suits—between FSBO sellers and agents by enacting laws that effectively bar an agent from collecting a commission unless there was some sort of written agreement with the seller.)

While holding eager agents at bay, set a time limit on your own brokering, exactly as you would with a professional broker. Give yourself 30, 60 or 90 days, depending on the current selling climate and how quickly you must sell your house. Then, during your time period, be clear and firm with agents seeking a listing: "No listings until I've taken a crack at it myself." Do your best to sell the home, but if you don't succeed, back off and turn the job over to an agent of your choice.

## GETTING HELP

You don't have to go it entirely alone to bring off a sale. There are a number of ways to get professional help and still pay less than full commission.

### Temporary listing contract

If you think a particular agent has a buyer who might not see or buy your house without the agent's cooperation, you might be persuaded to give the agent a shot at selling your house, but for less than a 6% commission. This calls for a short-term, custom-tailored listing agreement.

Tell the agent to come *alone* to your house (even if the prospective buyer just waits in the car at the curb) and sign a temporary listing agreement that contains the name of the agent, the amount of the commission (generally just 2% or 3%, since you've done most of the work yourself), the name of the prospective buyer and the asking price for this particular trans-action. The price will probably be higher than what you've been asking for a FSBO transaction, to cover the commission you're going to pay if the deal goes through.

You should limit the time an agent has to bring you a purchase offer from this buyer, so the agreement—covering only the particular named buyer—should be valid for only one or two days at most.

### Open listing: 3% deal for all agents

If, as described above, you are willing to pay 3% to any agent who brings in the final buyer and have made that known in your ad or when agents call you, the agents will ask you to draw up a listing agreement—called an open listing—that guarantees them their commission if the deal goes through.

You should be willing to sign such a listing, one for each agent. Unlike the agreement above, it need not identify a particular buyer. It can cover as long a period as you wish, but writing in a finite expiration date is essential, because you may not legally sign an exclusive listing agreement with one agent while you have any open listings like these still floating around valid.

## Discount agents and counselors

Some real estate brokers offer bare-bones service for about half the regular 6%-to-7% commission. Typically, discounters provide you with pricing guidance, signs, contract forms and help with closing. You do everything else, including showing the property.

There also may be real estate counselors or broker-consultants in your community who help owner-sellers for 1% or 2% of the selling price or work on an hourly basis. For names, check with large real estate firms in your area and watch for advertisements in the real estate section of the paper. In some communities, title companies will help you close the deal once you have a contract agreement with a buyer.

# 20

## Picking a Broker, Listing Your Home

$F$or most Americans, their home is their principal asset. If you want to turn the work of selling this asset over to a broker, choose one who will help you get the highest price for your home and perform the task efficiently, honestly and quickly.

You will pay the broker and his agent thousands of dollars at settlement. While any broker can list, advertise and show your home, brokers and agents—like lawyers, doctors and car dealers—come in every variety, bringing with them different economic backgrounds, personalities, resources and levels of skills and integrity. Two out of three sellers hire the first agent they contact. Needless to say, that's not the best way to do it.

Select one or two brokerage firms in your area with a reputation for integrity and a proven track record selling homes comparable to yours. Then interview at least three successful agents at those firms whose personalities and selling styles are compatible with yours.

Consider hiring a discount broker—a firm that will help you sell your house for less than a full 6% commission, in exchange for your doing some of the work that the listing agent normally does. (See the discussion in Chapter 19.)

### SELECTING THE FIRM

Find out how intensely the firm works your area. How many listings does the firm carry, both in and out of season? What percentage of those listings are sold by the firm's agents? One indicator is the frequency of the firm's name in the by-neighborhood listings in the Sunday paper and the number of the firm's signs you see in your area.

Check the company's reputation and experience with lenders, lawyers and former clients. When you sign a listing agreement, you are employing a firm or a broker to find a buyer for your property. If you pick a brokerage firm because you want to work with a particular agent, keep in mind that you are still relying on the firm's experience, contacts and reputation. While most of your contact may be with the agent, satisfy yourself that behind that agent is strong supervision and plenty of expertise. To whom will an agent turn for advice should problems arise? In most firms the managing broker is responsible for resolving financial problems, supervising complex contract preparation and counseling agents.

In your initial telephone contact, ask whether the 6% commission will be reduced under special circumstances—for example, if the buyer is found by the listing broker, with no sharing of commission with another firm. While brokerage commissions are officially negotiable, in practice, most firms hold tight to their stated commission. (See discussion below.)

Find out how the firm is staffed. How many agents are full-time? How many are part-time? How experienced is the group as a whole? Do most agents concentrate on selling homes, or do they dabble in commercial real estate and property management as well? Do agents have access to administrative and secretarial help?

How will telephone queries about your property be handled? Call the firm as though you were a prospective buyer, and ask a few friends to do the same. When you call as a seller, you're almost assured of a warm welcome; but the reception could be less enthusiastic for purchasers, especially in a seller's market when agents are busy.

Does a would-be buyer get an alert and enthusiastic response? How long does it take to get a call returned? How carefully are messages and phone numbers taken? Does the answering agent have listing information available, and is he or she able to tell you what you want to know about the property?

Does the firm participate in the local multiple listing service? An MLS provides a computerized master list of all the homes for sale in a marketplace through its member real estate companies. Agents use this information extensively to match up buyers and sellers.

Is the firm hooked into a nationwide referral system? If your home could be attractive to corporate transferees, find out how many referrals the office received during the past 12 months. How many referrals resulted in sales and what was the average selling price?

## FINDING THE BEST AGENT

Ask the head of the firm you select to give you the names of the agents in the office who have the most experience in your neighborhood and price range. An agent who does a lot of business with sellers in the area may work at developing a list of interested buyers, or may maintain close contact with agents who have such clients. Select one who knows the community's price history and one who has weathered bad years as well as profited during good ones. Look for an agent who can not only answer a buyer's questions about recently sold homes, but who frequently can say, "We made those sales."

Interview your former neighbors. Track down at least two who sold within the last six months to a year; ask them about the agent they used and those they chose not to use. The following is a list of suggested questions:

▶ How long was the house on the market?

▶ Did it sell for the original price, or did you have to reduce the price substantially?

▶ With how many agents did you have your home listed? If more than one, what happened to the other one(s)?

▶ Did the agent withdraw voluntarily, or did you refuse to renew the listing? Either way, why?

▶ Do you think your agent got you the best available deal in both price and terms, or did you accept the offer because you had to make a decision without more delay?

▶ Did the entire office push your home, or did the job fall almost entirely to the listing agent?

▶ Do you think your agent and his firm made it easy or hard for other firms to cooperate?

▶ Did the firm maintain a strong selling push, or did you have to keep prodding it?

▶ Do you think the property could have been sold faster? For more money?

▶ Did the agent see you through closing?

▶ Were the people you dealt with courteous?

▶ Did they call for appointments to show your home and call to cancel when they had a change of plans?

▶ Knowing what you know now, would you use the same agent again?

## INTERVIEWING THE AGENTS

To save time, you may wish to hold an informal open house for agents, during which several agents will come to tour your home at the same time. Later, select two or three to give you a full "listing presentation." The agent's presentation should include:

▶ Information about the agent's experience, education and background.

▶ Advice on repairs and other improvements that would make your home more appealing.

▶ Information about the housing market in general and current activity in your neighborhood.

▶ Market analysis showing all recent comparable sales in your area. An analysis should show properties currently on the market. It also should specify the selling price and date of sale for the sold homes, and date of listing for the unsold ones, along with detailed descriptions of each property.

▶ Suggested asking price, based on how quickly you wish to sell your home.

▶ Discussion of the kind of advertising and promotion to expect.

▶ "Net proceeds" sheet, illustrating what you might realize on the sale under varying financing arrangements and with various levels of commission.

▶ Explanation of various kinds of listings and listing agreements.

After all the presentations, select the one agent you want to do business with first. Your decision should be based on everything from professionalism and knowledge to the intangibles of personal chemistry.

You might very well receive from the agents you interview a wide range of suggested asking prices. You will be very tempted to list your home with the agent who confidently suggests the highest asking price. Take this with a grain of salt, and examine how the suggested price relates to comparable recent transactions.

Just as some agents will try to talk you into a low asking price to assure themselves a quick, easy sale (and sure commission), others will give you an inflated estimate of your house's value to get the initial listing. Only later, after your home has sat unsold for too long, will they suggest a price reduction.

## KINDS OF LISTINGS

After you select an agent, decide on one of the several kinds of listing agreements. A listing agreement, whether oral or written, exclusive or nonexclusive, is a legally enforceable contract. Review each prospective agent's listing agreement form while you are still going through the selection process. Once you've picked the agent you want to work with, you may want to modify certain parts of the contract.

With any kind of listing, if the agent brings you the deal that the listing calls for (full price and exact terms offered by a buyer who is ready, willing and able to buy), you are obliged to pay a commission *whether you accept the deal or not.*

These are the most frequently used arrangements:

▶ *Exclusive right to sell.* This is the most common agreement. The listing agent is entitled to a commission no matter who sells the property, including you. If another agent produces the buyer, you still owe only the one commission, which will be split between the listing broker and the broker who found the buyer. This type of agreement usually assures you the most service. The agent is guaranteed a commission if he produces a sale, and you have an agent to hold responsible for making all "reasonable" or "diligent" efforts to find a purchaser.

If your employer has guaranteed to buy your home at a discount if you can't get a better offer on the open market, be sure to amend an exclusive-right-to-sell agreement to prevent an agent from claiming a commission on your company's purchase.

▶ *Exclusive, or exclusive agency.* You don't pay a commission if you find a buyer without help from the agent. If you sign an agreement like this, you're in effect competing with your own listing agent; if you get direct queries about your property, handle them yourself and don't refer calls to your agent.

If you have a good prospect who expressed an interest in your home before you listed it with an agent, use this kind of agreement and add a clause that says you may sell the house to this named party—and any other whom you find yourself—without paying a commission.

▶ *Open.* You agree to pay a commission to any agent as long as he or she is the first to produce an acceptable buyer. Again, you don't owe any commission if you're first to find a buyer.

This type of listing is most common when there is no multiple listing service. It's also the kind of listing often used by sellers who want to do most of the selling work themselves but want the cooperation of agents in finding buyers.

The commission is typically half of the standard rate—say, 3%. The seller should notify agents of such an offer by putting the words "Brokers welcome at 3%" in newspaper ads. Then the seller signs a simple open-listing agreement with each of the agents who expresses an interest in bringing a buyer to see the home.

Make sure you specify an expiration date (not too distant) on every open listing, because you can't sign an exclusive listing with one agent if you have open listings still in force.

## ELEMENTS OF THE LISTING CONTRACT

### Expiration date

Knowing the average and median length of time it takes for homes to sell in your neighborhood should influence your choice of a listing expiration date. Thirty to 90 days is common. Generally, the shorter the better, but it isn't reasonable to insist on a 30-day listing when homes like yours are taking three to six months to sell.

A relatively short listing will give you the option of switching agents if friction develops with your first agent, or if you feel he or she isn't working hard to sell your home.

You can extend a listing beyond its original life, but don't inadvertently sign an agreement containing an automatic extension. If you wish, substitute a provision that extends the listing as much as 60 days if a buyer reneges on a signed sales contract.

You also may want to add a clause reinforcing your right to cancel the contract should the agent fail to do a good job. If you exercise that option, however, you may find you still are liable for certain expenses incurred by the agent. Moreover, in some listing contracts, you may have to pay a penalty for canceling.

### Protection period

If, after the listing expires, you sell your home to someone your former agent had a hand in finding, there may be a clause in the contract that entitles the agent to a commission anyway. Naturally, no agent wants to lose a commission because the listing agreement expires while he is still working with a prospective buyer.

Typically, protection clauses give commission rights to agents for 30 to 60 days after a contract ends. If a listing agreement contains such a provision, it also should provide, in fairness to the seller, that the agent give the seller the names of prospective buyers *before* the listing expires—and require written purchase offers from any such buyers within a reasonable time *after* the listing expires.

### Commission

Commissions are negotiable. They are not set by law or by industry rules—something most sellers don't realize. A listing agent usually gets a commission based on a percentage of the final sales price of the property—typically 6% to 7%.

As a practical matter you won't get very far negotiating a lower rate unless you have special circumstances that make your property more economical to sell than others. You can make a strong argument for a lower commission or other concessions in the following cases:

**Easy sale:** The property is fairly priced, and it's in the right location. The mortgage carries an attractive interest rate and is assumable, and the house is in immaculate condition.

**Volume discount:** You have other properties to put on the block with your home.

**Double score:** Another agent from the firm listing your property delivers a buyer, so the commission won't be shared with another broker.

**Scaled-back service:** You take on some of the burden of selling and lower the commission accordingly. You also may be able to find a "discount" real estate broker. In either case, be sure the listing contract is clear about what will be done for you in the way of advertising and promotion. Keep in mind that if the commission cut is too deep, cooperating brokers may not be interested in working for a share of an already small commission.

**Agent has a buyer at hand:** You pay less: the agent won't have to advertise, hold open the property or split the commission.

**The purchase contract or settlement is at risk:** An agent may be willing to make concessions to hold onto a piece of a deal that's on the verge of getting away.

For example, take a situation where the seller is dealing directly with a buyer whom the seller found; if that buyer's offer—which might net more for the seller—is accepted, the seller's listing agent won't get any commission on the sale. To compete against that buyer, an agent may have to present a considerably higher contract from another buyer and also shave the sales commission, to make the second contract net at least as much as the first one.

Another reason for a shaved commission might be a problem that develops on the way to settlement—say, the seller finding out he has to pay more mortgage discount points than he expected. If the deal is at stake, the agent might offer to make up the difference out of his or her own commission.

## Condition of property and what's for sale

The listing agreement should describe the general condition of the property. It should show what is being sold "as is" and what, if anything, will be repaired, removed, substituted or altered prior to settlement. The agreement should list each and every fixture that will be sold with the house, and those that will not.

Make the agent aware of problems or defects in the property. If the listing agreement doesn't adequately spell out the current condition of the structure, the appliances and the electrical, mechanical and plumbing systems, have it corrected or write a letter to the agent setting out the information.

### Marketing plan

Get the proposed marketing plan in writing as an addendum to the listing contract. It can serve as documentation should you feel the agent is not fulfilling his commitments. Arrange for weekly progress reports.

Know your tarket market. Ask the listing agent to give you a profile of your home's most likely buyer or buyers. Will they be first-time buyers, retirees or corporate transferees? What kind of income will they have?

The marketing strategy your agent proposes should be designed to reach those potential buyers. A comprehensive plan should include these elements:

**Advertising:** How often and where will your home be advertised? When your home is not being advertised, will the firm be advertising a comparable home so that interested buyers can also be referred to your property?

**Open houses:** What efforts will the agent make to bring interested buyers to your home? For example, will agents who deal with likely clients be sent an information sheet describing the property and date of the open house? Will ads and signs be used?

**Multiple listing service:** How promptly will your property be placed in the MLS? Ideally, it should go into the computer very quickly, and you should specify a deadline in the listing contract; some MLSs require their members to enter new listings within 24 hours of the signing of the contract.

Some brokers will try to keep a new listing out of the MLS computer for several days or more; that gives their own agents a first shot at selling the property "in house," so that the whole 6% commission is kept within the firm. Once agents at other firms see the listing in the computer and bring prospective buyers in to see the home, the odds increase that the listing broker will have to split the eventual commission with another broker (called the "co-op" broker or agent). You'll pay only the full commission in any event, and your interests are served by a fast sale.

**Agent tours:** An organized tour for other agents in the office should be arranged soon after you sign the listing. An open house for other agents from other firms is another useful sales tool.

**Spreading the word:** Will your agent inform your neighbors that you are selling? What other networks will he or she use?

**Financing:** Will your agent be able to work with interested buyers to locate financing?

## GET READY TO SELL

Your agent will set about the task of selling your house as soon as the ink is dry on a listing contract, so you had better be ready, too.

Ideally, your home will be ready to show immediately, but if it isn't, now is the time to do all the last-minute touch-ups and clean-ups described in Chapter 18.

From now until a sales contract is accepted, your home has to be ready to show on a moment's notice. It's difficult living in a home that's for sale, but its tidiness during an appointment or open house will have a lot of bearing on how fast it sells and for how much.

Try to have everyone out of the house when your agent brings a prospect to inspect it, even if that means gathering up the kids and your elderly parents and taking them all for a drive. This will enable the agent and house hunter to talk more candidly than if you're there, and the buyer will be able to visualize his or her lifestyle more easily if your kids aren't running around or making sandwiches in the kitchen.

Most importantly, you should be emotionally ready to deal with serious buyers. The signing of the listing contract and presentation of the first buyer's contract is not the time to discover that you have misgivings about selling or qualms about the asking price.

# 21

# Setting the Right Price

To set the right price on a home, sellers should combine objective evaluation of the property with a realistic assessment of current market conditions.

In good markets and bad, a seller is more likely to benefit by determining a fair value and sticking close to it than he is by asking an unrealistic figure and waiting for buyer response to sift out the "right" price. And when there are more sellers than buyers, setting the right price from the outset may be the only strategy that will work.

Underpricing deprives you of the full value you deserve. Unless you are in a frightful hurry, try to get full market value. Avoid over-eager or unethical agents who may suggest a price that will assure a quick and easy sale—one that won't require lots of advertising and showing.

## DANGERS OF OVERPRICING

If you wish, you could set a very fair price and refuse to bargain, but that is ill-advised. It would deter people who hate to pay full price for anything and like to think they're "getting a deal."

It's better to leave a little room for negotiation, by asking slightly more than you expect to get. How much more? Certainly not more than 5% to 10% above appraised value. If sales are brisk in your area, you might just be able to get top dollar.

What many sellers don't realize is that overpricing can result in their getting *less* for their house than if they priced it right to begin with. The reason is this: knowledgeable agents and buyers won't even put in a contract on a severely overpriced house. By the time the seller wises up to the overpricing, many of those qualified buyers will have bought other houses, decreasing market demand for the now properly priced property. The overpriced house may end up selling for less than it might have fetched a few months earlier.

Occasionally, an agent agrees to list a property for far more than it is worth—usually at the owner's insistence. The agent knows that, if the owner is serious about selling, the price will have to come down sooner or later. But sometimes an agent who is competing against other agents for a sales listing will give a seller an unrealistically high estimate of value, to ensure getting the listing. After the house sits on the market a while, the agent will suggest a new, lower price that is more in line with what the other agents suggested in the first place.

Some sellers who don't have to sell by any particular deadline ("unmotivated sellers," they're called) will cling for a long time to their overly high asking price—say, 15% higher than it should be. They probably won't get their asking price, and even if they do manage to sell a year later for the original price, it will be because a rising market finally caught up with their price.

They might think they were smart to hold firm, but in fact they were naive, ignoring the time value of money. In the year (or even six months) they clung to their high price, the rest of the real estate market probably wasn't standing still. The next home they buy may have gone up in value by at least the same margin, and possibly more. Even if they don't buy a replacement home, they have lost the earnings they would have received on the invested proceeds of an earlier sale—at least 6% per year, if very conservatively invested, and possibly much more, if invested in tax-free bonds or a rising stock market.

## STUDY THE COMPARABLES

You run the risk of either overpricing or underpricing if you settle on a price not based on solid information. Shop your competition. Whether you are using an agent or not, learn the offering and selling prices of similar properties. Find out how long each took to sell.

To be comparable, a house that sold has to be close to yours in age, style, size, condition and location. It also is important to know the terms under which a house was sold. A $100,000 all-cash-to-the-seller sale is very different from a $100,000 sale with $10,000 down and a $20,000 second mortgage taken back by the owner.

Timing is critical, too. If you are offering your home when sales are brisk and demand is high, you should be able to add something to the price.

Try to find at least three comparables no more than six months old. Information on home sales is available at the courthouse or city real estate tax office. In jurisdictions where there is a tax on the transfer of property, you can determine the price by the tax paid. For example, if the tax or fee is 0.1% of the sales price and the transfer fee is $88, then the price paid was $88 divided by .001, or $88,000. Sales prices of homes also are published in local or regional sections of newspapers.

You won't learn anything at the tax office about the terms of the sale, the style of the house or how long it was on the market. If you are going it alone, your best bet is to copy the names and contact the buyers and sellers yourself.

If you are listing your home with an agent, this kind of market research should be prepared and presented to you. Nevertheless, you owe it to yourself to ask questions and to be sure that properties being described as comparable to yours really are so.

## SELLER FINANCING?

The market for mortgage money will play a major role in what you can ask—and get—for your home.

In the short run, mortgage interest rates and home prices usually move in opposite directions; when mortgage rates soar, it dampens demand for homes, and real estate prices level off or even decline. (But not always: In the late '70s, inflation and interest rates headed up at a furious pace, but so did home prices . . . until the recession of 1981–82.)

The less a buyer has to pay in interest each month, the more house he can afford to buy—or to state it another way, the more he'll be able to pay for your property.

Conversely, when interest rates zoom up, not only are there fewer people out looking for houses, but those qualified buyers will be able to drive hard bargains on price.

As a seller, your ability to get the price you want when interest rates are high will depend on whether you've got something to offer by way of financing help.

Do you have a low-rate mortgage that a buyer could assume? That would be a big plus for the buyer and might justify a somewhat higher sale price. Look at your mortgage contract, or ask your lender if you're not sure. (All loans backed by the Federal Housing Administration and Veterans Administration are assumable.)

Are you willing to offer some cut-rate seller financing to assist the buyer in making a deal? If so, you can ask a slightly higher price for your house and stick to it (unless the eventual buyer doesn't need your offered financing).

Remember that most seller financing is, in effect, a discounting of the sale price, so if you're offering a cut-rate second mortgage (which you would have to discount even further to sell in the open market), you've got to get more from the buyer in nominal sale price to make up for it. (For more on seller financing, see the next chapter.)

## GET AN APPRAISAL?

If your idea of what your property is worth and the listing broker's recommendation don't coincide, an appraisal may help. An appraisal is an especially good idea for owners attempting to sell their homes themselves. An appraisal will cost roughly $200 or so, but it can be money very well spent.

Real estate appraising is part art, part experience and part science. As a result, opinions always are subject to honest dispute. Nonetheless, an appraisal prepared by an experienced professional comes as close to an objective evaluation as you are likely to get. Get the names of good appraisers from real estate agents, mortgage lenders or from professional associations of appraisers. (See the list in Appendix A.)

The value of your home falls within a range of prices. An appraiser uses his education and judgment to determine that range. Until recently, an appraiser probably would give you a market value figure based on his or her estimate of the highest price (within that range) that your property would bring.

In 1986, responding to widespread problems of sloppiness, incompetence and downright fraud in the real estate appraising industry, the Federal National Mortgage Association and the Federal Home Loan Mortgage Corporation began requiring appraisers to work with a new definition of market value on all loans the two groups purchased. The new definition of market value is the "most probable price which a property will bring." Appraisers also must adjust the value of properties being used as comparables to reflect any creative financing, sales concessions, seller contributions or buy-downs.

In many cases, these changes mean lower estimates of market value for sellers. A home appraisal today conceivably could result in a lower market value than one done in 1986, under the old rules.

If your home is in the moderate price range, you might want to consider a VA or FHA appraisal. VA and FHA appraisals are interchangeable. If you get a VA appraisal and then find a buyer who obtains an FHA loan, the FHA will accept your existing appraisal.

Obtaining a VA or FHA appraisal doesn't lock you into selling VA or FHA. Cost varies with the locality, but a typical charge for a single-family home is about $200; a condominium report costs slightly more. What you get with this type of appraisal is a certificate of reasonable value from the VA or a conditional commitment from FHA, rather than the more detailed report you'd expect from a private residential appraiser.

With an appraisal report in hand, you and the listing agent should be able to come to an agreement. The asking price you ultimately choose may well be higher than the appraised value. But, in most cases, it shouldn't be substantially higher. There's the rub. What is "substantially" higher in one community may be an accepted markup in another.

Go back to the comparables. How much of a spread was there between the original asking price and the actual selling price in each case? Is that the normal differential? Has anything occurred to warrant setting a higher margin?

Make your decision with confidence. You've got room to negotiate. You know your price is right.

## SPECIAL ADVICE FOR FSBO'S

If you're selling your house yourself, whether the job will be a bit of hard work or a protracted ordeal depends largely on how accurately you price the property.

It's imperative that the FSBO seller study comparables closely, and it's also desirable to have a recent appraisal. If your asking price is close to the appraisal, show the document to the prospective buyer.

Some FSBOs solicit pricing opinions from real estate agents, even though they don't intend to list the house with an agent. That may strike you as a bit shady, but look at it this way: If you can't make a sale in your time frame, you'll probably turn it over to a professional. Many agents will be willing to prepare a market analysis for a probable FSBO, because it gives them an opportunity to introduce themselves and their firm—and try to persuade the seller to use their services for a commission.

The heart of the FSBO's pricing decision is the motivation for selling on your own. Do you want a fast and easy sale—by offering your home for less than you'd be willing to sell it for if you were to pay an agent a 6% or 7% commission? Or do you want to sell it for top dollar and keep all of the saved commission for yourself?

The best deal is one that's good for both parties. You don't want to give away all of the saved commission to the buyer, but you shouldn't try to hog it all for yourself either. If you can show a prospective buyer that 1) the asking price is consistent with the market, 2) he'll save a little because there is no commission involved, and 3) you'll net a little more for the same reason—then you've both got a good deal, indeed.

# 22

# Negotiating With Buyers

$C$onflict between buyer and seller is inevitable. A buyer wants the most house for his money; a seller wants the most money for his house.

If you're working with an agent, rely on this professional to direct events toward a mutually beneficial conclusion. If you are going it alone, consider hiring an attorney to help with negotiating; otherwise, study up on the fine points of negotiating.

However you are selling your house, carefully read Chapter 8, to get a sense of what an informed, well-prepared buyer wants out of this negotiation and how he will try to get it.

## NEGOTIATING THROUGH AN AGENT

Buyers and sellers may find bargaining awkward and uncomfortable. Both are likely to be more frank and open when talking to a third party. For these reasons, an experienced agent often is successful where two-party, face-to-face negotiations fail.

You should be comfortable being utterly frank with your agent. Agents know sellers sometimes take positions they don't mean to hold to the end. Let your agent know what is most important to you. Be precise about what is and isn't acceptable. Make sure the agent has satisfied himself—and you—that the buyer is financially qualified to fulfill the contract offer; this can only be done by checking all the facts the buyer has submitted on a written financial-qualifications form.

Should a cooperating agent bring in a serious buyer, have the listing agent give him a briefing on your requirements as soon as possible. If that's not feasible, ask him to contact you before heading into a contract session.

As your agent should know, all serious negotiating should be done in writing, not verbally. Don't respond to trial balloons that the buyer sends up, hoping to find out your bottom limits on price and other terms. Ask that the buyer put his or her best offer in writing.

Don't jump at the first contract presented, especially if it's way below your expectations. Have the confidence that you've priced your home properly and that it's competitive with other houses on the market.

But don't regard your first offer too lightly, either—especially if it comes reasonably close to your goals. Experienced agents know that the first contracts on a well-priced house will usually be submitted by the most serious, well-qualified buyers—people who know their own needs and resources and who have studied the market carefully. A contract from this kind of buyer is well worth serious consideration and probably a counter-offer.

## CONSIDERING THE CONTRACT

Money, people and the law are primary elements in any real estate sales contract. If you provided the contract form to a purchaser, you should already be familiar with it. If a purchaser presents an offer on another form, you will need time to study it carefully. In either situation, you need to be sure the parties to the contract are legally competent to do business with you (for example, of legal age, mental competence, etc.).

To be valid, a contract must be in writing and be freely offered by the buyer and accepted by the seller. Money or other valuable consideration must be exchanged for the title to the property.

Any contract that passes your preliminary review and is a candidate for acceptance should be reviewed by your attorney, or be made contingent upon that review. See Chapter 8 for a discussion of contingencies commonly sought by purchasers, and decide in advance how you will respond to these conditions.

Consider the contract as a whole. Is it slanted in favor of the buyer? If so, consult with your attorney about making changes. To do that, analyze the document as a series of paragraphs or clauses, each written to benefit one party or the other. Take them one by one and make an orderly evaluation.

For example, most completed purchase and sale contracts can require you to sell your property. But what could you do should the buyer default? In an option contract, the buyer has an option to buy. If he doesn't, he stands to lose the earnest deposit (or option money), assuming of course that the seller is not at fault. On the other hand, in a specific-performance contract—the most common form of contract used in home sales—the seller can require the buyer to purchase the property or pay damages.

A small earnest deposit accompanying an option contract may be viewed with alarm by a seller. That same deposit, tied to a specific-performance contract offered by a well-heeled purchaser, may be viewed with less concern.

Beware of the contract that binds only you. Getting a seller to accept an offer that nails down the price and terms but leaves the buyer free to escape through a number of clauses is a favorite strategy of buyers.

Examine each contingency. Is each one clear and precise? Some contingencies are reasonable; others are less so.

## KEY ELEMENTS OF THE CONTRACT

### Price

Is the offering price right? There is nothing that evokes such an emotional response from a seller as the price offered. Try to keep an open mind on the price until you've studied the whole deal. Be realistic and objective. Was the price based on an independent appraisal or on a broker's market analysis? How long has the property been on the market? How many written offers have you received? Has the market changed?

Most properties don't bring full price. And price, by itself, usually doesn't make or break a deal.

### Condition of home and inspection

It is fair that the purchaser should have the opportunity to have your home inspected for soundness of construction and state of repair. Keep it fair by insisting that the person or firm to be used be named in the contract by professional designation, and set a time limit for the removal of the contingency—five or so working days.

Watch what you guarantee. Occasionally, a purchaser asks a seller to guarantee that the roof won't leak, the heating system won't go out or any number of other such assurances. Don't do it. If you do, you are not making a sale, you are taking on a partner. Do not undertake to remain responsible for your property once you have sold it.

As a rule, contract language determines what must be in working order at settlement. Have everything clearly spelled out, otherwise local law and custom may prevail. Say that only three of the four burners on your stove work, and you don't want to pay for repairs. Unless your contract states that the stove is being sold "as is"—with three burners, not four—you may end up paying for the repair at the settlement table.

Buyers often are willing to negotiate on the condition of the house. For example, if your home is a candidate for extensive upgrading, a prospective buyer who is planning renovations that include installing central air conditioning may be happy to bargain over the broken window unit, since it would be discarded anyway once work begins.

## Financing

If the contract is contingent on a buyer being able to obtain an acceptable loan, does the clause spell out what actions are required by the buyer? What interest rate and number of discount points does the buyer consider "acceptable"? Is there a time limit? What will happen if no loan is secured by the agreed-on deadline? How will the seller know when the buyer gets a loan commitment? How can the contingency be removed? Generally, you'll want to leave the buyer as few escape hatches as possible.

## Response deadline

You'll be asked to respond to a contract offer within a specified period of time—say, two or three days. Try to get as long a response time as possible. If you are presented with a desirable contract containing a deadline you are unable to meet—perhaps because your attorney or spouse is out of town—counter promptly with a more suitable one . . . and an explanation.

If you think you'll have other offers coming in, you'll want to buy as much time as possible to review them and perhaps use one offer to jack up another offer. Tell other interested parties (or have your agent tell them) that you've got a good offer on the table, and if they want a shot at this purchase, they had better move fast with an attractive offer.

It may benefit you to tell other parties what the highest offering price is, to get them to top it; but in other cases, it may be better not to name a price, in case the other bidder is willing to go much higher. If you try to bluff buyers by telling them you've been offered a price or contract you don't really have in hand, it might work—or it might backfire and scare off interested parties, leaving you with nothing.

While you are studying the offer, keep the buyer informed of your progress. A buyer left hanging may have second thoughts and may even withdraw the offer before you have a chance to accept or produce a counter-offer.

### Prior sale of buyer's home

Should you cooperate with a prospective purchaser who must sell a home before buying yours? Maybe. But that hinges the sale of a property you know—yours—on the sale of one you don't know—his.

Any such contingency clause should be carefully constructed and reviewed—if not written—by your attorney. Before getting to that point in the negotiations, however, seek the advice of a broker familiar with the area of your potential buyer's home. Assure yourself that the property is saleable and reasonably priced. Ask for a hefty earnest money deposit, or try for a non-refundable deposit should the deal fail.

### Settlement date and occupancy

If you're selling your home because you already have your next home under contract, try to get a settlement date that will enable you to take your sales proceeds to the closing of the purchase; that will make it unnecessary for you to get a bridge loan. Be realistic, however; the buyer of your home will probably need about 60 days to arrange his financing.

Most sold homes are delivered to the buyer empty and clean on settlement day. If you would like to stay on in your home after settlement, make this desire known to buyers and write it into the contract, suggesting a lease-back price that just covers the new owner's out-of-pocket costs (mortgage, taxes, utilities, insurance) for the time you remain there.

### Other conditions

Other contingencies address problems or events that may happen between the time the contract is signed and the time title is passed to the buyer. If your house burns down, what happens? Does the buyer have to buy and pay the agreed-on price? Can the whole deal be called off? Can a lower price be offered? What about insurance proceeds?

## TAKE BACK A MORTGAGE?

High interest rates and shortages of available mortgage money are always bad news for both home buyers and sellers. Be sure that any solution suggested to you—by whatever name—doesn't just shift the problem rather than solve it.

First of all, ask yourself whether you belong in the mortgage lending business. If you need your equity to make a down payment on another home, you may not be able to take back a mortgage. And even if you can afford to help your buyer with financing, you may not want to. Mortgage lending can be complicated. It involves two major phases: origination and servicing. Origination is setting up the loan—screening applicants, appraising the property and drawing up the papers. Servicing is collecting the monthly payments, dunning for delinquencies, sending annual statements and foreclosing when necessary.

There is considerable risk. Because seller mortgages are really worth much less than they appear, they generally are the equivalent of cutting the price. And because the interest rates and other terms of seller mortgages are almost invariably generous, these mortgages can be distinctly inferior to alternative investments.

Avoid these mistakes, common among seller financing:

**Too little down payment:** Don't take back a mortgage if the buyer has less than 20% equity in the property. Professional mortgage lenders prefer that the buyer have at least that much equity. This insures an adequate buffer in the event of foreclosure because it increases the probability that the property can be sold for enough to cover your loan. It also gives the borrower incentive to avoid foreclosure in the first place.

**No prepayment penalty:** When permitted by state law, professional lenders almost always impose a prepayment penalty. Sellers almost never do. Sellers hope the borrower will pay off the loan early and don't want to discourage the borrower in any way. Mortgage investors, on the other hand, see the prepayment penalty as providing the possibility of an even higher yield. Often they will pay less for a mortgage that has no prepayment penalty.

**Too low interest rate:** Sellers rarely ask enough, even on second mortgages. Lower-than-market interest rates reduce the return if you keep the loans and reduce the resale value if you sell it.

**Too long a term:** Keep the length of the loan as short as possible—one or two years if you can get it. Resist going over three years. The longer the term, the deeper the discount when you sell the loan.

**Skimpy credit check:** Too often, laymen tend to rely on appearances. If the buyer to whom they intend to extend a mortgage seems okay, they make the loan. Prospective buyers of that mortgage, however, are likely to ask for the credit report on the borrower. A credit report is inexpensive and relatively easy to obtain.

**Amateur loan documents:** Generally speaking, the best-drawn documents are the ones used by professional lenders. Ask a mortgage lender for copies of mortgage forms he uses. You should also have an attorney—one who has considerable experience in putting together mortgages. Ask a local professional mortgage lender for the name of the lawyer he uses.

**Allowing late payment:** Pros have learned that failure to crack down on chronic delinquents often leads to costly problems. Make sure your loan documents include a late charge, and enforce it to the letter.

## FORGING AN AGREEMENT

If you're selling through an agent, contracts will be presented to you through that agent, and you will counter all inadequate offers through the same agent.

Everything in the offering contract is negotiable. Decide what you want to give on and what doesn't matter that much to you. Changes can be inked in over or next to language on the contract, or a new contract can be drawn up from scratch. A draft contract can go back and forth between buyer and seller any number of times, but you'll both want to avoid an interminable negotiation, in which fatigue and disgust could jeopardize the whole deal.

When everyone has agreed to all the terms, initialed all changes and signed the contracts, you've got an agreement binding on all parties. All that remains is the removal of any contingency clauses, arranging of financing, clearing of title, and other steps on the road to settlement.

## SELLING ON YOUR OWN

The sale-by-owner seller will probably be doing his or her own negotiating with prospective buyers. However, some FSBOs hire an experienced real estate attorney to do this for them, paying the attorney a flat fee or hourly rate. If you've consulted an attorney to have your sample contract drawn up or to review a contract presented by a buyer, find out if this person will also do your negotiating for you.

If you have already agreed to pay a partial commission (say, 3%) on an open listing with any agent who brings in the successful buyer, you'll probably be dealing not with the buyer directly, but with the buyer's agent. Keep in mind that it is you, not the buyer, who will be paying the agent's commission. You may feel as if you're an adversary of that agent, but in fact the agent has a legal obligation to help you get the best possible deal on the sale; if things get tense, remind the agent of this simple fact.

If you're truly on your own—one on one with the buyer—keep all your dealings as professional and courteous as possible. Don't take anything personally; remember, the buyer has a right to try to pay as little as possible for your home, and you have a right to get as much as you can. It's a business deal, so try not to be offended by a low initial offer or any other tactic the buyer may try.

If an offer is to be made, both parties must be willing to ask for what they want, voice their objections and offer alternatives. Begin negotiations by seeking out areas of agreement. Find out what is attractive about your property, and build on that. Move on to issues that don't involve anyone's ego, such as the desired date of possession. (Normally, that's not a touchy issue, though, like everything else in a real estate sale, it can be.) Get the buyer thinking about moving in; it makes the whole purchase seem more real.

### Check the buyer's credentials

If the buyer intends to assume your current mortgage, you must be even more careful about verifying his or her financial stability and credit record. Under some circumstances, if the new owner defaults on the mortgage he assumes from you, you could be held liable.

In recent years there has been widespread mortgage fraud on FHA and VA loans assumed by crooks who purchased houses from desperate sellers with little or no money down; it has been most common in distressed local economies where home prices have fallen. The new owners often put tenants in the houses and collected rents, but made no payments on the assumed mortgages, inviting foreclosure. The FHA and VA have often tried to collect their losses from the original borrower. Both federal agencies are tightening their assumption credit checks, but the scam still poses a risk to unwary sellers.

All the legal fine print in the world can't make a good deal with a bad buyer. You could be back on square one if an impulsive or unprepared buyer is derailed by the first negative comment from a home inspector or mortgage lender. Make a judgment about a prospective buyer's commitment and financial capability before proceeding into a nitty-gritty examination of the purchase offer.

Ask for a net worth statement. How does the buyer intend to pay for the property? Has he or she been prequalified by an agent or lender? Where will the down payment come from? How knowledgeable is the buyer about market value, the neighborhood and so forth? Are the terms of the sale understood? Has the property been examined thoroughly? Ask these questions now. You have the right to know.

## Keep selling

When you sense your prospect is getting close to the contract-writing stage, keep selling. Now is not the time suddenly to begin acting the role of pleasant host or hostess, assuming the buyer will take it upon himself to do the rest. Avoid these common mistakes:

**Appearing too eager:** If the buyer feels you are overly eager, or too anxious to make a deal, you may lose a sale. He may become suspicious, or he may pressure you into making major concessions.

**Appearing too tough:** A good deal can slip through your hands if you are too rigid or unpleasant to work with. Try to be flexible and objective. If you can't agree over one point, keep pushing toward agreement in areas where you do see eye-to-eye. Try not to close the door on any one point completely; just put the matter off until later.

**Failing to empathize:** Try to see the buyer's side of things. Never become defensive. Be ready with all the information needed; be confident and patient.

If you reach a point where you recognize you must compromise or make a concession, get everything else agreed on in writing. Then, when you do concede the point, the deal essentially is locked in.

Once you have an accepted contract—fully signed and all changes initialed—stop talking! Stand up, shake hands and change the subject.

You have a contract and are on your way to settlement.

# 23

## Preparing for Settlement

Buyers may dread the arrival of closing day and the huge outlay of cash, yet still be eager to get it over with so they can move into their new home. Sellers, on the other hand, look forward to collecting their bounty, but their anticipation may be tinged with anxiety and sadness about giving up their home for good.

Most of the work between contract signing and closing falls on the buyer, who must get the house inspected quickly, arrange financing, and buy homeowner's and title insurance.

The seller has relatively little to do. If you agreed to have anything repaired before settlement, it must be done now. If a problem arises with the title to your home, it may involve you in some paper work, legal expense and delicate diplomacy. (As a seller, you should carefully read Chapter 12, "Getting a Good Title.")

If a title problem is intractable or so complicated it could threaten to delay settlement for a long time, your buyer may be tempted to try to void the contract. These anxieties might be calmed by you or a good attorney, but if the deal is on the rocks, have your attorney tell you what your rights are.

### KEEP YOURSELF INFORMED

The most important thing you need to do as seller is keep yourself informed of everything that is happening. If the buyer is having trouble getting a loan on the terms specified in the contract, you should know it; it could jeopardize the whole deal and end up putting your house back on the market. A day or so before closing, make sure all the papers are in place. The settlement agent was probably selected by the buyer, but you are free to bring your own attorney to the settlement appointment, at your expense.

Nothing is more tedious than sitting around a settlement table while the escrow officer telephones lenders, insurance companies, contractors and others for figures that should be at hand. A process that should take 45 minutes drags on for hours instead.

There should be no arguing over who pays what, because the contract and escrow instructions spell out everything. There should be no financial surprises, either. Your agent should have kept you up-to-date on what you could expect to net out of the transaction. You should have received an estimated net sheet when you signed the listing agreement, and another one along with each contract presentation. Prior to settlement, the escrow officer or settlement attorney should provide you with a copy of the settlement sheet. (See page 182 for an example of closing costs on a $100,000 home.)

If you are handling your own settlement, you can get an estimate at the time you arrange for closing, or "open escrow," whether it is with a title or abstract company or an abstract attorney.

Still, things can go wrong. Documents get misplaced or don't arrive in time, to name just two examples. Other areas where last-minute glitches or misunderstandings occur include:

▶ No-shows and too-lates: People who need to be present at closing should be kept informed of any change in the date, time or place. They should be reminded a week before closing, and again the day before.

If closing is being conducted by the buyer's attorney, and you want your attorney to be there to represent you, you no doubt cleared the initial date with him before signing the contract. However, if closing is delayed, or is changed for any reason, you'll need to clear it again. The same follow-through tactic should be used for each individual you are depending on to attend.

▶ Anyone named on the deed under which you hold title must sign the new deed by which you grant title. In many jurisdictions, if you have married since acquiring title, your spouse also will have to sign the deed. If your co-owner doesn't live nearby, allow time to have the deed signed and returned before settlement.

▶ Determine when you will be paid. Don't expect to walk away from the settlement table with a check in hand, but don't leave the question of when and how you will be paid undetermined.

Most settlement attorneys do not disburse checks until all the necessary documents have been recorded. If that's the case, when will the recording take place, and how often are checks made up? An additional delay in disbursement can occur if the lender wants to review settlement papers after it is over and then wait for the deed to be recorded before disbursing any funds.

If you are buying another property, consider having both settlements at the same office, scheduled back-to-back. That way, the timing of the disbursement is not a problem. You sign a paper authorizing the title company or attorney to assign the funds from your sale to your purchase.

## THE PAPERS YOU'LL NEED

For more detail on the settlement process, read Chapter 13, "Get Ready for Settlement." Here's a checklist of what will be needed to facilitate the closing:

▶ A copy of the sales contract and any documentation needed to show that contingencies have been removed or satisfied.

▶ All documents needed to complete the transfer of title. These usually are handled by the title insurance or abstract company and your attorney or closing officer. They may include: certificate of title, deed, correcting affidavits, quitclaim deeds, survey and title insurance policy or binder. Be sure the closing officer has the necessary papers showing that all judgments, liens and mortgages have been removed or satisfied.

▶ Homeowner's insurance policy. If the buyer plans to take over the unused portion of your hazard insurance, you'll need to make arrangements in advance so that all the paperwork will be completed on time.

▶ Prorations for on-going expenses, such as insurance premiums, property taxes, accrued interest on assumed loans, and utilities (if not shut off between owners). The proration date usually is determined by local custom but can be different if the contract so specifies.

▶ Receipts showing payment of latest water, electric and gas bills.

▶ A certificate from your lender indicating the mortgage balance and date to which interest has been prepaid. The closing officer usually obtains these figures calculated to the day of settlement.

# Appendix

## REAL ESTATE APPRAISERS GROUPS

There is no reliable estimate on the number of people working as appraisers; figures range from 100,000 to 300,000. Membership in one or more of the professional appraisers' organizations (which number more than a dozen) may indicate higher standards, or it may indicate little more than the ability to pay the price of membership.

The best of the appraisal groups confer certification based on continuing education requirements, ethical standards, and grievance and enforcement procedures. The following three are among those with the most rigorous standards for membership:

**American Institute of Real Estate Appraisers** (430 N. Michigan Ave., Chicago, IL 60611; 312-329-8559); membership: 6,000. Affiliated with the National Association of Realtors. Members use the designation MAI or RM after their names.

An appraiser using the designation MAI (member, Appraisal Institute) must have a college degree or its equivalent, at least five years appraising experience and must have submitted an income property demonstration report judged satisfactory by a committee of Institute peers. A residential member (RM) must have three years experience and also must have submitted a satisfactory report on residential property. In addition, members using either designation must have passed written examinations.

**National Society of Real Estate Appraisers** (1265 E. 105th St.,

Cleveland, OH 44108; 216-795-3445); this group designates members as master, senior or junior (MREA, CRA, RA) with five, three or two years of experience required, along with demonstration reports and approved courses. The top two rankings require qualifying interviews.

**Society of Real Estate Appraisers** (645 N. Michigan Ave., 9th Floor, Chicago, IL 60611; 312-346-7422); SREA designates its members as senior real estate analyst (SREA), senior real property appraiser (SRPA) and senior residential appraiser (SRA). All members are certified on the basis of training, examination and performance. All are qualified to do residential appraisals, but SRPAs and SREAs can appraise income property as well.

# Index